Through My Own Eyes

Through My Own Eyes

SINGLE MOTHERS AND
THE CULTURES OF POVERTY

Susan D. Holloway
Bruce Fuller
Marylee F. Rambaud
Costanza Eggers-Piérola

HARVARD UNIVERSITY PRESS
CAMBRIDGE, MASSACHUSETTS
LONDON, ENGLAND
1997

Copyright © 1997 by the President and Fellows of Harvard College
All rights reserved
Printed in the United States of America

Library of Congress Cataloging-in-Publication Data

Through my own eyes : single mothers and the cultures of poverty /
Susan D. Holloway . . . [et al.],
p. cm.
Includes bibliographical references and index.
ISBN 0-674-89122-8 (alk. paper)
1. Welfare recipients—Massachusetts—Boston. 2. Single mothers—
Massachusetts—Boston. 3. Poor women—Massachusetts—Boston.
4. Poverty—United States—Case Studies. 5. Family policy—
United States. I. Holloway, Susan D.
HV99.B6T48 1997
362.82′94′0974461—dc21   97-25240

*To the mothers, children, and teachers
who graciously welcomed us into their lives*

Contents

❀

Acknowledgments

❦

Several colleagues at the Harvard Graduate School of Education contributed to our ideas as we designed and carried out this project. We especially thank Robert A. LeVine. We profited greatly from his perspectives on child rearing in cultural context, as well as from his warmth, support, and enthusiasm. Others at HGSE who were a source of ideas and inspiration for this book include Sarah LeVine, Joseph Maxwell, Thomas Shaw, Judy Singer, and Catherine Snow. For providing valuable assistance during the course of the project, we thank Jeanne Adair, Veronica Guerrero-Mácia, and Petra Nicholson. Our appreciation extends as well to Harvard staff members Norma Diala, Erma Larson, Helen Rodriguez, and Paula White. We are grateful to Angela von der Lippe, the former behavioral sciences editor at Harvard University Press, who provided us with initial encouragement and assisted in shaping the book in its early stages, as well as to her successor, Elizabeth Knoll, who has ably moved the book through later stages. Kimberly Nelson and Christine Thorsteinsson have also been of valuable assistance in the editing process.

The Spencer Foundation provided primary support for our research. Rukmini Banerji, our project officer at Spencer, was wonderfully encouraging. Special thanks go to Deanna Gomby at the Packard Foundation's Center for the Future of Children, who provided initial support for survey work and parallel analyses that helped to strengthen our research program. The Lilly Endowment supported work on Chapter 8 and project dissemination activities.

Our families have provided all sorts of assistance throughout the process of conducting this research. Children have endured weekend trips to the office, partners have spent time fielding phone calls and faxes. They have all learned more than they ever thought they would about working mothers living in poverty. We are so grateful for their love and encouragement.

CHAPTER ONE

Empowering Strangers

❦

Imagine the last time a good friend behaved in an odd manner. Your spouse became angry for no clear reason. Your best friend suddenly hit her young child. At work your colleague acted aggressively, in cold disregard for others. How do you react to such startling behavior? You may respond with shock, dismay, or anger. You might search for the causes that are pushing your friend to behave erratically. Then you might muster the courage and candor necessary to ask her to disclose what caused her sudden, upsetting behavior—the reasons as seen through her own eyes. It is difficult to help a friend until you understand how she sees the problem, the causes, and how she envisions supportive remedies.

But when a *stranger* violates accepted scripts for how to behave, a different scenario unfolds. We will soon introduce you to Shirl, a black single mother who occasionally spanks her three-year-old son, Martin, when he wets his pants, and who refuses to let him play with dolls. You will meet Helena, who went back to work to get off welfare, then quit her full-time job to spend more time with her four-year-old daughter. You will get to know Kathy, who made good money working nights as a cocktail waitress but who, when she got into cocaine, had to give up her two-year-old son while she entered a residential drug rehab program. Such behavior on the part of strangers prompts all sorts of theories about their values and motivations. But observers rarely summon the energy to ask them for an explanation. Unlike diagnostics with friends, people seldom dig deeply to understand the context of and reasons for the actions of strangers.

Policy makers and scholars show a similar aversion to engaging in a dialogue with strangers who struggle in poverty, especially when they are single mothers with young children. Reformers and politicians form their own opinions about why low-income mothers don't return to work after having a baby. Teachers complain that single parents fail to read to their youngsters at home. These professionals, perceiving actions that are not in the family's best interests, offer their *own* diagnoses, claiming to understand the causes of such "reprehensible" actions. Intellectually they know that the behavior of single mothers in poverty is linked to the exigencies of their surrounding contexts. Yet at an emotional level they may feel that these behaviors and attitudes are just strange.

Concerned experts craft remedies based on these diagnoses from afar. Welfare reform comes in recurring waves from Washington every few years. Head Start and other preschool subsidies grow in fits and starts. Education and job-training programs are expanded for impoverished women. Fathers are pressed to fork over child-support payments. Yet activists and academics rarely listen carefully to how "the problem" is understood by the "victims." The behavior of parents within low-income families—from their attitudes toward work to the way they raise their children—remains strange in the eye of the beholder.

In writing this book we are motivated by a singular aim: to ensure that mothers and their young children living at the edge of poverty will no longer be faceless strangers. This book is an invitation to get to know fourteen of these women and to learn about their lives.

In recent years, debate has grown louder over the apparent deterioration of "family values," rising rates of births to single mothers, and the social and economic disintegration of the country's inner cities. Well-intentioned reformers on both the political Right and the political Left assign all kinds of bleak, even pathological meanings to these strangers' actions. After three decades of costly research *on* impoverished families, analysts have shed little empirical light *inside* their households. Rarely do we hear the voices of these women and see—

through their own eyes—how they view the struggle to hold a job, raise a young child, and negotiate the social welfare labyrinth.

One example from the recent literature on families in poverty is David Ellwood's *Poor Support*. An important analysis of poverty in America, it contains numerous charts describing the demographic ins and outs of poor households. Many of Ellwood's arguments, further developed after he became President Clinton's family poverty advisor, provided the starting points for welfare reform. But the book contains no evidence on how single mothers, who account for 95 percent of all welfare recipients, view their world and how they construct meaning and motivation within their daily lives. How can policy makers, welfare managers, and child-care experts claim to help impoverished families, in part through altering their social practices and cultural norms, when these parents remain strangers?

Since the Great Society's attempt to strengthen poor households, Americans have expressed wildly vacillating political sentiments over how, and even whether, to help poor families. Some on the political Left and moderates paint disturbing portraits of poor families with a very broad brush in order to justify calls for more jobs and more effective family supports. Alternatively, the conservative Right swerves between blaming poor families for their plight and advocating the use of tax credits and vouchers for the working poor, confident that inner-city parents are their own best guides out of poverty. Democrats and Republicans alike now speak of empowerment as the pivotal salvation, although they debate the meaning of the concept and fight over which level of government should deliver the poor from evil. Everyone is for empowerment. But empowering strangers? How can policy fixes hope to do that?

The American Family's Steady Demise

When it comes to addressing the problems of American families, many people make the mistake of assuming that the troubling statistics they read in the newspapers apply only to a small and remote segment of the population. They fail to recognize that the problems associated with economic uncertainty are strikingly close to home. Consider these facts:

- Nearly one-third of all infants are born to unmarried mothers, an eightfold increase since 1940. One in eight babies has a teenage mother. In many urban centers, such as New York City, Cleveland, and St. Louis, the majority of babies are now born to single parents.

- Almost two-thirds of all children will live with just one biological parent at some point before they reach age eighteen. Among children living with a single parent, one-third have no contact with their fathers.

- These strains on the family are found across diverse ethnic groups. The share of white marriages ending in divorce by middle age approaches the rate for blacks, more than one-third by age fifty. One-fifth of all Anglo mothers give birth out of wedlock. Twenty-nine percent of Latino families are headed by a single parent.

- Children living in single-parent homes are much more likely than children in two-parent homes to suffer from the constraints of poverty: almost half of all black and one-fourth of all white female-headed households live below the poverty line. The share of children living in poverty has crept steadily upward since the 1960s.

- Rising labor-force participation by women has placed enormous pressure on child-care and preschool systems. By 1990 more than half of all women with infants were working in the labor force. In 1996 more than half of all toddlers, age eighteen to twenty-four months, spent part of each week with a nonparental child-care provider. This proportion continues to rise. These sharp increases in demand have strained the supply and quality of child care.[1]

The recent War on Welfare illustrates that many politicians are also tempted to depict family poverty as limited to a marginal group of irresponsible parents. They argue that incentives to stay jobless and on welfare have eroded essential family values within low-income communities. What is needed, the theory goes, is "tough love," a swift kick to the backsides of single mothers to get them to move back into the workforce. But will family poverty go away simply by cutting benefits to those who are unemployed? The symptoms of family poverty are multiple and the causes difficult to remedy. As the clamor over family values and single parenthood grows louder, the political will to address family poverty has grown more fragile. Splashy political symbols rather than long-term solutions are the rule. The creation of a wedge between "us" and "them" scores political points. It further estranges single women in poverty from mainstream opportunities and from gaining simple respect. Meanwhile, the conditions of low-income families— whether residing in urban, suburban, or rural America—only grow worse.

Since the 1960s many policy makers have accumulated political capital by criticizing the absence of motivation or "family values" among impoverished individuals, rather than taking seriously the economic contexts and plural cultural patterns found within low-income groups. The popular notion of "empowerment" is rooted in the neoclassical belief that economic incentives—cash transfers, tax credits, and vouchers for welfare services—will coax the poor parent back to work. The sticking point is that millions of poor families are now headed by single women who have young children. Economic survival is an obvious goal for these women. But we will illuminate how they, just like middle-class mothers, worry about their children's need for parental involvement. Also, these women will express the fulfillment and warmth they feel as they raise their young children. Does this seem so strange? When affluent women decide to stay at home with their preschoolers, we express understanding and admiration. When a poor black woman or Latina engages in the same action, she's often accused of lacking a work ethic and displaying excessive "dependency."

The individual-centered discourse from both the Left and the Right over the causes of and antidotes to poverty ignores the power of the social context in which different poor families live. In this opening chapter we aim to place single mothers within their complex settings— what we call *competing cultures of poverty*. We highlight the fact that this particular study stems from emerging research on the varied pathways available to parents as they raise their children. These social channels can vary substantially among ethnic groups, among communities, and among kin networks within the same neighborhood. According to several women with whom we talked, for example, it was normatively accepted that they would stay on AFDC (Aid to Families with Dependent Children) while their children were young. But there was less agreement about the legitimacy of accepting assistance for more than a few months. Similarly, some women took it for granted that their own mothers or perhaps aunts were the best people to take care of their young children; others pushed to find a school-like setting in hopes of boosting their children's educational achievement.

There is no single culture of poverty. There are many. Some parents hold beliefs about the meaning of work and child rearing that lead to strategies for moving out of poverty. Other models lead to dead ends, offering no clear path out. The fourteen women in our study brought to light both sets of cultural routes.

Myths and Explanations of Single Mothers in Poverty

Casting stones at poor women has become a rewarding political sport. They have too many babies; they remain dependent upon welfare checks for too long; they don't properly prepare their children for entering school; they perpetuate poverty from generation to generation. But polls show that many voters are drawn to political leaders who call for a reinvigoration of traditional American virtues: personal responsibility, independence, and hard work. And these modern-day social monsters— single mothers, welfare recipients, and immigrants— are portrayed as failing to uphold such ideals.

Dominant Mythologies

To frame and define comparative points of reference for interpreting the fourteen women's stories, let us delineate the dominant mythologies that shape current representations of poor families.

Myth 1. Single mothers on welfare are all alike and they're not like us. Many Americans see themselves as members of the vast middle class, and draw a sharp line between themselves and those who fall into poverty. Impoverished single women were not always considered strangers, however: in previous decades they were often viewed sympathetically as unfortunate victims of spousal death or desertion. Ironically, government relief once aimed to ensure that mothers *not* work but stay at home with the children until they grew older.[2] Now single mothers in poverty are more often stigmatized and stereotyped, especially when they opt to stay home with their children. Even though about 60 percent of welfare recipients leave the rolls within two years, they are frequently identified as laggards or portrayed as eager to have more babies and lacking the motivation to piece together a better life. A leading Republican in the Congress recently voiced opposition to modest tax credits for working-poor families, arguing that recipients would just use the money "to buy TVs."

Early poverty scholars are partially to blame for such broad-brushed portraits of the poor. In the late 1950s, the anthropologist Oscar Lewis began studying poor families in Manhattan and Mexico. He began using an overarching term—*the culture of poverty*—to emphasize not only that family poverty is caused by economic hardship but that destructive social norms arise that calcify into stable personality traits reproduced in successive generations. According to this view, impoverished adults feel hopeless, perceive themselves as having no control over their lives, and expect little help or commitment from family or friends. Michael Harrington popularized this imagery of a monolithic culture of poverty in his book *The Other America* (1963), which strongly influenced the War on Poverty architects brought to Washington by President Kennedy. Harrington wrote, "Poverty in the United States is a culture, an institution, a way of life," and he argued that poor communities were populated by "those who, for reasons beyond their control, cannot help themselves" (pp. 22–23).[3] Academics and activists seized on this portrayal, designing social programs targeted on "culturally deprived" families and "disadvantaged" children who needed to become more like middle-class youngsters. Today medical terminology is often invoked to describe lower-class families: they exhibit "risk factors" that warrant "intervention" from public institutions.

According to the culture-of-poverty myth, the remedy for these "at-risk" families involves changing how they see work and how they raise their children. Through a panoply of services—delivered by welfare workers, Head Start teachers, counselors, and home visitors—the state will explain the right way to live, the optimal way of bringing up a child. In this way, the story goes, single mothers will be lifted up and out of the thick, constricting culture of poverty.

Myth 2. Single mothers will be motivated to join the mainstream only when job opportunities open up. Many Americans do not blame the female victims of poverty. They focus instead on inequalities that characterize the women's economic and social contexts. According to this second argument, poor families are not all that different from those in the middle class; they simply lack sufficient job opportunities and income. If the opportunity structure were more open and fair, poor and ethnic-minority parents would be able to pursue the American Dream. Unless they are invited into the mainstream, they will not play by the rules; there are few rewards for doing so.

This line of argument questions the assumption that culture is the culprit and asks whether the worsening of poverty isn't due to the steady decline of jobs and social vitality within America's central cities. A more textured and optimistic portrait of low-income families is sketched. Poor families seem more familiar; the underlying suggestion is that anyone would adapt in a similar way to the exigencies they face day in and day out. When job opportunities open up and racial discrimination is held at bay, poor parents will join the mainstream.

This contextual explanation requires that broad policy remedies be undertaken to create jobs and redistribute income. Affirmative action programs, for example, stem from a focus on structural barriers, particularly the unequal availability of jobs and high-quality educational opportunities in low-income communities. According to proponents of this view, such as the sociologist William Julius Wilson, when the windows of economic opportunity are opened more widely, poor parents will quickly move into the fresh air of jobs and social mobility.[4] Similarly, the mobilization of tax dollars to improve inner-city schools has yielded rising achievement scores among many black and Latino children.[5]

But these 1960s-style strategies have not been completely successful in alleviating poverty. In the 1980s more than eighteen million new jobs were created in the national economy, and spending on poverty programs rose 44 percent. But family poverty rates remained static, even rising in some years.[6] Economic growth has slowed but not stopped the rate at which families fall into poverty. The layers of social classes that have long characterized American society persist. The vast expansion of social services, educational opportunities, and other structural remedies has failed to combat successfully the family's decline. Why don't more families respond to positive supports provided by public agencies? In what ways is poverty perpetuated by deep-seated motivations and scripted behaviors of individual parents?

Myth 3. Government can empower single mothers by restructuring the incentives for remaining employed. Of late, the ways in which we portray low-income women have become entangled with many Americans' skepticism over whether bureaucratic government can effectively lift families out of poverty. The politically moderate position centers on empowering poor families to find their own pathways out of poverty. This policy remedy rests on the assumption that these parents are just as rational as those in the middle class. Economic incentives simply need to be arranged better to encourage work, marriage, and personal responsibility. Rather than building bigger welfare agencies to ameliorate the symptoms of family poverty, government should move income to those willing to work, reward initiative, and open up choices (by providing housing and child-care vouchers, for example). This strategy is built on the assumption that the latent resources and skills possessed by poor families will blossom if incentives are structured appropriately. Parents can rise out of the cultural quagmire and find their own route to the American Dream if they are rewarded for their effort. Within this view, the individual single mother or family unit is the exclusive object of attention; cultural norms and practices are given little consideration. This is a culture-less conception of individual motivation.

Over the past twenty-five years, this portrayal of the rational family in poverty has led to several important policy remedies. Income supplements for poor households with a working member began in the 1960s and were based on the ideas of Daniel Patrick Moynihan, then a poverty advisor in the Nixon White House. Based on the neoclassical assumption that the family will respond to economic carrots, tax credits are provided to parents who remain employed while struggling to stay above the poverty line. These tax credits, averaging $1,400 per household, aided more than 14 million working-poor families in 1996. Another remedy is federal child-care assistance in the form of vouchers awarded to single mothers who return to work or enter a job-training program. Other policies, from housing vouchers to opportunities for school choice, are being used to expand the options available to low-income families. This quiet, antibureaucratic revolution in poverty policy is built upon the economists' assumption that poor families will respond to clear incentives for being upwardly mobile—and become even more like the middle class.[7]

A second version of the empowerment paradigm focuses on disincentives. Under this variant, poor families are still viewed as rational economically, but social-welfare programs are seen as disincentives, discouraging the four million beneficiaries who are single mothers from going back to work. After the Republicans gained control of the Congress in 1994, a second claim gained credible-myth status (with no empirical evidence put forward): unmarried women have additional babies to obtain increases in their welfare checks. Even centrists like President Clinton backed a reform requiring teenage mothers to live at home as a condition for receiving welfare assistance, their argument being that providing independent income for young adults splits apart families. This version of empowerment emphasizes cutting "welfare dependency" and killing off the resulting contagion of negative behaviors that spread through poor neighborhoods. These arguments moved Congress in 1996 to eliminate the New Deal entitlement of aid to impoverished women, permitting states to cut AFDC spending 20 percent by the century's end.

Family empowerment without bureaucracy is a seductive myth. Ironically, conservatives, who tout the power of market forces to motivate the poor, have created a moralistic role for government. The empowerment model contains a mixed message: widen parents' choices while rewarding certain behaviors that are deemed to be in the public interest. Call it *guided empowerment*. When impoverished mothers return to work, enter job training, or enroll their youngsters in child-care organizations, they become eligible for additional benefits. The poor individual is now directly linked to the state and must abide by the moral signals dictated by government. The powerful cultural role of the individual's family, kin, and neighborhood is largely forgotten, reinforcing the policy maker's illusion that women's motivation can be manipulated from afar through economic incentives.

Context, Constraints, and Choices

Political support broadens when government—building on neoclassical, pro-choice assumptions—crafts policies that require less bureaucracy and espouse faith that poor individuals will respond to economic incentives. Policy makers and ordinary citizens focus on concrete choices that poor families should make: getting a job, selecting a good preschool, and raising a child "the right way." But getting to these choices depends upon the cultural models and available pathways that define and channel parents' actions. It also depends on the surrounding context: families who live in neighborhoods where shootings, child abuse, and drug deals are commonplace may be less likely to encourage their youngsters to be curious, to ask lots of questions, or to challenge adult authority. This book is dedicated to understanding how parents draw on cultural models available within their communities, making "choices" that are conditioned by the opportunities and barriers found within these settings. The voices of the fourteen women in this book are clear and strong: they illuminate the truthful elements of these theorized representations and expose their mythical sides as well.

In 1991 we selected fourteen low-income mothers in the Boston area who had at least one child under age five. All but one had relied on AFDC for several months following the birth of a child. Most drew AFDC benefits for less than two years. All but one had returned to work or school by the beginning of the study. Those successful in finding work nevertheless remained at or below the poverty line. Their involvement with the welfare system continued as they obtained such services as child-care subsidies, Head Start placement, and food stamps. A few had longer-term involvement with state agencies as a result of involvement with drugs or charges of child neglect. These fourteen women were pushing hard, despite stark financial constraints, to achieve a better life, hold down a job, and care for their children.

We visited the homes and workplaces of these women over a three-year period. We conducted wide-ranging interviews and participated in less formal conversations as well. We invited them to write in journals about their daily activities and feelings. At the end of this process we had more than 1,900 pages of transcribed conversations. The chapters that follow describe the lives of these fourteen mothers and report on the indigenous meanings that they assign to the human acts of working, raising young children, and negotiating the complex world of social welfare.

Next we turn to our framework for understanding the variable beliefs and assumptions about work and child rearing that serve as fundamental building blocks for these women's everyday actions. We describe how our approach departs sharply from the "culture-of-poverty" portrayals that characterized an earlier generation of scholarship. We will show how these fourteen women's models of belief and behavior guide their lives in two crucial domains, work and child rearing. We will highlight the dynamic qualities of these models as they are resculpted in response to pathways suggested by friends, kin, and caring community workers.

Discovering the Family's Cultural Foundations

Parenting involves *cultural processes*. We draw on the idea of *cultural models* to capture women's tacit conceptions of what constitutes "proper" approaches to finding work, raising one's child, and negotiating high-quality preschooling. These models or sequences of accepted actions are embedded in their roles as the sole breadwinner and primary parent. Cultural models are defined by Naomi Quinn and Dorothy Holland as "presupposed, taken-for-granted models of the world that are widely shared (although not necessarily to the exclusion of other, alternative models) by members of a society and that play an enormous role in their understanding of that world and their behavior in it."[8] This notion is linked to the anthropologist Ward Goodenough's original insight that individuals in all bounded cultural groups learn how to behave and speak in ways that make sense and appear legitimate to fellow members. One's membership and social standing depend on one's following these beliefs and expected forms of behavior. According to Quinn and Holland, cultural models "frame experience, supplying interpretations of that experience and inferences about it, and goals for action."[9]

These models pertain both to the individual's folk understanding about how reality works, and to how that person would like to influence desired outcomes in the future. Clifford Geertz sees these deep-seated cultural models as providing a map for what is "common sense" within a group—unquestioned, practical, and widely understood scripts that guide everyday motivations and actions.[10] They offer sequential, often scripted steps down a pathway that apparently leads to an intended outcome, be it maximizing the household's income, finding a safe place for one's infant, or strategizing over how one's child should be raised to get ahead in the future.

Cultural models are acquired or formulated by individuals within their immediate social contexts. The local community may be defined by ethnicity, immediate kin members and friends, or position in the social class structure. The cultural "scripts" or models that are most salient in local neighborhoods—for example, when to get on AFDC or what type of baby-sitter is the most trustworthy—may certainly vary *among* social classes or ethnic groups. But diverse, even competing cultural models circulate *within* the same low-income communities, offering alternative scripts and pathways that can be followed.

Sometimes tacit goals or beliefs become explicit. They are no longer taken for granted. We will discuss, for example, how these women debate, with kin and female friends, how long one can legitimately remain on AFDC after giving birth. The normative role played by fathers is contested in their communities. We will discuss how Aggie learned from a social worker to wait three minutes before yelling at her misbehaving son, and how Kathy came to see that the opportunities for play in her son's Head Start classroom actually led to learning. In these cases, taken-for-granted—that is, cultural—models became conscious and contested. Certain behavioral scripts became *declared models* in the sense that they were publicly debated and declared to be the best alternative.[11]

By following these fourteen women over time, we saw how novel cultural norms penetrate indigenous beliefs about work and child rearing. Low-income mothers frequently interact with coworkers on the job and with family professionals, including their welfare caseworkers and Head Start teachers. Through these interactions they are nudged to reflect on their roles as wage-earners and mothers. These new models do not always fit neatly with the old. Particular social norms, symbols, and forms of status sanctioned within the community come together in each family, composing competing cultures of poverty. The result for low-income women is neither unthinking reproduction of indigenous norms and practices nor mindless absorption of professional advice from welfare caseworkers and early childhood experts. We saw an active process in which beliefs and practices were co-constructed by these women and those in their environment.

A final issue emerged during the course of our conversations. Are cultural models bounded or organized in particular ways within the confines of ethnic boundaries? Does race matter? Is ethnic membership important in forecasting and understanding the core beliefs and commitments of low-income women? Many of the fourteen consciously pondered the "bicultural" character of their lives, roles, and child-rearing practices. The Latinas, in particular, reproduced some of the parenting practices tacitly expected in their neighborhoods, including speaking Spanish to their children and inculcating in them a deferential respect for adult authority. Because they were either first- or second-generation immigrants, they could easily compare the social norms found "back home" with those that dominate in the United States. But in the interests of bettering their lot in life, they also selected ideas and behaviors that better fit them and their children into middle-class Anglo institutions, from workplaces to preschools.

The African-American mothers we interviewed rarely attributed their beliefs and actions to racial or ethnic membership. We did hear about crucial social phenomena, such as very low expectations that fathers would participate meaningfully in children's lives, that were shared by all the black mothers. But these women themselves did not usually characterize their views as rooted in racial identity. In several chapters, we will return to this issue of whether ethnic boundaries distinguish particular cultural or declared models of action, or whether social-class similarities eclipse ethnic similarities.

A Single Culture of Poverty?

Claims about the cultural character of poor families have flowed freely in the myths and models created by politicians and scholars since the 1960s. The pivotal claim that poverty's ills are driven and reproduced over time by *cultural* rather than *economic* forces goes back to the early work of Oscar Lewis. In 1961 Lewis published the influential book *The Children of Sanchez*, which documented in vivid detail the plight of impoverished Mexican families. He described how parents struggled to feed and educate their young children amid squalor, disintegrating kin structures, and long-term economic depression. Five years later, Lewis published similar evidence from New York City's Puerto Rican community, showing how the deep-seated, cultural elements of poverty were reproduced across generations.

To this day, policy makers and researchers often use a culture-of-poverty lens to interpret the problems of poor families. This interpretive framework is a simple and seductive way of explaining their plight and the cultural forces that apparently constrain their lives. The founding principles of Head Start, articulated in 1965, reflected how pervasive the "cultural deprivation" imagery had become: "For the child of poverty there are clearly observable deficiencies in the processes which lay the foundation for a pattern of failure." One important book, published in 1965 by Benjamin Bloom and colleagues, had the telling title *Compensatory Education for Cultural Deprivation*.[12]

The culture-of-poverty imagery helped to mobilize the political will necessary in mounting the War on Poverty. But only a few policy makers or poverty researchers questioned whether the paradigm truly represented the actual lives of the families at which this war was aimed. In recent times the language of cultural deprivation has been softened, but it remains in the persistent use of such terms as "children at risk" and "disadvantaged." Leading family professionals rarely question whether their tacit conceptions of optimal child-rearing scripts should be universally applied to all families, or whether non–middle-class contexts require different cultural assumptions. They frequently assume that their scripts and values are *culture free* and functional in all local settings. Parents who raise children differently are often viewed as ignorant or irrational; they are seen as putting their children's development in jeopardy.

Cross-Cultural Windows into Diverse Families

A more penetrating—and empirically grounded—avenue of research began to take root during the late 1950s. This line of inquiry is now helping us push beyond culture-less and context-free portrayals of family action. It has focused on understanding how and why parents in different settings approach their roles as economic providers and parents in different ways. Pioneering anthropologists, including Beatrice and John Whiting and Robert and Sarah LeVine, began to study how mothers in various cultural contexts interacted with their infants and young children. These scholars were less interested in the dysfunctional facets of family processes under materially impoverished conditions than in how child-rearing practices were reproduced *and* how they were adapted to modernizing influences over time. They found that some cultural models guiding child socialization persisted in the face of rapid modernization while other family practices changed rapidly along with the economic transformations. In some indigenous communities, for instance, parents adopted the individualistic achievement orientation of colonial residents, encouraging their children to perform well within Western schools and become upwardly mobile within modernizing job structures.[13]

This approach to understanding the dynamics of parenting in poor communities contributed greatly to the expanding field of cultural psychology, which now focuses on ethnic or impoverished groups within industrialized societies as well. Three key assumptions distinguish cross-cultural family studies from the parallel culture-of-poverty line and its accompanying mythology. First, the effects of economic poverty are carefully disentangled from those of cultural practices. Many local communities are impoverished in material terms, but their cultural fabric remains strong and cohesive in terms of kinship support and strong parental commitments to children. Latino families in the United States are a case in point: despite high levels of poverty, most households remain intact. Cross-cultural family studies recognize that cultural practices can operate somewhat independently of economic conditions.

Second, cross-cultural family studies examine the linkages of features of the social and economic context to parental goals and parenting strategies. Barbara Rogoff, for example, has argued that the nature of mother-child communication in rural Guatemala is affected by the close proximity of children to their parents as they participate in their daily work, in contrast to North America, where work and family activities occur in separate locations.[14] William Corsaro examines connections between social structures and practices in preschools, describing how Italian youngsters are encouraged to develop skills in self-expression that are consonant with the collective commitments expected in Italian society.[15] However, most cultural psychologists do not take the functionalist view that *all* child-rearing practices derive from contextual or economic exigencies. They argue that cultural habits may persist even when they are not functional within a broader social context.

Third, traditional child-rearing practices are seen as potential contributors to positive outcomes for children, not as necessarily antithetical to the social rules of modern institutions. In Japan, for example, early child socialization at home and in preschools is often permissive—sharply violating Americans' belief in the efficacy of firm guidance during children's early years. But Japanese socialization produces children whose achievement in school is notably higher than that of Americans.[16]

In contrast to the assumptions of cultural psychologists, policy makers often assume that families should adopt middle-class social rules that are legitimated by academic experts and enforced in schools and workplaces. Seminars on "multiculturalism" abound, but most prescriptive writings are limited to strategies for promoting smooth relations among children of different ethnic backgrounds. The possibility that welfare or preschool professionals might actually *learn and build* from the cultural routines of parents outside the American middle class remains an exotic notion.

Rich and Competing Cultures of Poverty

The culture-of-poverty paradigm can help illuminate how family poverty and welfare dependency are reproduced over successive generations. But the model is of little utility in revealing success stories—the processes by which some families achieve upward mobility. In recent years, a growing number of scholars have challenged the culture-of-poverty model in order to learn why some parents in low-income communities succeed against the odds in propelling their children out of their impoverished communities. Elijah Anderson's long-term ethnographic study of inner-city Philadelphia shows that multiple family values and behavioral pathways operate within even the most economically depressed communities. Anderson documents how young African-American males struggle to choose between "street" and "decent" adult role models, and how kinship linkages vary in their strength and resourcefulness.[17] Hugh Mehan has described how students face choices between achievement-oriented peer groups and oppositional cliques that actively resist teachers and school authorities.[18]

Cross-cultural studies have also provided thoughtful descriptions of how low-income parents react to the *cultural agenda* advanced by preschool teachers, social workers, and other social service providers. Carole Joffe's path-breaking work in the 1970s detailed how the aims of white middle-class nursery school teachers in Berkeley conflicted sharply with low-income black parents' expectations about what their children should be learning at school.[19] Other kinds of cultural conflicts were explored by Caroline Zinsser in her recent study of child care within a working-class Italian community. The older Italian-American women who provided much of the family day care focused on providing a safe, clean, familiar environment. The younger generation of parents, as well as the professional newcomers to the community, expected child care that offered cognitive stimulation and preparation for school.[20] This evidence reveals sharp conflicts that can arise within a single community concerning assumptions of how children should be raised.

Plural Pathways out of Poverty

The salient cultural models that we describe—stemming from the voices of the fourteen women—display two countervailing properties. Some models are taken to be the "normal" or "obvious" ways children should be treated. They are widely understood and accepted by all adults within these women's communities.

But in counterpoint, a subset of these models is not taken for granted within the community. Rather, a number of alternative scripts may be available within the same context. Such contradictory models become subject to *conscious scrutiny* rather than to unthinking acceptance. To emphasize the process of evaluation and selection, we term these "declared models."[21] For example, our study illustrates that some of the fourteen women's cultural models pertaining to "how to be a mother" were reproductions of models acquired from their own parents. Most had been raised by employed mothers and expected to return to work well before their children entered school. But they also viewed AFDC as a legitimate means of temporary assistance after the birth of a child. Twelve of the fourteen women applied for welfare soon after they became pregnant. This sequence of actions was a highly credible model for mothers in their low-income communities. The moral significance of staying on AFDC for more than a few months was quite variable among the fourteen, however. Several voiced strong criticism of mothers who stayed on AFDC after having a baby instead of going back to work. Long-term reliance on welfare was not a widely supported model, and it prompted debate and disagreement within these communities.

We heard many stories about situations where the circulation of competing models of child rearing and the introduction of novel pathways for improving children's chances of academic success encouraged women to reflect on alternative routes out of poverty. The African-American mothers focused on how to get their youngsters into Boston's Metco initiative, a voluntary busing program that allows inner-city youngsters to attend suburban schools. Preschool teachers were often helpful in suggesting alternative approaches to disciplining children. One mother became more confident about setting limits for her son's behavior after his teacher challenged her to stop viewing his aggressiveness as an inborn, unchangeable personality trait. Another mother expressed relief when a Head Start teacher showed her alternatives to corporal punishment when trying to calm her four-year-old son. These alternative child-rearing practices and longer-term educational strategies were particularly significant because these women faced numerous constraints, mostly economic, on what they could do to improve their children's chances of success in life.

We do not mean to echo the dominant myth that most poor single mothers are radically different from wealthier parents. But the surroundings of low-income women with young children depart from typical middle-class contexts in many important respects. The fourteen women faced enormous pressure to maintain a minimal income, often through a combination of work and welfare. If scripted entrées into AFDC or child-care subsidies are highly credible in these neighborhoods, it is because these sources of income or services are necessary for basic survival. Undesirable alternatives include returning to abusive kin members or finding a homeless shelter, as a few of the fourteen will describe. Another common facet of their experience was the threat of violence. One mother removed her older child from the neighborhood primary school after a gunman entered the school on two different occasions and started shooting in the hallways. Several women reported concern over sexual abuse in child-care centers as a result of several highly publicized cases in the Boston area. The power of local surroundings, and the ways in which cultural models and credible pathways adapt to these contextual demands, should not be underestimated.

This book speaks to policy makers, professionals, educators, and community activists concerned with how to assist families living in poverty. Another audience is the growing number of child-care direc-

tors, teachers, and aides who work within Head Start and other preschool programs serving low-income parents. This increasingly includes public school administrators and teachers. As educators examine
the role of preschools in preparing children for later schooling, the
notion of "readiness" has become increasingly contentious. By portray-
ing the diversity of goals and values held by parents outside the middle
class, we challenge the received wisdom that making the poor look
more like "us" is the optimal remedy. Finally, we speak to researchers
and other academics interested in challenging current representations
of "the poor family." The dominant mythology about impoverished
households is becoming less tenable, but it still forms the foundation
for policy approaches that are often costly and ineffective. We hope
this book sensitively portrays what women in poverty see when they
reflect upon their daily lives and the choices that seem within their
reach. As you learn about the differing cultures of poverty through the
eyes of these fourteen women, you may come to feel that each woman
is no longer a stranger.

CHAPTER TWO

Fourteen Poor Women, Fourteen Rich Lives

Three of the fourteen women we interviewed will appear in this chapter. Their commitment to work and financial independence is striking, as are their child-rearing goals and their capacity simply to persevere. They begin by describing their circumstances, which are often marked by economic uncertainty and social fragility. The complexity of how they adapt and fight back, given the exigencies and uneven support found in their immediate surroundings, dispels the simplistic portrayals of the dominant mythology. These women display toughness, resilience, and resourcefulness.

In introducing Kathy, Selma, and Shirl, we highlight the areas of their lives upon which this book focuses: How do they define and pursue work? What are their goals and practices in raising their young children? How do they maneuver through the child-care and social-welfare maze? These important aspects of their lives are best understood against a broad backdrop—a complex pastiche drawn from their own biographies, their kin and social networks, and what they value in their own lives and in those of their children.

We begin by reviewing basic demographic characteristics of all fourteen women and their Boston-area neighborhoods. We then focus on three—Kathy, Selma, and Shirl—who exhibit the diversity of backgrounds and values we observed across the fourteen. Their stories reveal diverse understandings as to how they should organize their lives, particularly how they should see the two conflicting roles of mother and economic provider. Finally, we will outline the methods we used to select and get to know these fourteen women.

Mothers and Children in Competing Cultures of Poverty: An Overview

In 1991 we began a search for women living in poor or working-class sections of Boston. To find participants, we obtained referrals from child-care directors and staff in community agencies, and posted notices on bulletin boards in neighborhood schools. Within a few months we had enlisted fourteen women who were committed to talking with us on many different occasions over a long stretch of time. Each was paid following an interview or a home visit, as well as for keeping a written journal.

A brief sketch of the group can be found in Table 2.1. All but one went on AFDC just prior to giving birth. All but one subsequently went off welfare and joined the ranks of the working poor, meaning that they earned under $20,000 a year and drew some subsidies and services, such as housing vouchers or child-care subventions. When we first met these women, four lived with the father of their youngest child, the youngster on which our study focused. Three years later, two of these couples had split up and one father was living only sporadically with the family. Two of the fourteen women had lived in homeless shelters with their infants; one temporarily lost custody of her children during a period of drug addiction and subsequent rehabilitation. Another woman was involved with the Massachusetts Department of Social Services (DSS) throughout the three years of our study because she was accused of physically neglecting her son.

When we first visited these women in 1992, they ranged in age from twenty-three to thirty-five. Half of the fourteen had no more than a high school education. The other half had attended one year of community college or a vocational school. The youngest child of each woman—the "target child"—averaged three and one-half years of age.

ble 2.1   Fourteen mothers in poor Boston-area neighborhoods (basic characteristics at first contact, 1991–1992)

other's name	Age	Schooling in years	Target child's name	Child's gender and age
rican-American women				
Shirl	24	13	Martin	boy, age 2
Brenda	23	13	Cora	girl, age 3
Harriet	33	12	Shondra	girl, age 3
Jackie	30	11	Tiffany	girl, age 3
Pamela	26	13	Cedric	boy, age 4
Wilma	31	13	Janis	girl, age 2
nglo women				
Kathy	28	10	Darren	boy, age 3
Aggie	27	12	Fred	boy, age 4
Helena	31	11	Shawna	girl, age 3
Pat	35	13	Joshua	boy, age 4
atinas				
Selma	27	12	Zumary	girl, age 4
Beatriz	27	13	Jorge	boy, age 1
Delmy	29	14	Carla	girl, age 4
Sol	29	13	Elena	girl, age 2

Four Diverse Neighborhoods

The women lived in four economically depressed or working-class areas of Boston. At the beginning of the study, the six African-American mothers resided in either Dorchester or Roxbury. One of the Anglo mothers, Aggie, had moved from Dorchester to the western suburbs of Boston with a housing voucher just before our interviews began in 1992.

Dorchester is a diverse community, dotted with a mix of Victorians, "triple-deckers" in which three different families often reside, and old apartment buildings. Dorchester is a twenty-minute bus ride from the skyscrapers and plush hotels of downtown Boston. But the average income of Dorchester residents is quite low, with about half of all families earning less than $20,000 annually in the poorest sections (Table 2.2). Dorchester is becoming increasingly diverse ethnically: the poorest section is 80 percent black; the less impoverished area is 19 percent black.[1]

Table 2.2   Variable poverty levels in four Boston-area communities (zip code data, 1990 census)

Community zip code	Black residents (%)	Latino residents (%)	Households earning <$20,000 (%)	Households headed by single mothers (%)	Household head with no more than high school education (%)
Dorchester					
02121	90	12	47	25	41
02122	19	8	33	13	39
02124	59	9	35	18	37
02125	30	16	37	15	39
East Boston-Chelsea					
02128	2	17	44	10	51
02150	5	30	43	15	44
Roxbury					
02118	34	18	42	11	31
02119	73	21	52	24	40
02120	44	24	47	18	32
Somerville-East Cambridge					
02143	7	6	30	4	36
02144	4	3	24	3	30
02145	7	9	32	7	43

Source: Bureau of the Census (1993), *Census of Population and Housing: Equal Employment Opportunity File* (CD90-EEO, CD-ROM), Washington, D.C.

Roxbury is a more consistently depressed inner-city environment just south of the working-class Fenway Park area. The crime rate is very high. Roxbury residents live in old apartment buildings or public housing projects. The residents of Roxbury are also becoming more diverse. The poorest section, in which 52 percent of all families earn less than $20,000 each year, is split between black households (73 percent) and a rising number of Latino families (21 percent).

Two of the four Latina mothers lived in the East Boston-Chelsea area, an industrial and harbor community close to Logan Airport. Many immigrants from Latin America and the Caribbean have settled there. Spanish is heard on the streets and in the plentiful *bodegas*. Indeed, a language other than English is spoken in more than 40 percent of all households. But this dynamic culture is embedded in economic poverty. About half of all adult residents never went beyond high school. Almost one-fourth of all families live below the poverty line, and half of these are headed by women.

Three of the Anglo mothers and two Latinas lived just across the Charles River from Boston in working-class Somerville or sections of Cambridge near Central Square. Here the crime rate is about 25 percent above the statewide average. In Somerville about 10 percent of all households are below the poverty line. This area is more vibrant economically than Dorchester and Roxbury. Immigration into the Somerville area is changing the city's character; almost one-fourth of all residents are foreign born.

Kathy: Growing Up with Uncertainty

At age twenty-eight, Kathy is tall and thin, with long blond hair and eyes dramatically rimmed with black liner. She is an outspoken woman bubbling with frenetic energy: "I'm a hyper person, that's what keeps me happy. I like to move all the time." In the winter she's out building a snowman with her son Darren. In the summer she volunteers to drive a gaggle of toddlers to the beach. Fifteen minutes rarely go by without Kathy's lighting up a cigarette. She speaks quickly and has strong opinions on most topics. She punctuates her assertions with a dramatic wave of her hands. Her blue eyes dart about, accentuating the rapid pace of her ideas and commentaries. A toughness and resolve are evident in her mannerisms. Commenting about friends who are on welfare, she exclaimed:

Some people are slowpokes. Some people actually take . . . like the world just stops when you have a child. Like that's *more* motivation to me, to go out and do stuff. Like Angela my friend, she's like [whining voice], "How do you do it?" I'm like, "You get off your ass, you find a baby-sitter." You get a job, and you go for it.

Kathy grew up in one of the triple-decker houses that line the streets of her working-class neighborhood, just outside Boston proper. Her father, a jovial and supportive Irish Catholic, anchored Kathy's life when she was a child:

We were best friends, me and my father. He was my best friend. Everybody was in love with my father. My mother's friends would

all come over . . . they were having problems with their husbands.
My father was a model husband and father.

Devoted to his family, Kathy's father started a one-car cab company,
Betty's Taxi, named after his wife. Kathy reminisced about watching
her mother dress up every Saturday night to go dancing with her father.
When her parents left for the evening, Kathy would put on her
mother's high heels and pretend that *she* was the mother of her young
siblings.

Kathy was indeed forced to step into her mother's shoes at age ten,
when her father suffered a fatal heart attack. The family received no
pension from the company where he had been employed. Kathy's
mother found a job working evenings to support her eight children.
Kathy spoke with pride about how she helped manage the family during
those years, especially in the evenings when her mother was at work.

Before her father's death, Kathy and her siblings attended a Catholic
elementary school that served other working-class kids. The nuns and
teachers there "cared about you," according to Kathy. But after Kathy's
father died, her mother could no longer afford to pay the tuition and
shifted the older children to public schools. At age twelve Kathy entered a public middle school:

> Nobody cared about you. [At the Catholic school] we all were A
> students . . . A or B students. And bang! As soon as [we entered]
> public schools, I was just a kid among thirty kids. They didn't
> know my name, they didn't know who I was, didn't know my life,
> they didn't care.

Midway through high school, Kathy decided, "I'm going to work, I'm
not going to waste my time here." In a precipitous transition to adult-
hood, she began waitressing at a bar:

> They didn't know how old I was . . . I always looked older than I
> was. My mother never said, like, be home at 11:00 o'clock. And
> never told me what to do . . . 'cause I was, I'm an adult. My mother
> just appreciated the fact that I was alive, because I was helping her,
> you know what I mean? So I just did what I wanted. I was a very
> responsible kid. Like I wasn't out like going crazy at all.

While still a teenager, Kathy enrolled in an evening GED class. But the program collapsed because of budget cuts. So Kathy continued to work at cocktail bars, live at home, and cook for her younger brothers. At nineteen, she decided to look for a different job, becoming a nanny for a professional couple:

> The lady was great, we had a great relationship. I worked with her, in Boston. And she needed a person to take care of her kids, so I quit my [waitressing] job and moved in, took care of her four kids. And one of them was as old as me! They didn't know I was only nineteen. I said I was twenty-six.

A Young Mother, Learning to Survive

Kathy became pregnant at age twenty-four. She had gone "searching" for the right man to father her child:

> I always wanted to have a baby. I went, well, searching. I went searching for somebody that really worked, that did not gamble, and I found this person. [He] was a hard worker, and I just . . . right into him! [laughs, then sighs]. Yeah, that was too quick. But the only thing is, if I didn't have Darren [her son], I'd probably be dead, you know?

Kathy and Darren's father, Jack, took an apartment near her mother's home when Darren was a newborn. Jack came from the same working-class community as Kathy and was one of ten children. By the time Darren had turned two, Jack and Kathy's relationship had begun to deteriorate, and Kathy "kicked him out." He returned home to live with his parents. Commenting on their relationship, Kathy noted:

> We definitely get along good, as long as he stays where he is and I stay here. He left a year ago, and it was really hard. He thought he was coming back; I was like, let me have some time. I needed to be alone! Like I said, I've always been alone, always been. I take care of myself, nobody takes care of me. I can't stand it when somebody takes care of me . . . then I have to take care of him on top of it.

Kathy found another job as a nanny, earning just five dollars an hour. She was proud of being chosen out of the eighteen people interviewed: "I impressed her. I know everything about kids, and she could just see that I was so secure." But Kathy was not so secure. She began drinking heavily and snorting cocaine. Not long after Jack's departure, Kathy recalled, "I called the cops on myself." She went to a hospital and Darren went to live with his father and paternal grandparents for three months. In one conversation Kathy emphatically denied that Darren was harmed by her involvement with drugs: "I was abusing myself, not my child."

Kathy's survival—and the quality of Darren's life—became intertwined with the state. Social workers from DSS enrolled Kathy in a detoxification program and began to supervise Darren's care at his grandparents' home. Kathy successfully kicked cocaine within a few months. Darren was able to return to his mother's comfortable two-bedroom apartment in a safe area across the Charles River from Boston. DSS kept Kathy's case open, in part because doing so would eventually allow her to benefit from subsidized child care.

By the time Darren turned three, Kathy had returned to cocktail waitressing at one of Boston's prestigious hotels, where she could certainly make more than five dollars an hour. And when she "hustled," the tips were even higher.

Raising a Young Child

Throughout these years, Kathy worked at piecing together an elaborate patchwork of child care for her son. He stayed with various members of her family at night, and went to his paternal grandparents' house on the weekends. During our first interview, Kathy expressed concern about the effects that having so many care providers would have on Darren: "[He has] three different ways of being handled now. Must be confusing for him." After Darren's father began looking into preschools, Kathy followed his lead: "I wanted him [Darren] to learn something. I wanted him to go to school, because he wasn't around kids and [because] I live alone, and he needs more kids."

Darren's father was unsuccessful in finding a preschool with openings, and Kathy found no open slots at a Catholic center in her neighborhood. Frustrated and angry, she raised the issue with her DSS social worker, who arranged an opening in the Head Start center just three blocks from Kathy's apartment. This was an unanticipated benefit of being an active "DSS case":

> She [Kathy's social worker] works for the state, they have an "in" I guess. If you're involved with DSS, you have priority. So he's in there [Head Start center] for three years. I could be done with them [DSS], but I said I'll stay as long as I can keep him in, which is great . . . the school is great!

Head Start reserves a number of slots for DSS clients. If Kathy's case had been closed out, now almost a year following her apparently successful drug rehabilitation, she would not have been able to secure a place in Head Start for Darren.

With characteristic vigor and insight, Kathy reflected on how she was raising Darren. From her experience as a nanny with the Cambridge family, Kathy felt she had learned "how important structure and scheduling are in raising children." She contrasted this with the "chaotic" character of her own childhood home after her father's death. Kathy also talked of how these professional parents "got their brainy kids to use their minds," and she saw parallels with how Darren's Head Start classroom was organized:

> I like the way they have the day planned. They're always doing something with the kids. It's not like the kids are just ranting and running around. Every area in the room is set . . . a thing for the child's mind. You know what I mean? No matter what they're playing with, it's built on some kind of . . . I don't know, a good activity. He [Darren] likes it a lot. Comes home and tells me all these stories.

The sharpest contrast between middle-class forms of socialization and the working-class rules under which Kathy grew up appeared in the area of discipline. Kathy was conscious that her preference for physical punishment was not condoned by professionals:

> I don't think you should slap a kid in the face. But I definitely think that you can give him a couple of good slaps around to just

set him straight. I don't know, these days, boy you can't do that. [Taking on a mocking, sarcastic tone] It's like, you have to use your mind, you have to work through your mind. And I'm like, hah! a nice sock on the butt will work!

Kathy traced her views back to her own experiences as a child:

She [Kathy's mother] never beat me . . . but definitely the fear of God was in me when my mother came near me. I remember [my mother's] socking me with her hand. Like this [demonstrates] with her ring in my head, and it cut me.

During the final year of our time with Kathy, she was struggling to fit her "indigenous" views with these more middle-class conceptions. She talked about being more patient with Darren during his ear-piercing temper tantrums:

This fast-pace thing was hurting him. So now I'm trying to calm down. The [Head Start] teachers are so mellow, they're like robots. No, no, they're very mellow, and my whole family is hyper. They have the patience to deal with every little thing that he did that drives me out of my mind. Like kicking and screaming. I would just take him, and I'd hold his arms and I'd say, "Knock it off." Just look in his eyes, and he'd be mad. But now they talk him down. They talk him into . . . or try to read with him. Or they'll try to calm him down by saying you can just be upset, you have a right to be angry.

In our final conversation with Kathy, she revealed that she had quit her waitressing job in order to spend more time with Darren. She planned to go back on welfare and enter a job-training program. She was convinced that her current schedule was damaging to Darren, but she was ambivalent about leaving the world of work, which provided an outlet for her energy and a sense of stability:

It seems like I'm just going backwards. Let's put it this way: you gotta take three steps backwards to get one step ahead. If I go back on welfare—which is what I'm gonna do—but I always worked. I mean I can still work . . . but under the table.

Shirl: Growing Up with a Strong Mother

At age twenty-five, Shirl returned to live in her childhood home, a triple-decker that her mother has owned for twenty years in an old but relatively safe section of Dorchester. When we first visited Shirl, an animated and upbeat African-American woman, her mother and grandmother lived on the first floor of this well-kept house; her maternal uncle lived on the third floor. Shirl lived on the middle floor with her son Martin, whose father was serving a sentence for assault and battery in a Mississippi state prison. Her older son, Akeem, was living with his father in North Carolina. Much happened in Shirl's life from the time she was sixteen, when she was sent to live with an uncle in Georgia, and her return to Boston.

Shirl's mother, Millie, always provided the safety and security Shirl needed in her often chaotic life. Millie, one of seven children, was born with the aid of a midwife in rural North Carolina. Millie was forty-eight at our first contact with Shirl and had worked in the post office for seventeen years. Shirl recalled that her mother was a keen disciplinarian:

I thank God for that, because I'm not a slob now. I respect my elders, and I learned to. I'm not a person that goes from job to job, because I'm lazy at work or I don't want to do this. So, [I] do thank God for the way she brought me up.

Millie was also a constant source of support for Shirl, both materially and emotionally:

My mother, my mother's wonderful. Yeah, I mean, I've always had everything I wanted, except when I moped, and I couldn't have that, because she thought I was gonna kill myself [laughs]! But my mother, she's still good to me. I have to tell you the truth, I haven't bought Martin clothes since I've been back here. It's like, she doesn't care, she doesn't give me a chance to do stuff like that, you know. She bought his summer wardrobe already [giggles]. So, well, I guess she feels obligated or something.

When Shirl was growing up, Millie did not pull any punches. She was candid with Shirl and acted with a decisiveness that Shirl found admirable:

My best friend, when I was sixteen, was a prostitute? OK? And my mother thought that I was gonna . . . follow behind her. So, I had an uncle stationed in North Carolina and he was here visiting. My mother asked me if I wanted to go back with him to North Carolina to stay, and I said, "I don't know." I guess she made up my mind for me, because I came home, I had a new set of luggage. So, I'm assuming she made up my mind for me. And I ended up going to North Carolina. I finished high school down there.

In sharp contrast to her mother's protectiveness, the men that have passed through Shirl's life have been unreliable and sometimes violent. Shirl described her father as endearing but utterly irresponsible. By Shirl's count he had fathered nineteen children, just two of them with Millie:

No, never, I never remember living with my father. You know, they broke up. I don't even know why. You see, he's a big liar. I know that much . . . my brother's just like him, with these big extravagant lies, and my brother tells some big ones, believe me!
   He [Shirl's father] likes to be there in person, but financially he is not there for you. He's not gonna give you money. Actually, I've loaned him money that I've never gotten back.

Shirl complained that her father has seen her youngest son, Martin, age two, only four times since he was born.
   There were exceptions to her negative experiences with men. After giving birth to Akeem, Shirl moved to another uncle's house in Washington, D.C. He pushed her to find a job and child care, saying that he would not charge her rent *if* she went back to work. Shirl recognized how much she owed the family members who looked out for her: "I thank God for my relatives, because they do a lot for me . . . even now."

When Shirl became pregnant with her first son, she received a sobering lecture from her mother about the lifelong responsibility of caring for a child. Millie emphasized that "when a man gets ready to, he can get up and walk away, and you can't." Shirl decided to leave the baby's father and continued living with her uncle in Washington. "He [the baby's father] didn't know what he wanted to do with his life," Shirl explained, "and I didn't want to sit around waiting for him to make up his mind."

When she was in her early twenties, Shirl left Washington and headed south again, this time with a man who had inherited a family house in Arkansas. For a time after their son Martin was born, Shirl stayed home with him and Akeem. Later she began to work part time at a nearby convenience store:

> He [Martin's father] was working for a beer company, delivering, so he made pretty good money. Actually, I didn't have to work. But I didn't want to sit home and do nothing. I don't like to stay home . . . see, I don't like to have to ask him for what I want. I want to be able to get it when I want it.

Martin's father got into drugs and began to drink heavily. Shirl felt far away from home. She decided to head back to Boston with money that her mother had sent, "escaping" during the day while Martin's father was away at work. After coming home and finding that Shirl had fled, he went to her girlfriend's house: "He attacked her with a baseball bat and pulled a gun on her. He said he blamed her and my mother for my leaving him."

Martin's father was sent to prison for two years for aggravated assault. When we first met Shirl he was about to be released. She had obtained a restraining order forbidding him to contact Shirl and Martin, a prohibition he was violating with phone calls and letters.

The fact that the men in Shirl's life have rarely been trustworthy contributed to her evolving commitment to being strong and self-reliant:

> That's another reason why I'm so independent . . . I don't ever remember living with my father. That's one of the reasons why I have the attitude I have about working and taking care of myself

. . . because of my mother. She works, she's very independent, she has everything she wants. You know, I can get anything I want from her if I needed it. But she's my role model. I want to be exactly like her.

A Young Mother, Learning to Survive

When Shirl returned to her mother's house in Dorchester, she was twenty-three. Akeem was four, and Martin just under a year. She went on AFDC to supplement the household's total income. She used one free month of child care provided by welfare while she searched for work in Boston. Within two months, following a lead provided by a family member, she landed a job as a clerk in a downtown hospital. She was relieved to be off welfare again:

> I didn't want to be on welfare, I wanted to be working. I tell anybody that's having a baby, "Don't stop working!" [laughs] . . . I feel like you shouldn't put your life on hold for that long, when it is not necessary. By the time the kid is two . . . they have established their feelings towards you. No matter whether you send them to day care or not, they still know Mommy, they know what they feel for Mommy. You know? I feel like a woman should not have to sit at home and depend on the husband to be the breadwinner while you take care of the kids. That's just me. I'm very independent. I don't want to have to ask any man for anything!

The fact that Shirl had not formed a stable relationship with a partner who could contribute to her economic security led to occasional involvement with the welfare system. But she viewed having children as an act that signified coming of age, an act of strength, not dependence:

> I became a woman [when I had my first child]. That's when I became a woman. It was like, he [her first son] made me get myself together, get my priorities straight as far as what to do with my money. No more throwing my money away on clothes that I don't need, or [on] fast food. It was strictly grocery store, cooking at

home. You know, I got my values, my monetary values for one, from having a kid.

When Shirl received a child-care voucher, she placed Martin with a family day care provider used by the mother of her brother's children: "I figured if this girl trusted her [the child-care provider] to take care of my nieces and nephew, you know, I trusted. I didn't want to stick him [Martin] in a day care where nobody knew anything about them."

Shirl and Millie became close friends of Alison, the family day-care provider. Millie started inviting Alison and her husband, who often helped his wife care for the children, to Sunday family dinners. Alison began to bring Martin home at the end of the day, sometimes stopping off to get his hair cut or to buy him a small toy. According to Shirl, "She treats him like her own child!" Alison and her husband began to invite Shirl's family for Christmas dinners.

With her child-care arrangement in place, Shirl was soon attending medical transcription courses at the local community college, after obtaining financial aid. Determined to get ahead, Shirl made full use of all the public and private resources at her disposal. She was adept at finding sources of public support and expert in eligibility requirements. She also knew how to move to more stable forms of economic aid over time. When she heard, for example, that the governor of Massachusetts was attempting to cut child-care vouchers, she worked with the local child-care agency to obtain a subsidized "slot" with her family day-care provider.

Raising Two Young Children

Shirl forcefully articulated what was important to her about Martin's upbringing. She had very clear views about the importance of raising Martin using strict discipline tempered with abundant affection. One day we asked Shirl, "What's the most important thing in raising a child?" Here's how she responded, with characteristic verve and confidence:

Discipline! Discipline for one. You know, he has to learn, he has to respect me and his elders. I don't want him to get in school and, you know, just be back-talking the teachers and stuff like that.

I try and explain to him now that this person is an adult, you're a child. You can't talk to an adult like that. You have to listen. When an adult tells you, you have to listen. I try to explain that to him now.

What appears to middle-class eyes to be overly harsh treatment of Martin must be seen within the context of Shirl's frequent expressions of affection toward Martin, an endearing, verbal, and engaging young-ster. Shirl was always ready to tell us about the new thing that Martin had said that week. During one phone conversation, Shirl reported that she and Martin had been watching a special on TV about pregnancy and early childhood development. Martin posed the question, "Mommy, when I was in your belly did I wear sneakers?" Shirl laughed loud and long at the memory of this incident. In a discussion of discipline in the study's third year, Shirl commented, "I should hit him . . . but he's just too cute, I can't do it sometimes."

Shirl expected others to react to Martin the same way she did, and she emphasized the importance of a warm atmosphere in the child-care setting:

Alison treats him real nice. When she drops him off, he has to kiss her. I can tell by the way he acts to her that she treats him good. I can tell by his reaction. He took to her real well.

Shirl frequently expressed deep faith in education as a means of economic mobility. She felt that her emphasis on education was shared by Alison, who had furnished her family day-care home with small desks and organized preliteracy tasks for the six to eight children who were "enrolled." In one conversation, Shirl mentioned that sometimes she accidentally referred to Alison as a "baby-sitter" when talking to Martin:

I mean to say "school," but sometimes "baby-sitter" comes out. I prefer to call it a "school" . . . you know [it] prepares him, to let him know that eventually he is gonna have to go to an actual school . . . and plus they do the same stuff he would be doing in a school.

When Martin was two years and three months old, Shirl was already focusing on a learning agenda:

> She [Alison] doesn't just keep him, she teaches him. He comes home singin' little nursery rhymes, he counts, he says his ABCs. She teaches him well.

Nine months later, Shirl remarked on her son's progress:

> He still loves his day-care teacher [Alison]. Oh, he is so smart, you wouldn't believe it! The things he comes home and says to me, that he does at the day-care center! Martin knows his ABCs—all of them, and he can count to fifteen. All of this is because of her [Alison]. He came home one day and counted to ten, and I was like, "What?" I couldn't believe it. I helped him up to the fifteenth. He can count to fifteen now. They say a prayer in the morning.

The themes of respect, love, discipline, and intelligence all come together in the description Shirl presented of a typical Sunday afternoon at her mother's house:

> Everybody comes over; it's like a house full of people. And Martin knows *everybody's* name! He doesn't get anybody mixed up. He gets too much attention if you ask me. Martin is a trip. He's a little entertainer.

Finding a Better Life, Elsewhere

Soon after Akeem started kindergarten, a bullet pierced his school from a gunfight in the street. The perpetrator escaped and no one was hurt. Two weeks later he returned, began shooting, and was caught. Within a couple of weeks Shirl had removed Akeem from the school and shipped him south to his paternal grandparents' house in North Carolina, not unlike how her own mother had put her on the bus for the South. Indeed, Shirl's picture of a better life included moving back to the South:

When I was growing up in Dorchester it was fine. It was nothing like what it is now. When I was growing up you could get in a fight and not have to worry about getting shot. Everybody fought with their hands then.

I might go back to North Carolina. I'm gonna stay, you know, with some friends and see about finding a job. I'm saving my money, then I'm going back to North Carolina . . . because it's safer there. You don't have all this, like these kids get away with standing on these corners and stuff selling drugs. I mean the police know they're selling drugs, but they don't do nothing about it until after so long. In North Carolina they run you off in a minute. There's no gathering on a street corner. You can't do that . . . don't have to worry about anybody driving by shooting.

Shirl had clear plans about how to get ahead. She was also tapped into social networks, kin and friends who were working and knew about attainable jobs. Yet some days were filled with worries. Summarizing her life as a single parent of two children, she said, "It's hard. Taking care of kids is hard . . . 'specially working and going to school and taking care of a child." Shirl feared what Martin's father would do when he was released from prison. She missed Akeem even though she felt certain she had made the right decision in sending him to a safer place. She envisioned a clear pathway for moving ahead over time. And every day she felt support from her family and security in knowing that Martin was safe and flourishing.

Selma: Growing Up with Hard-Working Parents

Selma holds her body perfectly still when listening to someone talking. When asked a question, she stares directly at the speaker and allows a few seconds to elapse in silence. Then she begins to speak, and her soft words bring the listener sharply back to attention. Selma is a deliberate, thoughtful person.

We first met Selma, a twenty-seven-year-old woman of Puerto Rican parents, at her job in Roxbury. Selma was wearing a simple dress, and her hair was tied back in a small pony-tail. In her quiet, reflective manner she described her guiding principles for integrating her family and work life:

> I wanted to have some kind of career so I could give my children what they needed. I wanted them to have an example of what I wanted them to be like. I don't know if that's within me, or that's a learned thing. But I know if I have just one thing to do, it'll be so hard! But if I have ten things to do, I can do them all.

Selma had three daughters, ages five, six, and nine, when we first met her. The youngest, Zumary, was the focus of our conversations. The girls' father remained in the background throughout the three-year period. Occasionally he stayed with the family in their small apartment, located in a Roxbury housing project. He would sometimes buy groceries for the household; and he would occasionally pick Zumary up from child care, particularly after Selma encountered a gang fight on her way home from the center. But he remained on the periphery, physically and emotionally. Selma told us that one time he failed to show up for a family photo session, but later expressed regret when he saw the portrait of Selma and their three daughters, exclaiming, "God, I'm like a phantom here!"

As one of four daughters, all born in the United States, Selma was raised to believe deeply in education and hard work. Her mother did laundry at a hotel downtown until moving back to Puerto Rico in the year prior to our first contact: "She loves to work, too . . . having her own money." Selma reported that her father also held a blue-collar job but "drank on weekends and went out at night." Neither Selma's father nor her mother had completed high school before emigrating to their Boston *barrio*. Selma's mother later returned to school and obtained her GED. When Selma became pregnant at age eighteen, her parents were not happy; single motherhood was sure to interfere with their goal for Selma: getting a good education. In talking with us, Selma seemed to realize with increasing clarity how important educational achievement was to her parents:

> I don't understand how they instilled it [belief in education] in us. They never really talked to us, but [it was] a silent goal. I do

remember them saying how good it was when we had A's. You know, we got the handshake from my father. Or he would say things to his friends. I remember the [multiplication] times-tables . . . oh, that was awful! We would have to learn them by memory and tell him in his ear. He kept saying if we didn't get good grades, he was going to make a box of nails. Nails! And he was going to make us kneel on it! I can't believe I believed him!

Her parents' faith in education was linked to Selma's own conception of how to nurture strength and self-respect within her three daughters. In her journal she reported:

After work I go home, wait for the kids' father to drop them home. When they get home they give me all the papers they did today. I'm so tired, but I still have to, or want to, show them that all their work is wonderful, unique and out of this world.

Like Shirl, Selma translated her faith in education into specific practices. She talked about helping her girls with their homework, ensuring that it was correct and "neatly done." During one period she stopped all TV viewing, spent more time reading to them, and scheduled more library visits.

Selma reflected upon her own child-rearing practices in relation to the strict, "old-country" ways of her parents. She believed that raising youngsters in Puerto Rico was quite different from bringing up children in the heart of Roxbury:

I don't think they [Selma's parents] were ready to have kids. I mean they were probably ready to have kids in their country. They weren't ready to have kids in this country.

I am being more open with my daughters. They [Selma's parents] just had kids, they survived, and got help when there was a problem, because they didn't know how to handle it. There was no communication. If you want your kids to do something, I think you should explain to them why. They never did that.

Selma's siblings were upwardly mobile. Two of her sisters had obtained white-collar jobs, and one of them was attending business school at night. The third sister was on AFDC and lived in another Roxbury housing project, but Selma emphasized that this sister headed the parent advisory committee at her child's preschool. Selma believed that, in general, hard work and education paid off.

A Young Mother, Learning to Survive

Were you only to hear Selma's words and never see her surroundings, you would infer that she lived in a rich and stimulating community. In a sense she does. But Selma's heart and spirit sharply contrast with the visual images found in the heart of Roxbury. After driving by the elegant brick houses of the affluent Back Bay neighborhood, one reaches Fenway Park, and a few minutes later enters a desolate neighborhood. The streets are cluttered with litter and broken bottles. The corner stores look worn and decrepit. Row houses seem unkept or unoccupied. The housing project in which Selma and her children live is a gray, six-story building. Security is tight. In the stairwell, locked metal screens block the hallway at each landing. Whenever we entered her apartment for an interview, we looked forward to Selma's warmth and the smiling faces of her three little girls. Not once in three years did Selma decry her drab physical surroundings, which were eclipsed by the warmth of her bright, cozy apartment.

Selma has long been able to extract support and resources from her community. She grew up in the heart of Roxbury. Over the years she has engaged its inner workings—its community agencies, churches, and fellow families. As a child, Selma made use of a community agency that operated a health clinic. When she became pregnant with her first daughter, Selma left her parents' house to live with the father's family. The same clinic provided her with prenatal care as well as a layette and the essentials for the first month of her daughter Ada's life. Agency staff also made sure that Selma signed up for AFDC, then helped her enroll in a GED course, which she successfully finished (one-stop shopping for social and health services in the poor core of Roxbury).

After receiving her GED, Selma went to work as a receptionist for a Latino community organization. Selma left Ada in day care in her neighborhood, then headed north on the bus across the Charles River to Cambridge. For Selma, as for Kathy and Shirl, working was partly a moral issue:

I work because I need to. I have to survive, have to give [provide for] my kids' needs, too. It also gives me . . . I'm not a person that doesn't do stuff. I'm not idle.

Selma didn't like being on welfare and hated feeling that her daughters saw her as "dependent" on anyone else:

That's one of the things I've always said, that I wanted my kids to fend for themselves and not have to depend on anyone. That's very important. I hope I'm showing them that. I don't want them to get in a relationship with a man . . . or be dependent on a man. I want them to be, you know, proud of themselves and be comfortable with where they are and who they're with.

But Selma did recurrently depend upon social-welfare programs. The girls' father held jobs only occasionally, and so Selma couldn't rely on income from him. With each of her three pregnancies, she quit her job and went on AFDC for several months before negotiating child care and returning to work. Welfare payments and child-care vouchers inducted Selma into social networks that provided basic sustenance and social bonds:

We were on welfare first. That helped me to get that foot in the door and get my education [GED]. That was the only reason I got my second [child-care] slot and my third slot, because I had my first child there. Eventually I became good friends with the people there, and they were always looking out for me.

Selma also found spiritual and material support within the church. She was raised as a Catholic but became dissatisfied with "Sunday-only Catholics." She decided "to praise the Lord louder," and joined a Pentecostal church in Jamaica Plain that was started by her uncle. Her daughters sang in the choir each week and attended Bible school. Selma helped produce the church newsletter and led a Girl Scout group organized within the church. Fellow members were "like a family . . . any time you need them they are there." When her girls were just infants or toddlers, Selma could call a church member and "they would come over to help out."

Raising Three Young Children

Selma was torn between wanting to spend a lot of time with her three daughters and feeling committed to her social action projects, which usually included her job. She saw raising her daughters as the fulfillment of her most fundamental role. In her journal she wrote:

> What I liked most of this weekend was all the hugs and kisses I got from the girls. We cooked together sandwiches and Kool-aid and popcorn. And I enjoyed just the unhurried time we spent together because I made it a point not to go anywhere. One special moment was when watching the last part of a movie I turned to look at Zumary. She was watching the movie and the expressions that she made as she watched were priceless. I'd lose any finish of any movie to watch that face.

Selma preferred to work part time in order to have more time with the girls. At one point she had a run-in with her boss at the community agency and felt compelled to tell him, "I have kids, and I have to do this. This is my job, and I'm committed, and I do my work. But if my kids need me, I will be there."

At the same time, however, Selma's own conception of being a role model included getting her daughters involved in local organizations. The moral value that Selma attached to her own civic activism, especially aiding Roxbury's community groups and the church, carried over to how she thought her girls should learn to operate in their community:

> I want them to be aware of all the things that are around them. I want them to be active. You know how some people just live in a place, and they don't care about everyone else and the betterment of their surroundings? They just say, "Okay, I'm going to be here. I'm going to take care of my little corner, but I won't care whatever happens to anyone else." . . . I want them [her daughters] to be out there taking care of the children, of their surroundings, of the schools.
>
> We're not raising kids to be . . . I don't know if it is "upstanding," but it's some kind of citizen and that's what I want. I want

them to be out there. When someone is scared to even try they're never really going to learn.

Child Care and Community Activism

Selma has seen a lot of day-care options, having raised three children pretty much on her own, and having lived in different Roxbury neighborhoods. Selma recalls that after the birth of her eldest daughter, her social worker presented her with the name of one provider, not a list from which to choose. This day-care provider was "not Latina," but she gave Selma useful advice on getting her daughter to sleep or cooking things her daughter liked to eat. Another family day-care provider spent a lot of time doing homework with her own school-age child. Selma had "never thought about that before" and filed it away until her eldest entered first grade. Selma felt most comfortable with one Latina provider, and she often stayed at the woman's house to participate in activities with the four to five children in attendance.

Selma did worry at times. One day-care provider was pregnant and would leave the toddlers she was caring for with a neighbor when she had to go to the doctor. Another family day-care provider "would just take them at the door and not even let you in . . . I always liked to make the kids comfortable and not just leave them there."

When Zumary entered preschool, Selma threw herself into bettering the organization. By this time she had worked as a receptionist at a Latino agency, helped organize tenants in the projects around a variety of issues, and was working as an assistant at a multiservice Roxbury organization. Drawing on these skills, Selma joined the parents' advisory committee at the preschool and began to play a role in hiring new teachers. Staff morale and turnover had become a major problem, stemming in part from an ineffectual director:

> Every time a director [candidate] came and got interviewed, I would ask, "How do you feel about parent involvement?" I was going to be the first one that was going to be looking at them and trying to find out if they were going to be happy to see the parents get involved. I wanted them to make the parents feel comfortable, because that was one of the biggest problems, you just didn't feel comfortable.

Selma's child-care subsidy was reduced after she returned to work and left AFDC. With two daughters in the same preschool, Selma was paying about $300 a month on tuition, a sizable portion of her paycheck. Selma heard that the Boston public schools operated a small number of fully subsidized preschools through the Even Start program. She went to the downtown office and "got every kind of pamphlet that they had on every school," watched videotaped descriptions, and visited several in Roxbury and the South End.

Selma chose an Even Start preschool that offered many opportunities for parental involvement. The director organized breakfasts for parents and library nights, at which a book was given to each parent. Home reading activities were encouraged and formally structured:

> They always send notes home as to what she's done today . . . [whether] she's had a good day, a bad day. The notes she has to bring back, because I sign them. Sometimes I would go get them [at Zumary's previous child-care center] and maybe teachers in the morning weren't there. Something may have happened and I wouldn't have known.
>
> I've learned that . . . even if we are not invited to the school, we should always look and see what they're learning, what they're not learning. Become involved in it.

Selma's eager involvement typified her outward, engaged orientation to the world. Within this impoverished setting—a small apartment in a dreary housing project—Selma's perseverance and optimistic commitment to her community were all the more impressive. During our three years together, Selma repeatedly illustrated how her approach to the outside world was rubbing off on her three daughters:

> They are real good kids. They love meeting new people. Since they were born they've been going out the door. Like I remember as soon as Ada could put on her coat, she would [be] like, "Let's go!" And now they're like, "Well, what are we going to do next?" There's no time for them to just sit down and relax. Just sit here and just do nothing . . .
>
> Being a parent is one of the best things that I've ever had to do . . . you're almost forming their minds.

Getting to Know Strangers: A Methodological Note

Becoming comfortable with a new acquaintance—and coming to converse in an unguarded manner—takes a good deal of time. Initially these fourteen women saw us primarily as researchers from Harvard. Over the three years of meeting, our conversations became increasingly candid, at times painful and difficult, at times funny and joyful. We invested heavily in getting to know these women well. In turn, they came to trust us as careful, albeit inquisitive listeners. We used a few different methods and forms of dialogue to build this ease with one another. What follows is a brief outline of the research methods employed. Our qualitative methods are further detailed in technical articles.[2]

A minimum of three semi-structured interviews were conducted with each woman between July 1991 and May 1994.[3] By "semi-structured" we mean that a core set of questions was developed for each round of interviews, along with follow-up questions specific to the information garnered from the prior interview. Initial questions pertained to events leading up to involvement with the welfare system, the women's experiences going back to work or job training, and their negotiation of child-care arrangements. Subsequent conversations explored how they tried to be "good mothers," whether they perceived conflicts or convergence between working and child rearing, and how they handled discipline. Interviews were supplemented with less formal conversation and time spent in the households with the families.

Our research team conducted a debriefing exercise subsequent to each interview. These biweekly sessions aimed at making explicit our interpretations of each woman's own reports. When we felt confused or needed more details we explored the issue again at the next interview. Phone conversations were also used to clarify meanings and interpretations ("member checks," in Lincoln and Guba's parlance[4]). This process minimized the risk of making invalid interpretations that departed from the women's intended meaning.[5] Child-care providers were also visited and observed when access could be obtained. All interviews were audiotaped; several were also videotaped to allow further reflection on the women's contexts and perspectives. The body of evidence resulting from three years of data collection included 1,954 pages of transcribed conversations, as well as field notes from observations in homes, workplaces, and child-care settings.

The data were analyzed in three ways, beginning with the initial round of interviews. First, summary memos were written for each transcribed interview, including diagrams that mapped emerging themes and what we came to term the *leitmotif* for each woman: the central focus or motivating force that seemed to characterize how she organized her role as mother and principal provider for her child. These analytic memos allowed us to tailor questions for the second round of interviews, or prompted phone calls to check the validity of our tentative interpretations.[6] Second, a coding scheme was developed that included 17 major themes and 124 specific codes that were tagged onto the interview data (using software for narrative analysis). Third, once principal themes were identified for the book, we reread the transcripts and field notes for all 14 women, in part to analyze how their contexts and the demands placed upon them were shaping their cultural models. This process resulted in an additional 92 pages of thematically arranged "digests" of evidence.

These analytic procedures allowed us to feel comfortable in describing the cultural models that guided these fourteen women's beliefs and actions. We did not formally observe their behavior, and we recognize the limitation of relying solely upon interview data. Over the three-year period during which data were collected, however, we had many opportunities to explore the content of these cultural models as they were applied in a number of situations.

Our central aim was to understand the cultural models and scripts adhered to by these fourteen women. Caution is warranted in generalizing our findings to all low-income women. Because our sample was selected to focus on "working-poor" mothers who are employed, it is particularly important not to assume that these findings pertain to "hard-core unemployed" families.[7]

To preserve their anonymity, we use pseudonyms for all participants and their family members. We make extensive use of verbatim quotations from our interview transcripts in order to convey the mothers' and teachers' own descriptions of their lives, values, and aspirations. We use their exact words whenever possible, occasionally omitting words or phrases that are redundant or unclear. Omissions of more than one or two words are indicated by ellipses. We have not attempted to convey dialect or pronunciation, and we have made some corrections when the participants used variants of words that departed from standard English. Interviews conducted in Spanish have been translated into English.

Who We Are: The Origins of Our Perspective

When conducting a quantitative survey, it is easier to remain at a comfortable distance from the study participants, safely cushioned by the "hard, cold numbers" from any emotional involvement. In the intensive, qualitative work we undertook for this book, no such escape was possible. Convictions about "value-free" science are swept away when listening to a woman who was sexually abused by her stepfather explain her feelings of betrayal and anger. As our research team met over the three-year period, we found ways to expose and examine our responses. We wanted to learn from them and not allow them to distort our interpretations of the stories we were hearing. We did so by openly acknowledging our own values and perceptions about how parents should behave. We used staff meetings to express feelings of anger, for example, when parents were not protecting their children as we hoped they would from a harsh child-care provider or an irresponsible family member.

The four core members of our research group shared common attributes that contributed to a shared perspective on many issues. All of us are parents who have participated in the daily challenge of balancing work and child-rearing responsibilities. Each has faced the task of finding a trustworthy child-care provider, and we have all dealt with the drama of discovering that our child is sick on a day packed with meetings, or of awakening on a snowy morning when child care is canceled but work is not.

All of us have lived and worked for extended periods of time in countries outside the United States, collectively spanning the continents of Europe, South America, Asia, and Africa. We have all had the experience of parenting children in a culture foreign to our own; we have experienced flashes of insight that the parenting practices we had previously accepted as "natural" were in fact quite cultural in origin.

We are all professionally devoted to improving the welfare of poor families and children, although our training and experiences lead us to approach our work from different disciplinary perspectives. Susan Holloway was trained as a developmental psychologist with an emphasis on early childhood education. She has been deeply involved in work on parent and caregivers' beliefs about child rearing and on the effects of their behavior on children's development, examining these topics in the United States as well as in Mexico and Japan. Bruce Fuller is a sociologist with a particular interest in government policy and its effects on families and schools within impoverished settings. Marylee Rambaud is trained in sociology, human development, and qualitative methods; she has worked in French preschools and adult training programs in Europe and West Africa. Costanza Eggers-Piérola, originally from Argentina, has a background in educational curriculum and has worked in public elementary schools on issues involving bilingualism and learning within multicultural settings.

All members of the team participated in each phase of the project, from conceptualization through data collection, analysis, and writing, thus breaking down the dichotomy between data collectors and analysts who are one step removed from the participants and their daily context. The Latinas in the sample were interviewed by Eggers-Piérola in the language (English or Spanish) of their choice; roughly a quarter of the time she was accompanied by a second team member. The majority of all other interviews were led by Rambaud, either solely or accompanied by a second team member.

The author of Chapter 9, Bruce Johnson-Beykont, was not involved in the data collection and analysis of the mothers' data. But he served a valuable function by reading and reacting to manuscript drafts from the perspective of a "friendly outsider." Johnson-Beykont designed the study of preschool teachers reported in Chapter 9; he conducted the data collection and analysis himself, and authored the chapter. His perspective is informed by graduate training in human development as well as fifteen years of work as a teacher and director in preschool organizations.

Ultimately, our personal convictions about how children should be treated can never be totally erased from our writing on the topic. Indeed, a central point of our book is that these deep convictions should be acknowledged and respected rather than hastily swept aside by those who think their own perspectives are somehow more appropriate or scientifically valid. Our fundamental aim, however, has been to provide an unclouded view of the fourteen women we interviewed. We have benefited enormously from this intimate process and from the fact that they are, to us, no longer strangers.

CHAPTER THREE

Motherhood in Poverty

❧

I don't live in the best neighborhood, I don't live in the best apartment complex. But I can decide where my child is going to play and the people she is going to interact with. —*Helena*

All working mothers face a difficult juggling act as they struggle to balance the demands of being a mother with those of being a worker. Middle-class and affluent families are able to purchase services that augment their own labor. But poor single mothers can only dream of hiring a housecleaner, cannot afford to eat out, and must rely on buses and subways to get to work, to pick up their children at day care, and to go to the grocery store. On top of these economic exigencies, conflicting social demands are voiced by kin, friends, and welfare agencies: be a good mother *and* hold down a job, no matter how little it pays.

Current debates over poverty and single parenthood have focused on the small number of welfare recipients who neither hold nor are seeking a job. We have failed to ask those who are employed how they prioritize and manage their many responsibilities. This chapter focuses on several components of this question. First, and most fundamentally, what do these mothers think it means to be a mother—what are the defining attributes of the role? Although some experienced a sense of loss in leaving their infants, most were eager to return to work. But given that they must entrust their children's care to others, how do they carve out a role in child rearing for themselves? What expectations do they have for the amount and quality of time that they spend with their children? Most of the fourteen women in our sample live in dangerous neighborhoods characterized by scarce and underfunded support services. How do they perceive this immediate context and adapt to it in crafting their own identities as mothers?

A second set of issues deals with the role that mothers expect fathers to play in their children's lives. Popular media portray low-income fathers largely as irresponsible deadbeats. Scholars have failed to provide more texture to this overarching mythology, employing surveys that yield important yet partial information, like the proportion of fathers who deliver on child-support payments. During our three years with these women, the children's fathers appeared to hover in the background, surfacing occasionally in our conversations. What kind of relationship do these fathers maintain with their children, and how do mothers serve as the gatekeepers who define and control the fathers' access to their young children? Despite the many shortcomings that they identified in the men—and physical violence and drug problems feature predominantly among them—these women were anxious to find some way to help their children stay connected to their fathers.

Third, this chapter explores how these mothers see themselves as workers, as wage earners. At the time of the interviews, they were primarily employed in entry-level office positions. How important was this role of "working woman" to their identity and self-confidence? What were their reasons for working, or, in a few cases, for leaving the labor force? How are their career and child-care decisions founded upon their identities as mothers and workers, and how did they use available social support to help realize their goals?

A common thread running through all these questions is the issue of power and control—how do these women maintain a feeling of efficacy over their lives when they lack financial resources? Forms of coping that are associated with confidence and efficacy usually involve tackling problems directly and working toward logical solutions. For these women, such direct, problem-focused coping may not be feasible. They may not be able to challenge the status quo at work; nor can they exert much control over former partners. They cannot always protect their children from bad experiences. What alternatives did they see for themselves and how successfully were they coping with their family and work responsibilities? Did they resist societal forces—including racism and sexism—that pushed them into marginal positions? Empowerment requires a minimal and steady set of economic supports. But confidence and a solid feeling of efficacy—sensing that you can challenge or influence events in your own life—are necessary building blocks of empowerment. These cornerstones often crumble under the weight of poverty.

Helena and Shirl: Contrasting Views

Two women, Helena and Shirl, were selected to illustrate the themes running through this chapter. Of primary interest here are their divergent conceptions of what it means to be a mother, and the related views they hold on their identities as working women. Their strategies for balancing motherhood and work are also affected by their tacit expectations or cultural models for the appropriate role of extended family members in their children's lives. The superficial elements of Helena's and Shirl's lives are similar in many ways. Both grew up in households with strong mothers who contributed significantly to the family income. Both forged complicated relationships with their children's fathers, and each had to give up physical custody of a child for whom she could not provide. Yet the two conveyed very different views of their roles, and ultimately arrived at very different solutions for balancing motherhood and work.

For Helena, being a mother meant acting as her daughter's provider, protector, buffer, and companion. Lacking social support from her family and committed to an all-encompassing definition of motherhood, she ultimately felt compelled to seek a part-time rather than a full-time job, in spite of the financial constraints that decision imposed on the family. Shirl, by contrast, placed tremendous importance on her own financial independence, as noted in Chapter 2. Furthermore, she trusted her family day-care provider and her extended family to provide her son with affection and stimulation. She did not feel that he was deprived as a result of the limited amount of time she had available to spend with him, and she did not consider working less than full time.

Helena: "I don't ask for much"

Helena's serious—almost severe—demeanor initially appears to belie the sporadic turbulence and upheaval of her life. A descendant of Greek immigrants and Native Americans, she is slight of build, with large, dark eyes. Her short, cropped hair, face devoid of makeup, and somber clothing convey an impression of asceticism. But when she begins to speak of her family, her experiences with men, and her commitment to her daughter, the tremor in her voice reveals a woman of deep emotion.

Like many of the mothers in our study, Helena grew up in a large working-class family. Her memories of growing up with her three sisters were mostly negative. She portrayed her mother as exceedingly strict and remote, always busy with work, housecleaning, and occasional extramarital affairs. Helena reported that her father provided a good deal of care and warmth, but was cowed by his wife and unable to protect the children from her sometimes abusive treatment. He died when Helena was in her teens.

Helena was twenty when she had her first child. When her son was two, her husband left her, taking both cars and the furniture. Helena moved with her son to her mother's apartment. As she puts it: "So what was I going back to? I hadn't worked. I had no skills. I became a bum. I couldn't do anything." Her husband's sister offered to care for Helena's son until she "got on her feet." Helena reluctantly accepted and began working in "a sweatshop." Eventually her former husband took over the primary care of the child; by the time Helena was financially stable, she did not feel that she had the right to ask him to return her son.

Helena had an affair with a married man and gave birth to her daughter Shawna when she was twenty-seven. She had been working for a law firm, but she quit when she became pregnant. Estranged from her family, and with no financial resources, she moved into an emergency shelter for the homeless. After her daughter was born, she moved to a shelter for families and went on welfare. Four months later she received state funding for housing and moved into the apartment complex where her mother lived. Shawna's father contributed financial support, and her relationship with her family gradually improved. Helena pursued training in medical transcription and took a full-time job in a hospital, putting Shawna, then two years old, in a child-care center. Shawna stayed in the center for three years, until she began kindergarten at a local public school. Throughout these years, Helena worried about Shawna's lack of self-control and her aggressive behavior around her peers. She petitioned her boss for a reduction in work hours, but, unable to win any concessions, she finally quit. She then found part-time work as a cashier and began baby-sitting for her sister, happy that she could provide Shawna with more attention and generally make her daughter's life less hectic.

Shirl: "I'm trying to better myself"

Shirl laughed as she tried to count up how many stepbrothers and stepsisters she had. Was it eighteen or nineteen children her father had produced in forty-nine years? She suffered no illusions about her father, saying matter-of-factly, "He's a no-good person, you know. Not as far as robbing and stealing but, you know, in taking care of things he's supposed to do." Characteristically, she managed to stay on friendly terms with him ("I love him and I always will"). Indeed, Shirl's ability to see the good side of any situation helped her survive the violence and instability of her first two decades. She learned to maintain an elaborate social network to ensure that, unlike her father, she responsibly provides for herself and her two sons.

As we saw in Chapter 2, Shirl had her first son when she was nineteen years old. Martin was born when she was twenty-two. Shirl hastened to return to work after each pregnancy, in spite of the fact that her husband was making enough money to support the family. To Shirl, nothing is more important than independence: "I don't want to have to ask any man for anything!" When her husband began using drugs, Shirl took her children and fled to relatives in Boston. Her former husband was eventually imprisoned for assault, and Shirl dreaded his release, despite the fact that she had taken out a restraining order against him that prevented him from contacting her or the children.

In caring for Martin, adults other than Shirl were involved in activities that someone like Helena might see as a mother's responsibility. Shirl's mother dropped Martin off at the family day-care provider's house every morning, and the provider's husband often brought him home in the evening. Shirl's mother bought the boys' clothing and paid for Akeem's semi-annual visits from North Carolina. The provider sometimes washed Martin's clothes, gave him dinner, got him a haircut, and took him on outings to the Children's Museum or the aquarium ("I don't have to take him because she's done that!" remarked Shirl).

Martin spent a lot of time on the first floor with Shirl's aunt and her four children, and with his grandmother out in her new suburban home.

Shirl was thus more relaxed than Helena was about fulfilling her maternal responsibilities adequately when she was working full time. She had faith that the provider and her relatives were filling in the gaps, whereas Helena suspected that the well-meaning caregivers at her daughter's child-care center were overwhelmed with the problem children in the class. Helena also worried about the inadequate child-rearing skills, and lack of patience, that she perceived in her mother and her sisters. Helena's daughter was viewed as a problem child in school, whereas Shirl's son appeared to charm all those within his circle. All these factors, combined with Shirl's determination to stay independent of men, contributed to her commitment to being a full-time working mother.

The obstacles and opportunities faced by Helena and Shirl were common to all the women, and they illustrate the inevitable tradeoffs that poor mothers face in balancing child rearing and work. Simplistic maxims about what is best for children or for society fall by the wayside when we look through these women's eyes at the choices available to them.

What Does It Mean to Be a Mother?

All the mothers in the sample felt challenged at times to provide for their children even the most basic necessities—food, clothing, shelter, and safety. As we saw, Helena's daughter spent her first months in a shelter for homeless families, and Helena was forced by circumstances to relinquish custody of her son. Unwilling to expose her eldest son to community violence, Shirl sent him to live with his father in the South. Because of drug dependencies, Jackie and Kathy were not able to care for their children for a period of time. Aggie, found by DSS to have neglected her son, maintained custody but existed in an uneasy partnership with the state, which was making fundamental decisions about how and where her son should be cared for and educated.

The problem of sexual abuse also loomed large in their consideration of child care. To prevent their children from being sexually abused, several mothers avoided leaving them in the care of non–family members. Most of the mothers frequently asked their children whether anyone had "touched them," and warned them to have nothing to do with strangers. Brenda described how she instructed her daughter:

> I always say, "If anybody hits you, or if anybody touch you here, you know, possibly, you tell Mommy, you let Mommy know." So if someone hits her, she comes home and she'll tell me . . . I constantly ask her phone number. She knows her phone number, she knows where she lives, she knows her address . . . I tell her, "Don't talk to strangers. Don't take nothing from strangers. You know, they might try to take you away from Mommy and you will never see me again."

A common theme in the interviews with Helena was the negative effects of community violence on her child. Time and time again she attributed her daughter's tendency to be extremely aggressive to her experiences with violent children in her preschool and her neighborhood. For example, after describing a scene she witnessed in which several children (whom she describes as "animals") were fighting at the local park, Helena commented:

> I just don't want her exposed to that. She doesn't need to be. There are too many other places that we can go in the city. She doesn't need to be exposed to that. I don't live in the best neighborhood, I don't live in the best apartment complex, but I can decide where my child is going to play, and the people that she is going to interact with.

All the women were conscious of the dangers in their environment and strongly articulated the need to protect the children. They were extremely worried about random shootings as well as drug and gang activity. Many sought to leave the Boston area; Aggie moved to a middle-class suburb when her child was three years old, and by the end of the data-collection period, Harriet succeeded in buying a house outside the dangerous inner city. Pat, Shirl, Wilma, and Helena spoke of their plans to move to safer communities within a few years.

Related to the notion of protecting their children from danger is the feeling expressed by many women that they have to buffer their children from bad experiences and act as advocates for their well-being. Helena viewed most of her daughter's teachers as benign and well meaning but overwhelmed with their responsibilities. When she perceived that a teacher was not acting in the interests of her child, she did not hesitate to speak up strongly. For example, when the teachers at Shawna's child-care center were not careful to make her wear a hat in the sun, Helena quickly made her dissatisfaction known. Later, when her daughter was threatened with expulsion from her kindergarten gym class because of her aggressiveness, Helena resolved to intervene strongly:

> I decided to show the gym teacher that I am on top of it, that I will pop in every Friday morning, when Shawna has gym, and watch. So Shawna sees me there, and the gym teacher will see that I'm on top of it, as we can talk about any behaviors that are (voice trails off). I believe Shawna's behavior will improve if I show I am there, watching.

Helena's determination to act as Shawna's advocate was also spurred by her perception that even the people in her own family failed to give her daughter the type of love and attention that Helena felt she deserved. One sister, for example, didn't help Helena when she was pregnant and homeless, nor did she help baby-sit after Shawna was born. Helena gave up on this sister: "And with that type of attitude, I don't ask her to baby-sit. Because I don't want, I just don't want her to be around Shawna if she's going to be like that." Similarly, Helena's mother "just really didn't want to be involved" when Shawna was born.

Helena also resented the lack of attention paid to Shawna by her father, and felt she should protect Shawna from being hurt by him:

> He's a worm. You know, I don't wish him any harm. He's just, that's the way he is, and I've accepted that. But I don't want that type of person in my life. And if he's not going to be a constant factor in Shawna's life, then I don't want him involved at all. I don't want sporadic visits here and there, whenever he gets an hour or he decides to drop in. That's not the way it works. That's not how you raise a child. You're either there or you're not there.

Most mothers reported speaking up when they felt uncomfortable with something being done in their children's day-care centers. Delmy challenged what she perceived to be the unfair conclusion by her daughter's kindergarten teacher that she should be kept back a year. Aggie, the most uninvolved mother in the sample, described uncharacteristically vigorous attempts on her part to convince the teacher in her son's play-oriented kindergarten to introduce a more skill-based curriculum: "I have asked his teacher more than once to send extra papers home with him. You know, letters he can trace and stuff like that? And she won't even do that. And I have gone down there and I've asked her." Jackie was quite dissatisfied with the treatment her daughter received in her child-care center; she spoke to the teachers and directors on several occasion about harsh treatment and monotonous mandatory activities, and finally succeeded in having her daughter transferred to another classroom within the school.

Becoming an Advocate

How did these women develop the self-confidence to act as advocates for their children, sometimes even challenging the views and practices of professional educators? Delmy linked her assertiveness with the teacher to her own education level, emphasizing that she "knows her rights" because she is an educated person. Harriet and Selma, both of whom have three children, pointed out that they learned through bitter experience that it was important to speak up when there was a problem concerning their children. As Harriet put it:

> I got a big mouth, I guess. I paved Shondra's way, but how could I not say anything? How can you not pave the way? And I paved Allen's way by learning to talk. Learning how to talk for my kids and learning how to deal with adults when it comes to my kids.

Three of the women connected with DSS mentioned that they sensed from the teachers a disrespectful or dismissive attitude that they felt was based on the teachers' knowledge of the mothers' involvement with DSS. As a result, they lacked confidence that their opinions would be valued by the teachers. As Kathy pointed out:

I sense a weird feeling that has something to do with DSS. Like, that is something that bugs me. I wasn't abusing my child, you know? I was abusing myself . . . I just sensed something, and it was like, then I got mad. Because, don't judge me . . . I just felt like, they're going to be like twice as hard on me.

These comments reveal that some women were aware that teachers harbor critical thoughts about their competence as mothers. Although these mothers report resisting that characterization, it may be that the teachers' views—real or perceived—in some way undermined their feelings of efficacy as mothers. Susan Kontos and her colleagues report that child-care providers are indeed often contemptuous of parents, particularly single, low-income mothers.[1]

Becoming a Teacher and Moral Guide

Another important responsibility that many women defined as part of their duty as mothers was teaching their children basic concepts such as color and shape as well as literacy and numeracy skills. Given the emphasis they placed on getting a good education, the majority of the mothers we interviewed felt it was incumbent upon them to supplement the preschool programs, but, as we will discuss further in Chapter 8, not all of them felt competent or successful doing so. (They seemed to feel more competent teaching their children social behavior such as respect for adults, as we explore in Chapter 7.) Helena clearly believed that it was important for her to spend a lot of time with her daughter having fun as well as doing both formal and informal learning activities. She frequently mentioned all the things she was teaching Shawna, including learning to recognize numbers and letters, to tie her shoes, and to write her name. She also mentioned joining a book club, having her daughter help with the cooking, and taking her to the library and the park. This intense involvement contrasted with her own childhood, in which her mother was too busy and uninterested ("always in the background") to interact with Helena and her siblings.

Other women appeared to understand the importance of having an adult act as teacher and moral guide but did not have enough time to do as much as they would have liked. Shirl tried to engage Martin in rough play and sports to make up for the absence of his father. And she clearly monitored his activities and guided him toward her goals of educational achievement, nonaggression, and respect for authority. For example, she coordinated with the day-care provider to ensure that Martin's back talking and tantrums were punished; she didn't want him to lose out on educational opportunities because of behavioral problems. But she also acknowledged being too busy to spend a lot of time interacting with Martin, explaining that her family day-care provider has more time than she does to work on his literacy skills:

> Like when he's at home, you know, I get home from work, and I'm ironing my clothes, getting ready for the next day at work. You know, I'll give him paper and pencils to draw on, which is different, 'cause he sits there and he does it himself, you know. When he's there with her [provider] you know, she helps him, she does the, like she has the paper with a big *O* and a little *o* and all that, and then he has to copy that, and stuff like that. See, and I don't do that at home.

Others, like Pamela and Wilma, tried to be teachers but felt that their children weren't "catching on." Aggie was flatly unwilling to try to teach her son if the school wouldn't "do its part" by teaching him as well.

Providing Love and Attention

In addition to protecting, teaching, and guiding their children, these women were aware of the emotional side of parenting—both their need to connect with their children and their children's need for affection and parental involvement. We found significant differences among mothers with respect to their emotional connections with their children. Both Helena and Shirl, as we have seen, had intense, warm relations with their children. It is easy to be charmed by Shirl's infectious enthusiasm about her life with Martin. Shirl was clearly enchanted with him and was always ready with an anecdote describing another of his accomplishments or more of his shenanigans. As she put it, "Martin is real smart. He's no fool. Martin is no fool. I myself think he is smarter than most two-year-olds. I don't want to be bragging, don't think I'm bragging about my son, but if you met Martin, you would say the same thing!"

Because Shirl feels so secure about her role as mother, she is not worried about being away from Martin while she works. For Helena, motherhood was not such a carefree matter. She felt a tremendous responsibility to ensure that her daughter had a happy childhood. She tried to fulfill this responsibility by indulging Shawna with material possessions, accepting immature behavior, and buffering her from the harsher aspects of reality. For example, when the interviewer noted all the toys and art materials in Shawna's room, Helena replied: "I spoil her rotten [hugs child]. I really do. But nobody else is going to, so . . ."

Helena appeared to appreciate childish behavior and felt that a certain amount of indulgence is acceptable. When asked to describe the type of woman who would make an ideal baby-sitter, Helena remarked that an older person would be better because she would be more patient, "just accepting a child for a child, and not expecting them to be able to tie their own shoes or be able to get their own lunch."

Her view that a child should be allowed to be a child led her to feeling ambivalent about the lack of self-control exhibited by Shawna. On one hand, she realized that her daughter lacked self-control. Helena described a typical scene in which her daughter lost control at her aunt's house when she was five years old: "She is nuts over [aunt's boyfriend], she is like a little top spinning out of control, into a frenzy, and she can't control herself. I have to leave, we have to physically leave, put our coats on, so I can get her to calm down sometimes."

On the other hand, she felt reluctant to impose rules on Shawna, given that she "probably is a hyperactive child." For instance, she described an incident when five-year-old Shawna ignored her repeated requests to put her pajamas on, preferring "to dance around." Helena gave up, reasoning, "Instead of yelling at her, 'Come on now, what are you doing, let's go!' you know, I figure it's no big deal. So okay, 'Do your little jig.'"

Part of Helena's difficulty in establishing the boundaries of her own role may have been that she was consciously trying to depart from the child-rearing style of her own mother, which was very harsh, apparently to the point of being abusive. Helena remarked, "It's sad to say the things I remember [about childhood] are the times that my mother was just, you know, totally freaking out."

Helena was aware of her tendency to be what she calls "overprotective," and in early interviews she expressed the belief that having Shawna in child care was helpful because it encouraged Helena to stop worrying about keeping Shawna spotless. As a working mother, she was forced to relinquish some control over the household. When asked how having Shawna in child care had affected her ideas about child rearing, Helena remarked:

> Like I said before, just that I don't have to be as, this is the way it is and that is the way it's going to stay. Just very like no leniency at all. I think because I just don't have the time to be that strict.

Other mothers also reflected on the importance of creating a relaxed, warm atmosphere, particularly if they themselves had been abused or neglected as children. Jackie, shuttled between households as a child and abused by her stepfather, was adamant about allowing her children to "be children":

> The most important thing is that for her to live out her childhood, you know? To like, as I said before, it's important for me to allow both of my children in every way to remain a child. To be a child, and live out their childhood, not to put responsibilities on them too fast.

Similarly, Harriet, who perceived herself as the "ugly duckling" in a family of eight children, lived out her need to love and be loved through her own children, particularly her daughter:

> I felt unwanted coming up. I really did. And when I have my kids I just, like I tell my older son, I just wanted to love somebody. You know, I wanted somebody to love me, I want to have a family . . . You know, and I think, with my love and attention, with all the things that I always got a bearing on my boys, especially my boys, because it's you know, at this time in the world where things are so bad for these black young boys, that I'm always here. I'm always there.

The warm and loving involvement of most of the mothers was less obvious in the cases of Pat, Aggie, and Pamela. Pamela in particular was painfully conscious of her lack of maternal feelings and her impatience with her son:

> But sometimes I feel a little guilty, you know, sometimes that I don't have the patience, 'cause when I'm like, on vacation? Like I was on vacation, but I didn't go no place. I sent him to day care every day! (laughs) . . . I feel bad because I don't think I'm a mother type, you know?

Pamela carried around a substantial amount of guilt for neglecting her son, and the words of her mother appeared to ring in her ears: "You know, you're supposed to play with your kids!"

Aggie and Pat seemed less conscious that their conception of motherhood might be deemed inadequate by others. Pat manifested a certain detachment from her son, who spent a great deal of time with his father and paternal grandparents; he was picked up on Friday night by one of them and returned to Pat's apartment on Sunday night. When asked what she liked to do in her free time, she mentioned sleeping, bowling, bingo, watching television, and visiting friends—not activities that focused on Joshua. When asked what kinds of things she has taught her sons, she said, "Oh . . . always say 'please' and 'thank you.' Ah, I don't know, cleanliness, you know? I don't know, it just comes natural, I guess. I don't know!"

Although she spent a lot of time with him, Aggie appeared to take little pleasure in her son; throughout the interviews she complained about the burden of caring for him. As a new mother she felt "overwhelmed" by the dependent newborn. As he grew older she continued to feel trapped by his neediness and his misbehavior, at one point saying that if she didn't discipline him strictly he would "walk all over me, him being the boss and me being the prisoner." Whereas the preschool teachers liked the gregarious and self-sufficient little boy, Aggie could not stand his constant talking, claiming, "He drives everyone crazy . . . because he never shuts up." Because "he was with me all day long and he was driving me crazy," she arranged to put him in a family day-care home, even though she was unemployed.

Her basic lack of connection with Fred manifested itself in her limited understanding of her role as protector, teacher, and advocate as well. The primary reason she became involved with DSS was that she did not seek dental care for Fred's rotted teeth. When asked whether she agreed with the discipline strategies used by her family day-care provider, she remarked, "Alls I know is, nobody better be hitting my kid without me hitting him." Another example of her lack of attention to her son's needs was her decision to remove him from the family-care setting for the summer:

> I understand he's in the day care because I wanted him there, so that he's not with me all the time. But I also don't want to sit around in the summertime waiting for him to come home from school so I can go out! And then have to rush home so he can be ready for school the next morning. I wanted my summer free.

Thus wide variation is apparent in these women's conceptions of what it means to be a mother. Although all were concerned at some level with protecting their children from danger and abuse, the amount of attention and affection they gave their children differed widely.

Fathers: Help or Hindrance?

In our sample, the range of roles played by fathers was quite broad. In only one of the households—Beatriz's—was the target child's father living with the mother throughout the data-collection period. Nevertheless, most of these women expected, sought, and accepted active involvement from the fathers in caring for their children. They played an important role in shaping and monitoring the relationships of their children with the fathers. This role was a continuation of their basic mission to protect and advocate for their children, as well as to nurture their emotional stability.

On a practical level, fathers provided varying degrees of financial and instrumental support, and mothers were basically the ones who decided when and how to accept assistance. A number of the fathers cared for their children while the mothers were working. For example, Pat's (now estranged) husband cared for their son for two years while she worked; he was on workman's compensation after being injured on the job. After the couple split up and he moved back to his parents' house, he and his parents remained very involved, taking Joshua home after work on Friday and returning him to his mother's on Sunday night.

Similarly, Kathy's partner cared for their son for almost two years while she worked nights as a cocktail waitress. After the couple separated, he moved home with his parents, who continued to care for Darren every weekend.

Even though they themselves felt distant from these men, many of the mothers actively sought to maintain contact between their children and their children's fathers because of the children's emotional attachment. When asked what was most important in raising her child, Wilma replied:

> I want to give her all the love I can. I didn't grow up around my father, and I want her to—her father to be involved with her as much as possible. That's important to me.

Two of the fathers attempted to maintain a relationship with their children from prison. In Shirl's case, the father was very involved in caring for his son as an infant. During that period he became a drug addict, however. Shirl acknowledged that this man had "been there" for her son, and she realized that he would like to maintain closer contact with him. But she feared for her own safety and, as a result, had taken out a permanent restraining order against him. Pamela was also involved in an abusive relationship with her child's father. Because of his drug use, she would never allow Cedric's father to care for him when he was an infant. In spite of all these problems, she maintained a relationship with her son's father, who had been in prison since she left him. She struggled to articulate why she continued to maintain the ties:

> I kinda want to make sure my son always has his father, even though my mother says, "Just cut the ties . . ." His father loves him and always—even when he comes out and wants to see him, and he'll buy him something, buy him a bike, all that, and know, I know in my heart that if he got himself together that he would be very active in his [child's] life, 'cause this is his only kid and he always loved him. He got—he got pictures—and each time anybody's, he always talks about his son.

She regularly took her son to visit his father in prison, and conveyed the sense that Cedric was very aware of his father's presence.

Jackie also acknowledged the attachment her children felt to their fathers. In spite of the extensive abuse she suffered at his hands, she allowed her son's father to call his child from prison in California. She explained, "I didn't want to feel like I was totally knocking [my son] off from his father, and what I did, I told him, 'OK, you can call him and you call collect,' and I mean I felt like that was fair."

Helena acted as a buffer, limiting her daughter's exposure to her father because she felt that he was too undependable to provide any benefit. Helena was very bitter that he appeared more interested in his son Scott than in Shawna:

> He sees Scott every Sunday, picks him up from nine to twelve, spends every Sunday with him, and then the woman that he's involved with, she has a child, and he's over there with that child all the time. It's like [Shawna] is sort of pushed over to the side. And I don't like that. It's like, this is his first-born, she is just as much a child of his as Scott is, or this other woman that he's involved with. It gets me really angry. It's just like, she is not going to be treated like that. She's done nothing to him. There is no reason for him to treat her like that. So I would just as soon not have him around her.

Three conclusions can be drawn about the role of men in these women's lives. First, mothers played a very large role in controlling and monitoring fathers' interactions with their children. Second, when the fathers' own families—particularly their mothers—were involved in the children's care, the fathers had more contact with their children than when the fathers were acting on their own. This suggests that strategies for increasing fathers' involvement in child rearing should include exploring and strengthening their family networks. Third, it was striking how little these mothers expected of men—either as fathers or as partners. Many had experienced numerous abusive relationships with men, and though some had active social lives that included men, they rarely brought up the possibility of marriage when talking of their dreams and expectations for the future. It appeared that their plans for themselves and their children were developed under the assumption, tacit or explicit, that they and they alone would be responsible for making things happen.

Making Things Happen: What Helps, What Hurts

In determining whether women are able to carry out their notions of what it means to be a mother, three key factors must be examined: their views concerning work, their relations with extended family members, and the nature of their child-care settings. We turn first to women's conceptions of work. For most of the women in our study, work was essential to feeling independent of men, building a stable economic future, and creating a community for stimulation and companionship. Shirl expressed the view of many when she talked about the importance of work in freeing her from unhealthy dependence on men:

> I feel like a woman should not have to sit at home and depend on the husband to be the breadwinner while you take care of the kids. That's just me. I'm not like that. I'm very independent. I don't want to have to ask any man for anything!

When Martin was born, she decided to return to work quickly, even though her husband offered to support her and let her stay at home. In short, as she put it, "I say that to myself now, if I hit the Megabucks [lottery] I would still work."

Harriet not only needed to feel independent but also wanted to model that independence for her children:

> You don't see me laying around here being Miss Slob, you know, watching soap operas and popping bon bons in my mouth and not worrying about if you got a dinner on the stove or the house is clean. I'm trying to give you [her children] something here.

Many of the women were also attracted to work as a means of gaining more skills and improving their stations in life. Shirl was taking courses at a community college to "better" herself. The theme of self-improvement came through particularly strongly from the immigrant mothers in the sample. Beatriz, for example, made it clear that she worked hard to rise above her initial position as a housekeeper:

When I had [my older son] I worked as a housekeeper. I worked for four years but in the mornings I always went to study English for two or three hours and then after I continued to do cleaning from four to midnight and during the morning I continued to study English.

These women sacrificed to achieve their goals. Sol decided not to marry the father of her daughter because she feared that the relationship would interfere with her professional goals:

I became pregnant, then I didn't get together with him, because I didn't want a commitment, so we didn't live together . . . I didn't want to have the responsibility because I wanted to study—and thanks to—I continued studying.

Delmy felt that in traditional societies women are prevented from feeling the self-fulfillment (*realizarse*) that comes with achieving professional goals:

You feel like you have no rights if you cannot become fulfilled . . . You're not complete, you haven't achieved your goals. You have your goals and you have to achieve them, like all human beings have their own goals. And at the end you have to feel good, that you have done what you have always wanted to do.

Even though these women were not employed in high-status jobs, the majority appeared to enjoy working. Helena said she loved her job and was very happy to go back to work after her time at home with Shawna: "I didn't realize how much I missed it. I just liked being with adults and the interaction." In spite of liking it, however, she eventually quit when work got in the way of her ability to care for Shawna. Kathy expressed a lot of enthusiasm for her waitressing job, even though she, too, eventually quit in order to spend more time with her son: "That's what I like to do! I like physical—I'm very fast-paced, I'm a hyper person. That's what keeps me happy. I like to move, all the time. I love it."

Working and Parenting

All the women except Aggie felt that working was important for self-improvement and stimulation, so they were motivated to continue. How successful they were in doing so depended heavily on the support they received from extended family and child-care providers. Helena did not have dependable family support. Shirl represented a contrasting case; assisted by a dedicated family day-care worker and a stable family network, she was able to maintain a full-time job, particularly since she saw her motherly role as providing guidance and love, but not necessarily a lot of day-to-day interaction.

Roughly half of the women were similar to Shirl in that they felt little tension between their family and professional responsibilities. Most of them felt fully supported by their families and child-care providers. For example, Wilma never worried about missing work when her daughter or her provider became ill:

> I've never had to take time off work because she's [daughter] been sick. And the two people that I work for, they've really been great, if I have to take her to the doctor or anything. . . . When [my provider] is out sick, fortunately my sister's at home . . . but if my sister wasn't available, they have alternative day care, where they've got other people that I could have taken her to.

Brenda's situation was even more similar to Shirl's. Living in her parents' home, on AFDC, she had few problems attending school and raising her daughter. For Brenda, being a single mother and going to school "is hard sometimes, but it's all right. I like it. I have my family and I have a lot of help from my family, so that makes it even better."

When a feeling of conflict arises, it may be because— as in Helena's case—a woman feels that maintaining a full-time job prevents her from spending enough time with her children. Both Harriet and Selma were deeply committed to being fully present in their children's lives. They both valued communication and active involvement in schooling and recreation. Selma decided to work part time when her third daughter was born for the following reasons:

> I really wanted to spend some time with Zumary when she was a baby. And I realized how much I lost with the other two . . . It's

awful! I remember when I used to leave them at [the provider's] house. I would sit there with them a bit, watch TV with them, then I would leave, and . . . I would still have a hard time doing that, 'cause I remember the six-month-old . . . she would crawl all the way to the door, and I would have to hurry up and close it so that she wouldn't get out, and I would cry and cry.

Kathy quit the cocktail waitressing job she loved because her son was so distressed at never being with her:

He just missed me so much. 'Cause I was working every night . . . that's why I quit my job. So he's getting so adjusted to the fact that I'm around and don't go to work at night now. It's nice, we sit home and we watch movies together. We can actually eat dinner together and I don't have a baby-sitter in my house three nights a week.

Except for Wilma, whose employers were generous in giving her time off when her daughter was sick, the women portrayed their employers as insensitive to their family needs. Helena's original employer did not support her request for part-time work, nor did he excuse her when her daughter's schedule interfered with work. Pat described dragging herself back to work after a gall bladder operation because her boss considered her indispensable as the main secretary in his law office. A frequent theme concerned the issue of timing—how to leave work at the end of the day and make it to the child-care center without incurring a late pick-up fee. For those who relied on the bus to get from work to the child-care setting, this was a source of anxiety, particularly in the winter, when transportation was often slow and unpredictable. Neither employers nor center personnel seemed able to help ease this problem. In contrast, the mothers noted the flexibility of pick-up times among family day-care providers.

The cost and stability of child care were also important factors in determining how successfully women balance child care and work. For the women with child-care slots, which were more or less guaranteed as long as child care was needed, the financial problem was less acute. But for those with a voucher, the decision to work sometimes appeared not to make financial sense. Beatriz described her own situation when faced with the likelihood that her voucher would not be renewed after one year:

> I was talking with my mother and I was saying, "Imagine, I make about $260 a week, and if I pay $140 in baby-sitting and spend $20 a week on gas, plus in food and things, $20. What's left is $80. It's worth not working." . . . It's best for me to go on welfare, at least for a while, right? I would have money, work less, right?

For Beatriz, the difficulty of financing child care led to a continual struggle over how to maintain a job.

Psychologists like Ellen Hock have tended to construe mothers' beliefs about their roles as parents and workers in terms of the construct "maternal separation anxiety."[2] The focus of their work is mothers' perceptions of how their infants respond to separation from them, how sensitively other caregivers can care for the infants, how separation affects the mothers themselves, and the mothers' views concerning work and its importance in their lives. These studies show that a moderate amount of maternal anxiety is associated with a secure attachment between mother and infant. Mothers who treat the separation experience very lightly, as well as those who perceive it as extremely traumatic, are likely to have less secure attachments to their infants.

Recent work suggests that the construct of maternal separation anxiety may describe white middle-class parents but not necessarily those outside the mainstream. Robin Harwood found little evidence that Puerto Rican mothers view attachment (and the effects of separation) as a major issue in mother-infant relations.[3] Even middle-class American Mormon mothers—in spite of their tradition of staying at home with large families—do not show the same concerns about the effects of separation upon their children as do non-Mormons.[4]

Our study suggests that mothers did have concerns about leaving their young children with providers, but that these concerns did not focus primarily on threats to the children's basic attachment to their mothers. Of all the mothers, only Shirl alluded to the attachment controversy, dismissing the fear that a child won't know "who Mommy is" if she returns to work. Rather, these mothers feared that negative elements in the environment would harm their children in ways that they couldn't control. Thus they worried incessantly about sexual abuse and violence in family day care and center care. Some, such as Helena and Pat, worried when their children were exposed to other children who were overly aggressive or otherwise emotionally and socially incompetent. They worried about the effects on their children of having fathers who flitted in and out of their lives. They worried about teachers who were harsh, incompetent, or rejecting. These concerns led them to conceptualize their roles first and foremost as protectors and buffers, and galvanized them to act strategically on their children's behalf.

Several of these women did acknowledge that long daily separations from their children were painful. Harriet wistfully imagined what it would be like to stay at home, with time to make a nice hot breakfast for her children and read them stories. Mothers such as Harriet and Helena, who focused heavily on their roles as companions and teachers, missed these small moments of daily interaction. Other mothers, such as Pamela and Pat, were more detached and did not report feeling traumatized by leaving their children while they went to work.

Ultimately, however, the pull to work or study at least part time was stronger than the pull to stay home for all but one mother. These women's descriptions of work and its meaning defy the stereotype of the impoverished woman as—in Harriet's words—"Miss Slob, popping bon bons in her mouth." Work is a means not only of survival but also of self-betterment, independence, stimulation, and companionship. Thus the desire to work was the least variable element in the equation describing the balance of work and motherhood. These women did not express feelings of futility or alienation from a system in which the cards seemed stacked against them; rather, they attempted through work and through their identities as nurturers and protectors to improve incrementally their own status and that of their children. Dorinne Kondo describes this complex interplay between resistance and reproduction of societal norms in which people "inevitably participate in their own oppressions, buying into hegemonic ideologies even as they struggle against those oppressions and those ideologies."[5]

The symbolic construction of work and motherhood must be seen within the context of women's lives. These elements of a child's "developmental niche"—cultural models and child-rearing practices plus the elements of the social and physical setting—clearly work together in determining whether mothers can find child-care arrangements that meet their emotional and material needs.[6] As we saw, there was a lot of variation in the extent to which family and providers afforded the support that mothers needed to pull off their complex balancing act. Mothers such as Shirl, Pat, and Brenda, who were strongly supported by extended family and their child-care providers, had made stable and rewarding employment and education arrangements. Others, such as Helena and Selma, whose extended families were not particularly helpful and who had strong feelings about their primary role as mothers, had moved to less stable, part-time jobs. And for those few without a satisfactory means of funding child care—such as Beatriz—the prospect of returning to welfare remained a preoccupation.

These mothers responded to their social reality by weaving together elements of resistance and accommodation, depending upon the circumstances and resources available. Elements of resistance included developing job skills to remain economically independent of men and the state, and ignoring advice and recommendations regarding their children if the source was not trusted and credible. This form of resistance is neither extreme nor pervasive. Rather, these women engage in what Kondo characterizes as "multiple, mobile points of potential resistance." Significantly, they remain largely within the parameters of "legitimate" society (with occasional unexpected journeys into homelessness or drug addiction).

These mothers recognized that in the dangerous and unpredictable worlds in which they lived they were not going to be able to create a fairy-tale existence for their children. Yet they constantly battled to create a safe zone where their children could be protected from danger, where educational opportunities were provided, where loving family was available, and where material needs were met. In the words of Selma, when she was asked whether she would have changed anything about the way she had raised her three daughters: "No, I don't think so. I think I did the best with what I had."

CHAPTER FOUR

Conceptions of Children's Behavior

❧

The nature of evil in children has long been a topic of debate. In the West, romantics like Rousseau saw the child as inherently good and susceptible to evil only when exposed to it by adults. The countervailing Calvinist position, exemplified by John Wesley, argued that children were born with the potential for evil as a result of Original Sin. Elements of these conflicting beliefs are still present in parents' views of their children. Advocates of corporal punishment still justify physical chastisement, as did Wesley, on the ground that adults need to exorcise a child's evil tendencies before they get out of control. When it comes to tacit assumptions about the child's inner character, our beliefs change quite slowly.[1]

The philosopher John Locke, writing in the late seventeenth century, argued that the social environment played a role in shaping a child's character. Around the turn of the century, Freud and his followers emphasized the importance of parents in channeling the child's primary biological impulses. The environmentalist position has found very strong advocates in modern times, including among behavioral psychologists such as B. F. Skinner. One implication of this position is that parents are held responsible for the actions and character of their children. If a child does poorly in school, lacks self-confidence, or fights with peers, environmentalists blame the parents. If a child excels or is a model of good comportment, parents receive a lot of the credit.

In the past fifteen years or so, the primacy of the environmentalist position has eroded somewhat in research on family socialization. It has become popular to describe socialization as "bidirectional," acknowledging that the child's personality will affect caregivers' socialization priorities and methods. Research on infant temperament has revealed that babies vary in their moods, their level of social activity, and their sensitivity to outside stimuli. Parents respond differently to a fussy, "difficult" infant than to one who is quiet and complacent, a "good baby."

There is also some evidence in mainstream culture that environmentalism is on the wane. The bellwether of social mores, Ann Landers, is more and more likely to sympathize with parents whose children turned out to have problems, despite the fact that the parents baked cookies, drove car pools, and coached softball teams. This post-1950s shift toward recognizing that children's basic personalities do play a role in their socialization reflects the fact that parents today often feel they cannot control their children's varied social experiences— because they are in competition with peers, the media, and pop culture.

Our research picks up on the notion that it is not enough to study what mothers think and do as if they were operating in a vacuum. We must recognize that parents are *reactive* as well as proactive in the socialization adventure—and in large part they are reacting to actions and characteristics of their children. Furthermore, we must acknowledge that the actions of their children are filtered through mothers' own cultural models. Mothers' expectations and values shape what they tend to see and not see in their children, and the meanings they attach to behavior that catches their attention. In this chapter we look at the children of the women we interviewed through their mothers' eyes. Our first objective was simply to find out how the fourteen mothers described their children. We know the terms that researchers use to classify children, but which elements of their children's character are important to these mothers; what did they pick up on and what did they ignore?

Second, we wanted to know how the women evaluated the characteristics they perceived in their children. What did they like about their children and what did they feel upset and worried about? Because we are embedded in our own cultural milieu, we tend to take for granted everyone shares our views about which kinds of behavior are atic and which are acceptable. Yet textured descriptions of socialization in other cultures reveal that what is considered misbehavior depends upon the values of the society.

We were curious to discover how these descriptions and evaluations differed according to the child's gender. Although some of the more obvious forms of gender stereotyping may have disappeared from the home and classroom, many studies find that it still exists in more subtle forms, often outside the consciousness of the parent. We were curious to learn more about gender stereotyping among the women in our sample. What did they see as typical of boy or girl behaviors and how did their own children fit into those expectations? As Wilma put it, these women were "fiercely independent." Most of them were taking on the traditionally male role of primary breadwinner. Some of them had been raised in families headed by working single mothers. These factors made it seem unlikely that they would attempt to inculcate stereotypical behavior in their own children. By contrast, other women, especially the Latinas, described growing up in families where gender roles were quite traditional. Furthermore, it was unclear whether or not the women saw being employed and financially independent as incompatible with other forms of "traditional female behavior." Perhaps their conception of appropriate gender behavior was differentiated—even fragmented or inconsistent—rather than dichotomized into two internally consistent categories of "traditional" versus "liberated."

We also became interested in how mothers' understandings of their children changed over time. As their children emerged from the mysterious silence of infancy and became garrulous toddlers and preschoolers, what did mothers discover about them? We were able to witness the unfolding of their children's personalities through the mothers' perceptions. As the children moved into the world of extended family and outside caregivers, mothers themselves began to see how others viewed their children. They saw their children reflected in the "looking glass" formed by the perceptions of others, and these reflected images became increasingly important elements of their dynamic construal of their children. The sociologists William Corsaro and Kathleen Brown Rosier documented the experiences of Zeena, a low-income African-American girl, as she moved from a preschool serving children similar to her to a kindergarten populated by children from white, middle-class families. Zeena's behavior was seen as appropriate by teachers in the preschool but deemed immature and overly aggressive by the teacher in the middle-class kindergarten. The authors witnessed Zeena's mother struggling with the new evaluations of her daughter, and described how she incorporated images of her child derived from the "looking glass" provided by others.[2] We asked the women in our group when and how they took into account the views of others in constructing images of their children. When were mothers likely to agree with the views of outsiders, and when did they refuse to incorporate outsiders' perspectives?

Cultural Models

Four clusters of cultural models emerged from the descriptions that mothers gave us of their children. The first cluster centered on the issue of dependence—the emotional side of the mother-child relationship. All the mothers were preoccupied with their children's need for affection and involvement with them; all recognized the changes in the intensity and nature of those needs as the children matured. The second cluster dealt with the children's social behavior in a more general sense. This cluster contained models or tacit understandings of the children's relation to the wider world beyond the mother-child dyad, including the characteristics of aggressiveness, bossiness, stubbornness, and gregariousness. The third cluster dealt with the children's intellectual skills, and the fourth dealt with their conformity (or lack of conformity) with gender stereotypes.

These clusters roughly corresponded to the children's ages. Mothers dealt more with issues of dependency when their children were infants. Social behavior and its control became a hot topic when the children were toddlers. As the children approached school age, mothers focused more on their intellectual skills. Gender issues, though perhaps the least closely attached to a particular age, appeared to become more salient as the children reached preschool age.

In this chapter we introduce Beatriz and Wilma. They struggle with the same questions as do all the mothers: Should I encourage my child to be more independent? Why won't my rambunctious toddler listen to me when I tell her something? Is my child ready to handle the challenges of elementary school? Yet Beatriz and Wilma differ from each other in important respects. For instance, Beatriz was very concerned about her son's headstrong behavior but felt it was inevitable that first-born boys would defy their mothers. Wilma wasn't so likely to attribute her daughter's misbehavior to uncontrollable forces like birth order, and she was more sanguine about having a positive effect on her development.

WILMA: CONFIDENT WORKER, CARING MOTHER

Our first conversation with Wilma occurred in the cafeteria of the tony law firm where she works as a legal secretary. Poised, smiling, and carefully dressed, she projected an image of someone who "has her eye on the prize" and knows she will get it. Wilma, thirty-one at the time of our first interview, was born in Barbados. Her parents split up when she was thirteen, and her father moved to the United States. Wilma had bitter memories of her father, particularly his unwillingness to help the family after he came to America, while they were still living in poverty in Barbados. She and her mother, a nurse's aide, moved to the United States when Wilma was eighteen. She attended high school and one year of college in Boston and became an American citizen. Wilma settled into a relationship with an American man, and gave birth to a daughter, Janis. After thirteen years of living together, the couple split up. Wilma remained on good terms with him, and he continued to be involved in caring for Janis, who was three years old at the time of the breakup. Wilma's family lived nearby and provided child care and other assistance from time to time.

Wilma was successful in mobilizing social services to supplement her income. She went on welfare during the last months of her pregnancy, but returned to work at the law firm when her daughter was nine months old. She located a family day-care provider with the help of a resource and referral agency that furnished a list of providers in her area. She received a subsidized voucher for child care, but it expired when Janis was four. At around that time, Wilma became concerned that she wasn't learning enough at the family day-care home and placed her in a center run by a charitable organization. Wilma expressed satisfaction with the center, which was more academically oriented and a little cheaper than family day care.

BEATRIZ: THE CHALLENGE OF RAISING TWO YOUNG BOYS

Beatriz grew up in a middle-class family—mother, father, and three children—in El Salvador. She attended high school, where she took secretarial courses. When Beatriz was seventeen, her mother came to the United States and took a job in the kitchen of a large hotel. Beatriz and her brothers followed two years later, leaving their father alone in El Salvador. Shortly after arriving in Boston, Beatriz became involved with a man from El Salvador who worked as a car mechanic. They had two sons. Beatriz was the only woman in the sample who lived with her children's father throughout the study.

After her first child was born, Beatriz worked as a housekeeper at a hotel from 4 P.M. to midnight. In the morning she attended English classes. For the first couple of years she relied on her family for child care, but she eventually enrolled her son in Head Start. She attempted to get a scholarship to take business classes, but was told she made too much money to qualify for the program. Determined not to spend her life cleaning hotel rooms, she made a decision to go on welfare and soon thereafter received financial support to study. Her second son, Jorge, was born four years after her first. When he was seven months old she began working as a receptionist. She put Jorge in family day care and was very happy with the provider, Isabel, a Honduran woman who used to be an elementary school teacher. After school, Beatriz's older son also was cared for by Isabel. Beatriz received a voucher to offset the cost of their care; at the time of our first interview, the cost to her was $50 per month. Beatriz noted with satisfaction that Isabel continued to take education classes. She felt that Isabel was able to provide the children with a rich educational experience, and to give her valuable insights into raising them. She also approved of the active role Isabel's husband played in caring for the children, especially since she believed that her active boys needed a man's guidance. By the last interview, Beatriz had been told that her voucher would soon expire, bringing her child-care costs to $140 per week for the two children. She was contemplating quitting her job and going back on welfare.

Dependence and Independence

Each of the mothers we interviewed had considered the effects of day care on her child's feelings of dependence. All mothers sought some sort of balance between dependence and independence, but to most, the perfect balance proved to be quite elusive.

These women felt a lot of love for their children; in fact, love was a defining characteristic of their relationships. Wilma reported on how physically affectionate her daughter was and laughingly predicted that Janis would eventually complain about being told "zillions" of times how much Wilma loved her. For Beatriz, motherhood was "very beautiful . . . a really wonderful experience." As we saw in Chapter 3, this love and dedication to their children was the driving force behind the mothers' constant struggle to protect, provide for, guide, and educate their children.

Yet most of the women found themselves at times chafing under the burden of their children's dependency. Many of the children had no siblings, and few had to "share" their mothers with men. Many children became accustomed to sleeping with their mothers. Wilma, for example, had allowed her daughter to sleep with her until she was three and a half. At that point, anticipating the possibility of a new boyfriend, she tried to get her to sleep in her own bed, but Janis begged to be allowed back in with her mother. Wilma expressed uncertainty about how to proceed, noting that her family day-care provider had originally encouraged the bed sharing. Other mothers also expressed dismay that their children thought of themselves as their mothers' peers. One of the mothers, Jackie, reported that her daughter, Tiffany, seemed to think she could stay up as late as her mother because "oh we friends and we hanging out." Kathy's relationship with her son also was one of companionship among "equals." She worried that he was not "child-like," preferring to style his hair, wear fancy clothes and cologne, and be with her: "He sleeps with me, and he says, he'll lay down during the day and he'll have his arms up under his head and he'll go, 'Ahh I had a pretty good day today, how about you, Ma?'" Kathy was relieved that after entering a Head Start program, Darren seemed to take on more child-like qualities. Pamela had begun to regret her original decision to let Cedric sleep with her out of protectiveness: "When we moved out from his father's . . . it was a bad time and since that time I always wanted to have him close. Then he just grew up, next thing I know, he's still in my bed. He's four and now I want him out!"

For a number of the mothers and children, the daily separation that came when mothers left for work was difficult. The mothers empathized with their children's sadness and tried to understand the situation from a child's viewpoint. Beatriz interpreted Jorge's separation behavior as normal for his age: "Children have stages you know. Now at times he cries in the morning. He says he doesn't want to go, but that's because he wants to go with me. But before he didn't cry. Perhaps he knows he's at the stage that he knows he's going to be left and he doesn't want that."

Many of the mothers felt that their children would become less dependent after attending child care. For example, Helena remarked, "I don't think she is as dependent on me as she was when we were here by ourselves. I couldn't go out, just because we were with each other so much. It was very hard for me to leave her, because she didn't want me to go."

For two of the mothers, Pamela and Aggie, the dependence of their children was overwhelming. Over and over again they talked about their struggle to accommodate the demands of their sons and to get them to, as Aggie often put it, "give her her space." When her son Fred was born, Aggie felt a sense of panic at having "this little person to take care of, who depends on you for everything." Because she did not re-enter the workforce after he was born, she spent more time with Fred than the other mothers in our study spent with their children, a situation that made her feel like his "prisoner."

Pamela was even more aware than Aggie was that her parenting was seen as inadequate by others. Although haunted by her mother's criticism of her lack of involvement with Cedric, Pamela told herself that Cedric did not really need as much attention as other children:

> I always say God gave me the right kid, because I couldn't take those kids that you know, you have to sit down and spend a lot of time with him. 'Cause weekends, he makes his own bowl of cereal, puts in his movies . . . He does everything on his own. He's very independent.

For Pamela and Aggie, becoming independent meant becoming more separate and perhaps more disconnected from their children. Even though she could appreciate her son's independence, Pamela expressed surprise and some remorse when describing an incident in which three-year-old Cedric opted to spend the afternoon with some people he barely knew rather than come home with her.

For most mothers, however, children's independence was defined primarily in terms of learning self-help skills like dressing themselves in the morning. These skills can be nurtured even when emotional ties remain strong between parent and child. Most of the mothers felt that the child-care providers were helping their children become independent by teaching them self-help skills. For Beatriz, it was a mystery how Isabel managed to get her sons to do things that they refused to do at home:

> If while he's eating something falls on the floor, he picks it up, and puts the dish away. Then he gets a rag and wipes up the spill . . . And that's because she teaches them. She just looks at them and says, "Okay, now we are going to eat," and each child knows that he has to go to the living room and get his chair and take it to the kitchen, like the big kids. Stuff that if I cared for him maybe he wouldn't do . . . Or sometimes she punishes them. She gives them "time out" and he stays quietly. When I tell him, he ignores me!

Wilma is perhaps more typical of the fourteen mothers than Beatriz is in that she tried to teach Janis independence skills at home, as well as expecting her to learn them at school. Most of the women mentioned giving their children responsibilities around the house, particularly cleaning their rooms, bathing, and helping with food preparation. For example, Wilma mentioned encouraging Janis to pick up her dirty clothes at night and was teaching her, at age three and a half, to make her bed: "She doesn't do it very neatly, but I'll go on and make a big deal, and I'll say, 'Oh honey, your Mommy is so proud of you, you did a good job.'" Kathy was teaching Darren to clear his dishes after he ate so that he wouldn't be like her lazy brother. She regretted that she did not have enough time to "let him cut the carrots for three hours" when he wanted to help her make dinner.

These women felt that becoming independent had many benefits for their children. Harriet observed her daughter's emerging independence as a source of pride, amusement, and evidence of intelligence:

> I think she really likes the action [involved in going to child care]. Getting up in the morning, going outside, getting on the bus—you know, the action! I think she really likes that, because when that bus comes, [imitating daughter], "Don't touch me! I want to walk up these stairs by myself! I wanna find my own seat!"

Selma also saw independence as beneficial in building self-esteem. She felt that when she moved from a low-quality preschool to a very good kindergarten, Zumary became more outspoken, "expressing herself a little bit more fully," and less dependent on her older sister, having learned that "she could be okay by herself." In terms of academics, Zumary was also learning "that she can do things for herself."

Yet it was not always easy for these mothers to determine exactly how to balance the encouragement of independence with an awareness of their children's still limited competencies. Wilma drew the line when Janis's teacher "evaluated" her at age four and determined that Janis should learn to tie her shoes and zip her coat. To Wilma, it appeared that the teacher only wanted to save herself some work: "I guess there's so many kids in the room, it's too much of a responsibility to go around changing everybody's shoes." Not seeing any benefit to Janis, Wilma resolved to ignore the teacher's suggestion: "I think, to tie a shoelace, that's difficult for a four-year-old . . . and I'm not going to force that on her."

On one hand, Wilma was adamant that she needed to be less protective than her parents had been of her. She felt that as a result of being "sheltered" she was insecure and too introverted to deal with a wide variety of people and situations. She felt that outside experiences were important: "I don't think you can learn everything there is to learn from your parents. You have to go out and experience other things. You have to be around other people, and she [Janis] has to learn to interact with other people." On the other hand, she worried intensely about Janis's welfare, reporting that she felt nervous and guilty even leaving her with her own mother: "I felt like I had deserted her or something." She desperately wanted Janis to have better educational opportunities than those provided by the Boston public schools, but she was too nervous to let her be bused to the suburbs.

Living with Toddlers

As their infants grew into fast-moving toddlers, these women became aware of new characteristics heretofore buried in inscrutable cries and gurgling. The words that women used to describe their children during this time reflected the challenging ways in which the youngsters asserted their individual wills and minds in a social world. The mothers characterized their children in terms of their willingness to conform to adult wishes, the amount of talking they did, and how they got along with peers. They also marveled at their children's sheer energy, sometimes despairing as to whether there was any hope of guiding it into constructive channels. They discussed the rewards as well as the frustrations of dealing with children at this age. For Wilma, the difficulties revolved around getting her daughter to move quickly and smoothly through daily routines like brushing her teeth:

> I hate going shopping with her . . . I end up, well I end up yelling and screaming . . . Sometimes I just let them [Janis and her cousin] go off and do whatever they want to do, 'cause after a while it gets frustrating . . . And it's just like at home, too, the hardest thing is to get her to go to bed at night. Every night I yell and I scream at her because she doesn't like to go to bed . . . I try to be strict and make her go to bed at nine o'clock but then she starts yelling and screaming, "I don't want to go to bed." And then I'll go take her out [of bed] . . . When she's over at my sister's house, my sister said, "Come to bed," she'll just go sit in her lap, she's sitting real quiet and next thing you know, she's sleeping. But she gives me the hardest time.

Many of the mothers reported similar issues. Shirl discussed her strategies for getting Martin to sit down on the bus. Pamela and Helena worried about their children's aggression toward other children at the day-care center. Jackie described Tiffany as bossy and controlling at times. These issues cut across social class lines and are faced by any parent whose child is learning the boundaries of appropriate behavior.

What varied considerably among mothers were the *explanations* they gave for why their children displayed particular characteristics; in scholarly lingo, these explanations are called causal attributions because they refer to the causes to which parents attribute certain characteristics or behaviors of their children. These explanations about causality tended to cluster into two general categories. In one category were explanations that refer to stable attributes of the child—elements of the child's personality or character that might lead him or her to behave in a particular way. In the second category were explanations that refer to elements of the environment, such as the behavior of other kids in the classroom or parents' actions toward the child. Researchers have found that when parents attribute their children's misbehavior to their natures or personalities, they tend to become more angry and more harsh in their reactions than when they think that children misbehaved because of some circumstance in their environment.[3] Such reactions are rooted in the philosophy that children have the potential for evil and that these inborn tendencies must be vigorously stamped out by vigilant parents.

Some of the women in our group bore out this general finding. Beatriz believed that a child's misbehavior was a result of his or her basic character. Here is Beatriz's perspective on the ongoing problems she had with the disrespectful behavior of her older son, Eduardo, who was six when we first started talking with Beatriz:

> But I do punish Eduardo more, because, since he always pays less attention to the mother. Just today I punished him, because I told him not to go outside, because the little one [Jorge] wants to go out, and he can't unless I go out, because it's dangerous. And he didn't pay me any attention, he just went out. And I had just come in [from work], was taking my clothes off, so I just put my clothes on and went to bring him in. I punished him with a belt. He has a very bad character.

In trying to determine why Eduardo misbehaved, Beatriz looked to the problematic formation of his character. She believed that he did not learn as many social skills as Jorge had because he had less early experience in child care:

> Eduardo, he was reared alone, with me, because, that is, with no other children around. And I think it changes, when children are involved with more children, they manage faster, develop more . . . I don't think Jorge is more intelligent than Eduardo at his age, no. But that he's around more children, and sees what the others are doing.

Beatriz felt that Eduardo misbehaved on purpose, even though he understood what behavior was appropriate in a particular situation. She even attributed his many questions to a motive to annoy her:

Eduardo . . . is very intelligent in his studies . . . Sometimes he drives me crazy, he never stops asking. Then Rolando [Eduardo's father] tells me, "That's good," he tells me. Yes, I know. But at times, perhaps, I'm not in the mood for it . . . Sometimes he asks things he already knows. If he doesn't know, that's OK. But sometimes you've already told him, and told him many times, and he knows it, and he asks.

Beatriz frequently discussed with Isabel the problems she had with Eduardo. Isabel tried to convince her that part of Eduardo's misbehavior was related to his age. But though she respected Isabel for having taken many courses in child development, Beatriz did not seem convinced that Eduardo would change as he grew older:

Jorge is a very active, intelligent child. Eduardo has a strong character . . . Jorge [misbehaves] maybe because of his age, but Eduardo, no. I think if I lived alone, do you think I could raise him well? I think he needs a man's discipline. He misbehaves with me. [With his father, he is] a totally different person. He screams at me if I tell him to do something. He says, "Noooo!" So I punish him. I give him a couple of good whacks. But I spank him and he still doesn't do what I tell him. I think it has to do with the strength of character. All the first-born kids in El Salvador are like that . . . Sometimes I don't know what to do.

As her comment reveals, Beatriz felt very little confidence in her own ability to deal with Eduardo. She felt that mothers were particularly unlikely to be effective in getting their children to behave: "It's that children with their mothers are different . . . And her [Isabel], without speaking harshly, she gets them to pay attention. It's because children are like that. I imagine all children are like that." With this type of reasoning, Beatriz had painted herself into a corner. She perceived her children, particularly Eduardo, as acting on the basis of their gender, birth order, and basic character, and reacting to adults along prescribed scripts. She left herself no options for taking a proactive stance.

WILMA: "SHE HAS TO SHARE THINGS"

Wilma, by contrast, was likely to view her problems with Janis as amenable to intervention. For one thing, unlike Beatriz, she had bought into the notion that cognitive limitations in young children's reasoning, as well as lack of experience, contribute to problems they may be having at a particular age. Wilma felt very strongly that Janis should be nice to other people, and repeatedly expressed concern about her unwillingness to share her toys. Her comments reveal that she attributed this failure to share to immaturity rather than to a character deficiency. When asked in the first interview how Janis was getting on in family day care, Wilma mentioned the problem of not sharing and said, "I think that's probably her age. I don't think she has [the idea] that she has to share things. She sees that as hers, and you know, she doesn't want anybody to play with it."

Wilma did not always attribute misbehavior to immaturity, however. At times she felt that Janis misbehaved on purpose, as when she reported Janis's pulling things off the kitchen counter "just to aggravate me." In that incident, Wilma reacted strongly: "And then she'll wait till I scream at her, and then she'll leave it alone. I do fly off the handle sometimes . . . It's just stress, this having to get home and fix dinner and clean her up and have everything that I'm supposed to do done by a certain time." Wilma did not attempt to defend her response to Janis's misbehavior, but rather acknowledged that she lost control during this stressful period in the early evening. Most of the time, Wilma reported, Janis was obedient: "I can tell her something once, and it's very rare that she not listen to me or do it again."

Our conversations with the women on their children's emerging social skills made clear that there is a link between the explanations the mothers give for their children's behavior and their reactions to it. A number of mothers were similar to Beatriz in seeing their children's behavior as stemming from their idiosyncratic personalities, and these were the mothers who appeared to become angry and to use more physical punishment when their children misbehaved. Kathy, for example, described her son Darren as "slick" and "street smart." She continually felt challenged to stay a step ahead of him, because she believed that he tried to manipulate people: "He'll run you into the ground. He knows exactly how to use you, use your mind." As we will see in Chapter 6, Kathy often resorted to "a nice sock on the butt" when she felt that he was trying to pull one over on her. Shirl also emphasized the personality of her son and the role it played in directing his behavior. She tended to be much more positive than Kathy was about her son, describing him as "a trip" and "an entertainer." When he misbehaved, however, it was because of *who he was*, not because of the circumstances he was in or the influence of other people:

> Martin is basically a fresh mouth. It's like he never really does anything bad. It's like running off at the mouth. It's his mouth. Yeah. It's Martin's mouth. He's too smart! Like I said, he's too smart.

Shirl confessed to being too lax when it came to discipline ("I should hit him more than I do"), but she did give Martin "a few good whacks . . . when he deserves it."

Some of the women attributed misbehavior to a wide variety of causes, going beyond the children's own personalities to examine how they as mothers affected their children, and how the children's previous experiences and current circumstances played a role. Like Wilma, these mothers were less likely to punish their children physically. Helena was forever trying to understand the causes of her daughter's aggression at school. She recognized the role that Shawna's intense personality played in her physical outbursts, but she also paid close attention to the role of peers in modeling and provoking aggression. She monitored the effectiveness of Shawna's teachers and social worker in responding to these incidents. Helena did not use physical punishment, but rather attempted to intervene by changing or improving her daughter's environment, including monitoring the type of children to whom she was exposed, quitting full-time work, talking with teachers, and trying to treat Shawna with more respect.

Thoughts about Intelligence

One striking finding in our study was the enthusiasm that the mothers expressed over the intellectual skills of their children. Not a single woman described her child as slow-witted or delayed in cognitive development; most thought their children were exceptionally smart. As we will see in Chapter 7, their optimism about their children's intelligence fit a strong desire to see them begin engaging in formal learning experiences as preschoolers in preparation for "real school."

Mothers tended to use two criteria in determining whether their children were smart. One was how much their children talked and the other was how the children were evaluated by their child-care providers. Their conception of intelligence was co-constructed, that is, formed by their own assessments and indicators invoked by child-care staff. As we have seen, Shirl found Martin's constant talking stressful at times, but she nevertheless viewed it as an indicator of his intelligence. Delmy saw this verbal inquisitiveness in an even more positive light, saying about her daughter Carla: "She's very advanced. She talks, very sociable, plays with the other children. If she doesn't understand the English, she'll ask for the Spanish . . . What I like best about her is that she asks—she doesn't keep quiet—she asks." These views were bolstered by positive feedback from the children's teachers. Harriet reported that Shondra's teachers felt she was very smart and begged Harriet not to send Shondra to public school. Even Pat, who did not exude praise for her son Joshua, picked up the kindergarten teacher's view that he was "advanced" for his age, and reported that he had been selected along with a few other children to learn to read.

The mothers did tend to be critical of their children when they appeared unable to pay attention during school activities. Wilma's views were affected by an evaluation of her daughter conducted at the preschool: "For the most part she's done good. The only thing is her attention span. The teacher says I have to work on that, that she's not very attentive." Wilma mentioned some frustration in trying to teach her daughter to spell, mainly because of her daughter's apparent lack of attention. Helena had also received feedback about Shawna's inability to pay attention during circle time. Helena found this inconsistent with her own observations of Shawna at home, where she seemed to concentrate on her projects for hours at a time, but she was willing to accept the teacher's perspective:

I do have to rely on their judgment and not [necessarily] go along with what they say, but if they suggest something and they say, "Well this is what Shawna is doing and we think it would be beneficial if she got this kind of help," and if I know what her behavior is and I feel it's going to help, fine. I'll take the suggestion and I'll try it out. You know, I'm open to ideas.

In the area of attention, the mothers were generally open to the perspectives and suggestions of professionals, particularly when their own views corroborated those of the teachers.

Thoughts about Gender

The issue of gender came up sporadically in our conversations. In general, the women's views reflected the confusion many people in today's society feel about how boys and girls should differ, and what the best pathway is for parents when it comes to socializing their children. For the most part, the mothers seemed to support gender stereotypes in how they dressed their children and in the toys and other materials they provided. Wilma, for example, told us that she and Janis had a running battle over whether or not Janis could wear pants to the family day-care provider's house:

> Janis and I end up fighting in the morning to get her dressed. She doesn't like to wear dresses. She'll say, "Mommy, I don't wanna wear a dress. I want to wear pants!" And I'll say to her, "Why? Do the other kids at the day care wear pants?" Most of them wear pants, but for some reason I always put her into a dress. 'Cause you know, a dress looks cute!

Wilma recognized that Janis could play more easily in pants, and so she didn't mind that the family day-care provider changed her into old jeans. At the end of the day, the provider cleaned her up and changed her back into her dress. For Wilma, it was important that Janis look good, and she appreciated the provider's sensitivity to her preferences: Janis "hardly every comes back home dirty or with food all over her."

Wilma wanted Janis to develop strengths in areas that were traditionally considered female as well as some that were considered more masculine. Her overwhelming goal for Janis was that she learn to be a nice person who respects others. At the same time, she also wanted her to have "respect for herself" and to be confident and outspoken enough "to deal with any kind of situation." Wilma contrasted her goals for Janis with her own tendency to be shy and unassertive. She felt that among other things, her lack of self-respect had led her to remain in a thirteen-year relationship with a man who did not treat her well, and she wanted to make sure that Janis would be strong enough to avoid such harmful relationships. She was vigilant about possible gender inequities in the classroom, and indignantly recounted an instance in which she had noticed Janis's preschool teacher calling on boys before the girls: "And I had seen, a couple of weeks ago on TV, where the teacher wasn't conscious that she was calling on the boys. And I did see it! In that room!" Although she did not follow up on the issue with the teacher, she underlined for us her expectations for Janis: "I expect her to be treated fairly, no matter because she is a female, you know. She has sense and she's just as smart as a boy, maybe smarter!"

Many of the mothers seemed to be following Wilma's path of emphasizing some gender-related characteristics in their girls while still expecting equity in treatment and opportunities at school. Harriet had always felt ugly as a girl, and as the seventh child in the family, she was always dressed in strange combinations of hand-me-downs. As an adult, she paid no attention to her appearance—refusing to worry about her hair or to wear makeup. But her daughter, she reported with some surprise, "was all girl" and wanted "to look pretty . . . not ugly," and Harriet was willing to help her out. Harriet did not see this as inconsistent with Shondra's goal of being a doctor when she grew up, and she was very supportive of her daughter's education. Like Wilma, Harriet wanted her daughter to grow up being respectful and helpful to others, and at the same time to be a strong, independent woman. Harriet acknowledged that Shondra had a forceful personality but noted that she and Shondra's father were encouraging that: "We're teaching her to be proud of who she is. She's got a lot going for her, and that's her father and me all the time, telling her to be proud and do her best. But she will protect herself."

Mothers of boys also brought up gender issues, but less frequently. Some of the mothers felt that boys were more likely than girls to be aggressive and mischievous; as we saw with Beatriz, boyhood was equated with activity and rebellion. Shirl also expected Martin to be active and set out for herself the task of wrestling with him because he was not able to roughhouse with his father. For Pamela, boyish aggression was not desirable. Having been abused by a violent boyfriend, she was anxious to prevent Cedric from falling into the pattern of aggressive men. She revealed how guilty she felt about telling Cedric to deal with a bully by fighting back, because she later came to believe that she had encouraged Cedric himself to become a bully.

Several of the mothers discussed the issue of sexuality in their children's lives. Wilma mentioned several times that her daughter seemed more responsive to men than to women, and Wilma wasn't sure if this was a problem. Jackie also felt that her daughter was attracted to men, saying she had a "big seductive issue about her" just as she, Jackie, did. Jackie disapproved of and worried about this hypothesized orientation, and she complained to Tiffany's day-care teachers when she came home from school doing hip thrusts to the tune of songs with lyrics like "sex me up." A victim of sexual abuse by her stepfather, Jackie wanted to be sure that Tiffany learned to respect herself and her body. Harriet had noted without anxiety her daughter's preoccupation with understanding male and female anatomy as well as the physiological changes that occur during sexual maturation. But she was very worried about sexual abuse in day care, even to the point of expressing suspicion over the intentions of her daughter's male cousin during the time she spent in the care of her aunt.

Some child-care workers suspected that Cedric, Pamela's son, had been subjected to some sort of sexual abuse, and one of them recommended to Pamela that he be evaluated. Pamela recounted how humiliated and outraged she had been by the clumsy attempt at intervention, which occurred during the evening pick-up time in front of other parents and children. She angrily rejected the provider's suggestion, and did not report to us any concern that there might be validity to the suspicions.

In general, these mothers were struggling with the same issues that confront many middle-class parents. Those with girls, in particular, were gradually developing a sense of how to balance elements of traditional gender identification with the new challenges and opportunities open to women in this society. At the same time, the nature of their communities affected their perspective on some aspects of the debate. Some were particularly exhilarated by the freedom they experienced in the United States compared with the restrictions in their home cultures. Others had grown up in female-headed households and took working and parenting for granted. For these two groups of women, in particular, the need to encourage their daughters to realize their potential was not questioned. Their concerns were more centered on issues of sexuality, even when their children were only preschoolers.

% When these low-income mothers speak about their children, we see that their perceptions and concerns are ones shared by most parents, regardless of their social class. During the course of our study, they were dealing with the seemingly endless energy of toddlers, rapid fluctuation in their preschoolers between egocentrism and social impulses to be empathetic and caring, and wondering what it means in today's world to be a girl or a boy. But their own contexts put a spin on these reflections, making them different from the conclusions of more affluent parents. The primary lesson that comes through in the candid revelations by Wilma and Beatriz is just how difficult it is to be a mother in a decaying neighborhood, with limited funds and competing demands on one's time. Wilma expressed a lot of love for Janis, was carefully pursuing educational experiences for her, and was working hard to ensure that she maintained a relationship with her father. But many factors impinged on her ability to raise Janis exactly as she wanted, and thus her image of Janis and her potential was shaped by these barriers and constraints. We saw, for example, how difficult it was for mothers to encourage their children to be independent when they were constantly worried about their safety. How do you celebrate a child's growing sense of curiosity and self-confidence when you cannot let him leave the apartment unescorted? How do you view a child's relentless questions at the end of the work day when you still have a full menu of cooking, cleaning, and preparations for the next day?

What came through equally clearly in our sample was that gaining access to financial resources isn't the sole answer to these mothers' daily battle to be good parents. We saw that family day-care providers and teachers were relied upon heavily for their perceptions of children, and were quite instrumental in shaping the ways that mothers saw their children. As Helena mentioned, when teachers remarked on something that was also of concern to her as a mother, she was receptive to comments and suggestions that they might have. We saw Isabel make some headway in shaking Beatriz's conviction that Eduardo's misbehavior was the inevitable result of his "bad character." Wilma and others took seriously the evaluations conducted by teachers and tried to respond to areas exposed as weak points. Although family members could also provide useful insights, preschool teachers and providers were particularly important in bringing in new ideas and views from the early childhood field. To the mothers, the perspective that those such as Isabel, fresh from her courses on child development, brought to the table was welcome and helpful in breaking through seeming impasses.

The fourteen mothers were selective in how they used and evaluated professional advice. When it did not match their perceptions, or was proffered in a heavy-handed, insulting manner—as when Cedric's teacher publicly advised Pamela that he needed to be evaluated—the suggestions were rejected. Wilma rebuffed the teacher's suggestion that she teach Janis to tie her own shoes because she saw the teacher as acting from her own interests, not those of Janis. It may seem obvious that parents will take advice only when the source is credible and the suggestions are in line with their own goals for their children, but it is a lesson that must be learned over and over. Professional knowledge and accumulated expertise can be of great value, but only when they are assimilated into the parent's own views through the active process of exchange and co-construction.

The respect that these mothers had for their children's formidable intellectual skills defies the stereotype of low-income parents as dismissive of their children's intellects, or of only valuing qualities peripheral to mainstream definitions of success. It helps us understand why mothers are so receptive to programs that claim to build up children's readiness for academic work. But the predominant response of many educators and social workers is to decry parents for pushing their children prematurely into academically oriented programs. Instead of criticizing parents for not understanding how young children learn, we need to support their interest and involvement.

These conversations revealed a variety of cultural models for why children behave "well" in some situations and stray off the path in others. Careful thought needs to be given to the tendency of some parents to assume that their children's difficulties spring from stable personality traits or "bad character." Mothers who are trapped in the perception that their own actions would make no difference in bringing children under control might welcome suggestions on how to open up their thinking about the multiple causes of behavior. In helping women sort through factors that very likely influence their children's behavior, there is not necessarily one right or wrong answer. But engaging in an open dialogue about the subject—as well as about other contentious issues such as appropriate gender roles and the nature of children's sexuality—can provide a guiding framework that enables mothers to make decisions that are in their children's best interest.

CHAPTER FIVE

Cultural Models of Child Rearing

My child has to learn to live in both cultures, same as me. —*Delmy*

Like most parents, the mothers in our study voiced their opinions on how best to raise their children. Socialization—how to "raise them right"—was a topic that all fourteen women eagerly discussed with friends and kin members. In some of our conversations, we could glean elements of cultural models that were truly tacit, or taken for granted; in these instances mothers enacted a cultural model unquestioningly, with no alternative in mind. More often, however, it was the contested elements of socialization that were discussed—a process resulting in what we call "declared models" because they have been constructed after conscious examination of stated knowledge and principles.

In forming declared models of socialization, these women drew from various sources, including traditional models of child rearing that may have guided their own parents. The individual process of synthesizing and producing declared models of socialization resulted in variation among the women in how they handled issues such as discipline. For instance, a few of the women believed in spanking their children for misbehaving, whereas others were opposed to this form of discipline. Some mothers inculcated in their children obedience to adult authority. Others resisted this method of maintaining order, either because they had bad memories of harsh treatment in their own childhood or because they were learning through experience and observation that they could converse and reason with their children. Many of their socialization practices were the subject of explicit debate and contention as they asked themselves questions such as, Should I let my daughter wear old blue jeans and get dirty at preschool? Does my son talk back to adults when I'm not around? What should I do when his teacher reports that he's been hitting other children? For women such as Delmy, who grew up in Latin America, the challenge was to combine elements of traditional child rearing with methods she observed in her contemporary setting. Hence her statement, featured at the beginning of this chapter, indicating that she and her daughter had to figure out a way to coexist in two cultures.

Over time, each mother was exposed to advice from many people about how to raise her child right. Mothers received advice from their friends and families, as well as the opinions of professionals—primarily preschool teachers and social workers. Many of the women reconsidered beliefs that were initially taken for granted. Often their own experiences or reflections prompted alterations in beliefs or behavior. We became curious about the range of cultural models about which mothers were conscious and reflective. And we were particularly interested in observing the dynamic process that occurs as a child attending day care returns home with novel ways of behaving.

In this chapter, we discuss the goals that these mothers had for their children, and their reflections on the strategies that seemed effective and those that didn't. In Chapter 6, we turn specifically to the area of discipline and explore how mothers instilled the concept of respect for others in their children.

Nurturing Individual Strength and Collective Obligation

The women were concerned with raising their children to be independent and self-reliant, but at the same time were focused on inculcating in them a sense of respect, deference to adult authority, and a spirit of obligation to family. For some, a comfortable synthesis was relatively easy to achieve, whereas for others this was a difficult dilemma. Some mothers who had benefited from welfare wanted to make sure their children hadn't absorbed a message of overreliance on the system. They were already urging their three- and four-year-olds to be independent and self-sufficient. Some had seen rebellious adolescents in their immediate neighborhoods. By encouraging their own children to become independent, they hoped to make them less susceptible to destructive social norms. Yet most mothers also were pushing their children to be deferential to adult authority, to avoid any expression of disrespect. Collective obligations among family members, old and young, were commonly emphasized.

This pivotal area of early socialization plays out somewhat differently for Latino, African-American, and Anglo families. Latinas often come from families with a traditional spirit of collective obligation and subordination of self to the group's welfare. African-American parents also prioritize belonging to the broader kinship network and community.[1] But considerable variation existed among mothers in our sample in how they *blended* individualistic and communal socialization practices. The Latinas valued warm, supportive social relations. But they also expressed their goal of *realizarse*, or reaching their own potential, as well as encouraging their children to do so. They were consciously preparing their children to operate and get ahead in an Anglo-dominated society that they saw as individualistic.

The African-American mothers wanted to nurture a sense of love, trust, and family obligation in their young children. These mothers also knew that their children must become strong individuals in order to survive the risks and demands of inner-city life. They were intent on making their sons and daughters independent and resilient. They knew that if their children were to improve their position in society, they would need to be able to get ahead individually and not be dragged down or led astray by peers engaged in antisocial or self-destructive behavior.

Preparing Children for Two Worlds

The anthropologist Oscar Lewis, studying impoverished Mexican and Puerto Rican families, gave us the stereotyped images of child rearing in the "culture of poverty": practices that contributed to a lack of individual initiative, a "traditional" feeling of fatalism, and loss of control over one's own fate. Lewis's work echoed the century-old dichotomy between *traditional communalism* and *modern individualism*. Early sociologists, such as Ferdinand Tönnies and Emile Durkheim—looking through Western European eyes—argued that industrializing societies were raising children to be independent, unfettered by traditional bonds to the family, church, or village authorities.[2] Modern schooling in Europe contributed to breaking down collective obligations, preparing children to fit into an industrializing economy and coalescing nation-state.

Western psychology often perpetuates an individualistic orientation in its theories of child development. Most perspectives emphasize intra-individual processes that naturally unfold, à la Piaget's constructivist conception of how young children learn. Others focus on how the young child's self-confidence, self-esteem, and curiosity should be nurtured to strengthen his or her ability to work independently and compete successfully later in school. Child-care professionals in the West are often concerned by parenting or preschool practices that demand deference to adult authority, didactic teaching, or socialization that limits blossoming of curiosity and self-expression.

In the last decade, the notion that individualism is a social construction rather than a biological given has penetrated the thinking of a small number of Western social scientists. Patricia Greenfield and Rodney Cocking use the interdependence vs. independence polarity as the organizing rubric for investigating the development of ethnic-minority children in the United States.[3] They urge us to remember that interdependence or collectivism is the predominant belief system of some 70 percent of the world's population. It may be that the benefits of a more collectivist orientation are also becoming apparent to Western scholars who have begun to study Asian children, finding that they frequently outperform American students on achievement tests while miraculously remaining respectful of their parents.[4]

Perhaps it is fair to say that the academic world is waking up to a message that American conservatives have been pushing for a while—individualism has potential costs in the form of less community cohesion, less willingness to sacrifice for the good of one's children, and loss of meaning or spiritual direction. Notable commentators, such as the sociologist James Coleman and the political analyst Francis Fukuyama, have begun to write about how the trust and social capital (support) inherent in traditional, obligatory bonds are not so bad and may even yield both economic and social benefits for families and economies.[5]

But the world cannot be placed neatly into dichotomies. The bilateral distinction between individualism and collectivism may have run its course as an introductory heuristic to understanding cultural differences. American scholars have tried neatly to place entire ethnic groups on a one-dimensional spectrum: in this overly simplified scheme, middle-class Anglo parents raise independent and outspoken children; Latino or Italian-American parents raise youngsters who subordinate self to the welfare of the family or collective group. These superficial categorizations do not take account of the active process by which values and child-rearing strategies are co-constructed by actors in a pluralistic society.

Recent research indicates two important ways in which individualistic and collective world views come together. First, individualistic norms may be encouraged by parents within a collectivist framework. For example, a child's ability to do well in school may be nurtured and assessed in terms of his or her contributions to the family. Secondly, it appears that when nonmainstream groups are committed to their own cultural values and practices, parents may consciously prepare their children for two different worlds. Concha Delgado-Gaitan's research on Latino families, for instance, shows how Mexican-American families in California marshaled time and resources to enable the children to perform independently within formal school settings. Yet parents continued to expect their children to maintain a traditional attitude of respect toward adult family members.[6] In fact, even within middle-class, nonimmigrant families, it is clear that a parent's adherence to collective or individualistic norms will depend not only upon the individual but also upon the situation. By using the concept of cultural models, we can begin to move away from the overgeneralizations engendered by the use of macroframeworks like individualism and collectivism.

Delmy's Model: "Be the best you can be"

In this chapter we will explore in detail the views of Delmy, an immigrant from El Salvador who was thirty at the time of our first interview. Delmy's portrait is highlighted because she exemplified the way in which many women were trying to accommodate a "mainstream" orientation toward individualism with more traditional values such as demonstrating respect for elders and contributing to the community's welfare. Delmy grew up in a close-knit family of fourteen children. She considered her family background to be middle class by the standards of El Salvador. Her mother stayed home with the children and her father worked as a medical assistant. Although her father did not believe that women should work outside the home, he valued educational achievement and sent all his children to Catholic school. Searching for better economic opportunities, he moved to the United States when Delmy was six, and some members of her family eventually followed him. Delmy attended college briefly in El Salvador. After coming to the United States at age seventeen, she enrolled in night classes in various community colleges, working toward the goal of becoming certified as a teacher in a bilingual classroom.

After coming to the United States, Delmy married a Salvadoran who worked as a computer technician. Several years after the birth of their daughter Carla, the couple separated. Delmy expressed her strong desire to keep her former husband involved with Carla's care, and he continued to baby-sit her at least two times a week and take her on outings on Saturdays. Meanwhile, Delmy remained strongly attached to her siblings and her mother, who was seventy-four.

When Carla was six months old, Delmy began working part time as a substitute in a child-care center. She relied on her mother and sister-in-law to care for Carla. Through her sister, Delmy heard about a position as a teacher's assistant at a local elementary school. After landing the job, she placed Carla in a preschool program housed in the same school. She was happy with the program and was glad to be so close to Carla. Delmy originally paid the full tuition of $435 per month, but was eventually able, with the persistent help of the preschool director, to apply for a scholarship that reduced her costs to $285. Eventually, Carla moved on to kindergarten, which her teacher suggested that she repeat. Delmy initially disagreed strongly with this proposal, but eventually ceded to the teacher's opinion that Carla would benefit from having another year to obtain the social and intellectual skills needed to succeed in first grade.

Delmy's quiet voice and gentle demeanor give the impression that she would have trouble charting an ambitious course out of poverty. But as we will see, she was strongly committed to her goal of developing professional skills and using them to create a better life for herself and Carla. She was thoughtful about how to blend the traditional values of her childhood, particularly the sense of belonging and mutual obligation that existed among family members, with an American sense of striving for professional development and personal fulfillment.

Raising Children to Contribute to the Family

Most of the fourteen women came from, and remained embedded within, strong extended families. Delmy, Sol, Beatriz, Wilma, and Selma had immigrated with the help of friends and kin members; those who arrived first arranged housing and job opportunities for later arrivals. Among the nonimmigrants, Brenda and Shirl lived in homes with their mothers or aunts; kin support was always available. This physical and economic interdependence was paralleled by socialization practices that inculcated in children a feeling of *belonging* and the belief that, as a member of the family, the child had concrete *obligations* to the family. To achieve these two valued outcomes of collectivism, mothers attempted to instill in their young children respect for adult authority, close contact and involvement with kin members, and a sense of obligation to the group's interest. Collective commitment and responsibility often extended to groups outside the family, including church members or other poor families.

According to the Latinas in the sample, children learned to become responsible family members through a process of *educación*. This term goes beyond the English word *education* to refer to the act of guiding the intellectual and moral development of the child. It denotes influences from a sphere larger than the school—encompassing the family, community, and religious guidance. Having *educación* means knowing how to behave in society, how to be respectful, cooperative, and considerate toward others. Although it is sometimes translated as "learning manners," the term *educación* connotes values, not simply socially acceptable behaviors.

Routes to Belonging

"Familism," or a prioritized orientation toward family, is an aspect of interdependence that underlies most of the women's constructs of child rearing. The family network protects each member and serves as both a resource and a source of support. These mothers relied extensively on their network of family and friends to augment their own efforts. Many women received financial support from their families, as well as help with child care. Family gatherings were the core of weekends and evenings for several of the mothers. Accordingly, the mothers sought to pass on to their children this sense that the family is the deepest,

most dependable source of personal support. Harriet articulated her
theory that the absence of family support is the principal cause of
delinquent behavior:

> The whole thing is having a family, having a family life. I believe
> that if a lot of these kids had a family that they could say, "Hey, I
> know my mom loves me, and I know my dad may not be here,
> but I know he loves me . . . I have aunts and uncles I can go talk
> to," there wouldn't be any gangs, you know?

Delmy, herself a member of the early childhood profession, nevertheless underlined the importance of family life in her decision to limit
the amount of time her daughter Carla spent in center-based care:

> [Being in child care all day] is too much for a child. It's too much
> because a child needs a family life. So I know that sometimes you
> can't give them that because you work, but since my mother was
> telling me that she could [take care of Carla] and my husband also
> told me, then I said I'd better not take that option [full-day child
> care] unless it was the last option I had.

Several of these mothers were conscious that their children's sense
of identity and belonging was being created not only within their
families but within their cultural communities as well. Delmy talked a
lot about her hope that her daughter would remain bicultural, and not
let American social norms overtake her Latino upbringing and language. Delmy's own mother required her grandchildren to speak Spanish when they visited her, and Delmy agreed with her on the issue of
language:

> Yes, they have to know [Spanish]. Because if they don't know, they
> will be ignorant of many things and think that English is the best
> thing in the world. I know that to survive here we have to learn
> it, but we also have to maintain Spanish.

The Latina mothers were more explicit than those from other ethnic
groups in their discussions of the sense of belonging that comes from
recognizing one's role in an ethnic or cultural community. However,
one of the African-American mothers, Shirl, also wanted her child to

grow up knowledgeable and proud of his cultural heritage. She hoped that he could attend a school with an Afrocentric curriculum because "that's something that needs more than to just be talked about, as far as teaching him. I can't teach him that, just by telling him. I'd rather have him see for himself." A number of other black mothers were explicit about the role of the religious community as a place of caring and belonging.

Contributing to the Family

Most of the women believed that even the smallest child had a moral obligation to begin contributing something to the welfare of others. For these mothers, "proper" behavior included learning how to behave socially, how to be respectful of elders, and how to fulfill moral responsibility to the needy. Wilma talked a lot about how to ensure that her daughter would grow up to be a "good person":

> I think about it all the time. I want her to grow up to be a good person, somebody who cares about other people, who is not selfish, not into themselves, giving. I don't know, just kind.

Wilma judged her daughter's character in terms of her capacity to interact with others:

> A good person to me is somebody who's kind, who cares about other people and not just themselves. Loving, understanding. I'm not very outgoing, and I think sometimes that kind of hampers me a little bit. I find it hard to relate to other people sometimes. I don't want that for her. I want her to be able to deal with any kind of situation.

Harriet saw "doing the right thing" as combating the negativity and hate that she observed in her impoverished community:

> Cooperation is basic to life itself. You can't get along in life if you don't have those traits. This is so important, to share and cooperation. 'Cause if you grow up selfish, you get angry and you have hate in your heart. If you know how to cooperate, you'll know how to live.

Delmy and Selma both emphasized their moral obligation to contribute to the betterment of their communities. Delmy clearly stated the importance of working in a field where she could make a contribution to society:

> I want another job, [but] I also want to feel good as a human being, working in a classroom and helping needy people in my community. I see much that is needed: people that could help, but with their whole heart. I dream of having my classroom in order to be able to do that . . . I'm going to help. I want to fulfill my obligation *[cumplir]* in all that. I want to be useful.

To Selma, facilitating her daughters' moral socialization and connection with the immediate community was an important aspect of child rearing. She modeled this involvement through her work with the preschool and elementary school, the tenants' organizations, and the church. Her goal was raising her daughters to be "upstanding citizens" who cared about others:

> I want them to be aware of all the things that are around them. I want them to be active. Well, you know how some people just live in a place and they don't care about everyone else and the betterment of their surroundings? They just say, "Okay, I'm going to be here. I'm going to take care of my little corner, but I won't care whatever happens to anyone else." I want them to be aware of everyone else's feelings. We're not raising kids to be, I don't know if it's upstanding but it's some kind of citizen and that's what I want. I want them to be out there taking care of the children, of their surroundings, of the schools.

One of the highest priorities held by these mothers was seeing that they, and their children, did not neglect their responsibility to their communities. As Delmy said, "[I want her] to be very hard working and want her to enjoy helping other children because, like I say to her, 'There are other people who aren't as happy as we are.'"

A number of the women had a dual motivation for teaching their children to "do the right thing." Some of their conceptions of right and wrong were motivated by the *moral sense* that each individual has a personal responsibility to care for others, as we saw in the remarks of Wilma, Selma, Delmy, and Harriet. But we also saw that women derived *instrumental* support from family and community members, and they were aware that in order to draw this support they had to contribute their own resources as well. The examples of reciprocal cooperation among kin members and close friends are numerous and often involve child care or support for youngsters. Delmy's mother, brother, sisters, and friends intervened to help her continue her studies, obtain a job, and find subsidized child care. The staff in her daughter's child-care center went beyond the boundary of their official roles, keeping Delmy informed about scholarships and housing options once her husband left. Delmy herself was very supportive of her mother, visiting her frequently and cleaning her house every weekend. Within these contexts, cooperation and mutual support were modeled daily— and became an explicit part of how to socialize the next generation.

In talking about their children's socialization, several mothers emphasized that the children must give to others if they expect to get something in return. For example, Wilma believed that sharing would make her daughter a better person, but she also emphasized the personal reward that Janis would reap from sharing: "It's just important for her to share. I'm sure she'd want people to share with her, so she has to reciprocate!" When children ignore family interests, violating a core collective dictate, the consequences can be sharp and clear. Shirl reported how her brother, then in his early twenties, failed to pay rent to his mother or provide in-kind services. He was asked to move out, since other kin members were all providing the mother with some cash in compensation for staying in the family house.

Independence as Self-Reliance and Personal Development

As we saw in Chapter 4, these mothers implicitly acted from the assumption that their children would change over time, forming a character or personality partially shaped by the mother's actions. They also focused on their children's individual capacities, skills, and social habits—child-specific virtues somewhat detached from any particular social context. When asked about their aims in raising their children, many described wanting to create a child who was independent and reported telling their children to "be a leader, not a follower" or to "be the best you can be."

As the fourteen mothers turned to the topic of nurturing independence in their preschool-age children, two distinct cultural models emerged. Most of the mothers expected their children to become self-reliant members of the community, not dependent upon anyone else to get ahead economically. Additionally, some mothers saw independence as the way to stay safe in a dangerous world; they wanted their children to be savvy loners who did not tangle with the wrong people.

Delmy argued that providing the best opportunities would allow her daughter, Carla, to get ahead:

> I want the best for her. I want her to be in the best place, where she will be able to learn best, where she will feel best and where she can choose, not to have just one alternative. Because when one only has one alternative, you go and fail, because you don't see many ways. [I hope] she will be a professional, have a college education . . . that she better herself *[se supere]* as a woman, also . . . a professional woman.

Delmy knew that she was departing from child-rearing norms back home in El Salvador. But to survive and get ahead in American society, she believed that her emphasis on independence was the better alternative:

> The most important thing is to teach them to survive here, so they can be independent . . . because we Latinos, especially Latina mothers, we perhaps protect our children too much. On the other hand, Americans are different . . . they bring them up more independent . . . I know it's our own love that makes us do it, but we have to leave them on their own also, so they can survive.

Selma's views were concordant with those of Delmy. She believed that being independent enabled her daughter to manage well in different situations, including child-care settings and preschools. Selma linked self-reliance with acquiring important cognitive and affective capabilities:

> I think she needs to believe that she can do things for herself, have that confidence, because that's just going to take her, that's going

to make her feel more comfortable, you know, learning, doing her work.

While Delmy and Wilma implied that parents can nurture independence by being less protective of their children, mothers also felt that independence was achieved by expanding the child's world to include interactions with people outside the immediate family. Brenda, the mother of four-year-old Cora, articulated a model in which the child's peers are seen as important in nurturing self-reliance and self-confidence:

> I feel that she should be in the preschool to be around other children. When she's at home with me, she gets more and more dependent on me, instead of trying to do things for herself . . . waiting for me to do them for her. They see other children doing it, so it makes them more aggressive to walk and talk, imitate other children . . . try to be like them, then they're proud.

Wilma shared this belief, stating that her daughter Janis's development of a confident and independent self stemmed not only from her attachment to her parents, but also from her interaction with others:

> I don't think you can learn everything there is to learn from your parents. You have to go out and experience other things, you have to be around other people, and she has to learn to interact with other people.

Only Beatriz expressed worried ambivalence over socializing her child to be independent, decrying the liberal freedom afforded youths by Anglo parents. Her preference was to return home to Latin America before her children were too heavily influenced by North American socialization. She emphasized the traditional connotations of being *independiente*, including arrogance and egocentrism.

Another powerful way for children to learn independence is through observing their mothers, and these women were very conscious of acting as role models for their children. They were proud of their survival skills and, even more, of their ambitions to create a better life for themselves and their children. A personal goal for Delmy was to realize her own potential, and she was pushing strongly to create opportunities for herself as well as for her daughter:

> Traditionally, in Salvador, women can't work. But I think it's very important. Here I've become aware, because it's another culture, here there is a need, because of the economic aspect, which is important for survival, and the fulfillment aspect. Professionally, we, and not just men, we have rights . . . You feel like you have no rights if you can't become fulfilled . . . you're not complete if you haven't achieved your goals . . . in the end, you have to feel good that you have done what you have always wanted to do.

Sol also wanted to better her position through schooling; like Delmy, she was quite aware that she served as a role model for her youngsters. She emphasized that she wanted her two children to be "responsible" and pointed out that "my own son, he sees me studying, and he says he's proud, because [he knows] it's not easy." She reported that her younger toddler, Elena, tried to stay awake at night, lying next to Sol as she studied, or pretending to work on her own homework. Both Sol and Delmy believed that some child-care workers perceived Latinas as uneducated or uninvolved with their children. This stereotyping may have intensified their zeal to develop themselves professionally.

The emphasis on perseverance and getting ahead through hard work was not limited to the Latina women. Harriet—also reflecting on her ability to set a good example for her children—described how she talks to them about work:

> [I'd say to my children,] "When you get older, and there's going to be mornings when you're laying in that bed, and you're going to say, 'God, I don't feel like going to work today.' And you're going to think about mommy, and you're going to say, 'God, mama got up every day. Let me get out of this bed and go do what I have to do.' That should give you the gumption to get up and say, 'If mom can do it . . . I can do it.'" That's what I'm hoping that is rubbing off on my kids. That get up and go, you want to do, be somebody, do something. You know, I'm hoping that'll rub off on them.

For several of the women, the impetus to gain skills and create opportunities for their children was ultimately motivated by collectivist as well as individualistic goals. For example, as we saw earlier, Selma and Delmy were both dedicated to raising their children to be, in Selma's words, "upstanding citizens."

Independence for Self-Protection

Another cultural model for encouraging independence stems from a different set of motivations. Some mothers looked out into neighborhoods with errant youths and destructive temptations. A good number of the fourteen had themselves used drugs, been victims of violence, or dropped out of school. As we saw in Chapter 3, mothers relied on a variety of strategies to protect their children from danger. Eleven of the fourteen mentioned the immediate safety of their children as a major factor influencing their child-care and living choices. An important protective strategy mentioned by several mothers was to nurture a sense of independence in their young children—so that they would not conform later to negative peer expectations. Kathy, for example, expressed her agreement with how the Head Start teachers pushed her four-year-old son, Danny, to be a leader and not a follower. She had concluded that other people often tended to drag her down, and she intended to teach Danny how to avoid such influences:

> I want him to be very independent, so he's secure with himself, a loner. I think that it's better to be happy alone. Soon as he gets [older] I want him to feel secure just being alone. Not alone but on his own. Like he doesn't have to follow every kid around.

Jackie was already dealing with signs that her preadolescent son was involved with the "wrong" crowd:

> My main concern right now falls under my son, because my son is really attracted to the . . . what is it? I would call it negativity, the games, the "yo, man's," the loudness. The message that I want my son to know is that you have to put protection around yourself, you can't be around negative people. You can't be a follower. You need to be a leader.

It is important to note that both these models of independence were shaped by the features of the women's immediate social contexts. For these women, independence was not linked to developing cognitive capacity or self-esteem in the abstract, as it is in the theories of middle-class professionals. Rather, the exigencies of impoverished contexts appear to have prompted these particular models of socializing independence.

"Taking the Best from Each World"

Many parents—regardless of their social class or ethnic background—work hard to accommodate the goals of nurturing individual strength and fostering a spirit of collective obligation and respect for authority. The fourteen mothers saw danger in adhering too strongly to one pole in this emotional dialectic. Black mothers worried about losing their children to the streets and the defiant peer groups that dominate them. Latina mothers worried about losing their children to an irreverent and individualistic Anglo mainstream that undercuts the family's long-term interests and the moral character of their offspring.

Yet the bicultural path is also not without potholes. The incongruities among cultural values were at times quite clear to the mothers. Delmy placed the collectivist orientation of her own upbringing in Salvador alongside the more individualistic norms she observed in the classrooms in which she had worked. She believed that she could choose the strong aspects of each form of early socialization for her daughter and avoid mindless conformity to less desirable elements:

> Learning another culture teaches one a lot. You have two cultures, you have to maintain the other one, but in certain aspects, not all aspects. Because when you have two cultures, you can take the best from each and leave behind the worst. Even if it's traditional. There are things that don't go. There's many people who can't adapt. They think that they can survive with only our [Latino] culture here. The truth is that you can't. You have to grab something from here also. If not, you are lost.

Delmy chose to keep some aspects of the "traditional way." This proved difficult at times, particularly when Carla came into contact with conflicting social norms in her preschool:

When *la niña* [Carla] arrived there, I found that we educate children in a different way [in El Salvador]. [At the preschool] they're more liberal. Because our culture is fairly conservative, it implies much respect. And you have your children educated in a certain way. But in the preschool they don't want to pay attention. It's due to the fact that they're in another model, they see other things, and so they adapt themselves to that. Afterwards it's a little hard to discipline them because of that . . . the children here see what the other children are doing and want to do the same, and so it's difficult to impose these rules. Maybe a little less strict. But we try to treat our children the same over there, even though I know it's hard, because they want to be like the Americans.

Delmy was an active agent in crafting declared models of socialization that were rooted in collective family obligations and clear authority; yet she had strayed from traditional models, permitting Carla to operate and feel comfortable in more liberal social settings such as the preschool classroom. She was appropriating, interpreting, and adjusting the cultural models of socialization that stem from each world.

This recrafting of socialization models was often motivated by direct comparisons with these women's own mothers. The area in which women most consciously compared themselves with their mothers was that of behavioral control. Most of the women wanted to loosen the reins of authority, allowing their children more freedom and opportunities for personal expression than they had as children. Delmy felt that her own parents were too strict and protective of their daughters. This may have been functional back in El Salvador, but "when you arrive [in the United States] and see another world, you feel very different, shy. You feel limited." Selma spoke about how her parents rarely talked openly with her about problems, especially when she was an adolescent. This lack of communication was very difficult when the family moved to the United States:

They weren't ready to have kids in this country. I am being more open with my daughters. They [my parents] just had kids, they survived, and got help when there was a problem, because they really didn't know how to deal with it. There was no communication, there was, you know, if you want your kids to do some-

thing, I think you should explain to them why. They never did
that.

Helena and Jackie were also moving toward middle-class Anglo
norms, focusing more on individualism, with permissiveness in some
situations. Jackie, the resilient black woman who was abandoned by her
mother and abused by her stepfather, felt that she had to face too much
responsibility during a very tough childhood:

> It was just crazy because I felt like I was the black sheep of the
> family. I felt like I was the slave. I was brought there to be a slave,
> to take care of this kid [her stepsibling], to clean the house, and
> cook, and you know it's like I didn't have the opportunity to
> continue to be a child.

Helena rejected the strict upbringing she had experienced as a child:

> I don't have to be as, "This is the way it is and that is the way it's
> going to stay," like no leniency at all. I think because I just don't
> have the time to be that strict. I remember a lot of my childhood
> just being miserable. And that's the biggest thing . . . I'd never
> want my child to look back and say what I am saying. And, I mean,
> you're a child. Enjoy it!

A few of the fourteen remained committed to reproducing their
mothers' socialization practices. Brenda remained tied to the cultural
model of authority and discipline under which she was raised, emphasizing and agreeing with her mother's philosophy: "If she said, 'no,'
she meant no! There were no ifs or buts about it!"

The Pros and Cons of Individualistic Strength

The struggle to accommodate individualistic and collective interests
left some mothers feeling ambivalent. As Helena's daughter, Shannon,
developed a stronger personality, Helena found herself caught between
two conflicting desires:

> She can be very sensitive at times when she wants to be, very aware
> of other people's feelings. I think she's a good person, I really do.

I mean at times she drives me nuts. But it's . . . I think she's going to be okay. I mean it's not even the kind of person I want her to be [feisty and assertive]. But I do want her to be her own person. I want her to be very secure in the way she feels.

Similarly, Harriet mentioned the conflict between fostering an assertive, individualistic character in her daughter and promoting her family goal of sharing. Even though Harriet urged her children to "share! share! share!," her daughter often refused to share materials with her brothers, demanding, "Leave me alone or I'll slap you!" Harriet justified this assertiveness as being necessary for survival and as providing independence from conformity:

We're always teaching her, "Use your head!" We're teaching her to be proud of who she is. She's got a lot going for her. That's her father and me all the time, telling her to be proud and do her best. But she will protect herself. She's really smart, she's smart as a whip. I'm so happy, she'll be going places with her life.

Jackie also expressed ambivalence about her daughter's self-assertion. Even though she wanted her daughter to be "pretty much strong-minded," she admitted to sometimes wondering what she had let herself in for:

It's like Dr. Jekyll and Mr. Hyde or something . . . I think it's mostly trying to be in control of every situation . . . She's real bossy. She's like me. I'm real big power and control, big time. Sometimes I look at her and it's like, oh, I don't like her!

These women's words help us to understand their struggle to instill both individualistic and collective values in their offspring. Çidem Kagitçibaşi challenges the assumption that parents who begin to incorporate individualistic values consonant with achieving in modern times must necessarily forsake more traditional collective benefits and obligations.[7] She makes the case that collective values such as interdependency and kin networking are inherent in American as well as non-Western modern societies, and that these values can coexist with individualistic orientations also developed within families. The nature of this coexistence is well illustrated by these fourteen mothers, who grappled on a daily basis with moving up financially while trying to nurture their ties with family and community. Education, independence, *educación*, and family life work together to provide the structure that supports and inspires the children to develop what Delmy calls a "mission" in life.

The question that remains is whether these working mothers will be able to uphold the discipline, respect, and collective orientation they value. It's unclear whether the lines between *educación* and *education* will become blurred the more the children are socialized into an individualistic educational experience. Many place hope in reform efforts that encourage children to reflect on the sociocultural nature of knowledge and see how their contributions are used within the classroom community. Bryk and his colleagues are part of the movement to strengthen the feeling of community within schools, equipping students with "technical competencies to function in the twenty-first century while also encouraging a sense of hopefulness and safety in confronting the unknown and a sense of belonging in a large, complex, and highly specialized society."[8]

The context of these mothers' lives and their perceptions of what it means to *realizarse*, or realize their full potential, in an urban American environment have affected their lives, beliefs, and practices. This is not to say that all these mothers consciously undertake all their actions in terms of a rubric of higher socialization goals, but it is clear that they try to visualize what place their children will have in the world and formulate paths to help them get there. Parents want to prepare their children to survive within their environment, and therefore focus on instilling the behaviors and skills necessary to survival. We would argue, however, that they are not guided solely by what is functional in current society. Their perceptions of the environment influence their child-rearing beliefs and practices in combination with cultural norms and critical reflection.

CHAPTER SIX

Discipline and Obedience

I think respect is the number one thing. Respect with parents, and respect for people around you. Kids are not being taught that today. Showing respect for themselves and to be obedient. I think all children should be taught how to behave. —*Harriet*

To many parents, discipline is virtually synonymous with child rearing itself. Adults vividly remember incidents when they were disciplined by their parents, and most have firm beliefs about how their own children should be handled when they misbehave. Beliefs about discipline are debated in the media as well as among families and friends, and often one parent—or professional—will judge the discipline strategies of other parents without delving deeply into their world view or appreciating their values. The way that low-income parents discipline their children has been an endless source of commentary by those who take an interest in the welfare of families.[1] In this chapter we focus on understanding what mothers mean when they talk about the need for respect, and we explore how this value influences the ways they conceptualize and enact child discipline.

As a result of active debate among lay observers and professionals, opinions on two dimensions of discipline have fluctuated over the past century: the emotions that parents display and the amount of control they exert over their children. Norms regarding parental emotions have shifted continually: at one end of the pendulum is a model of warm, loving parenting; at the other end is a model of strict, cool parenting. The issue of control has also been viewed from a variety of perspectives, as one generation favors granting freedom à la Rousseau while the next endorses vigilance and control.

In several studies conducted in Berkeley, California, Diana Baumrind found that parents who were warm and democratic but also firm in setting limits—a pattern she labeled *authoritative*—had children who were capable of both self-assertion and interpersonal competence. Worst off were children of *permissive* parents (warm but laissez-faire in their control of the child) or *rejecting* parents (lacking in both warmth and control). Children whose parents were *authoritarian* (relatively cold and strict) fared less well than children whose parents were authoritative but not as badly as those who were permissive or rejecting. Most of the families in Baumrind's sample were middle class and white.[2]

But do the effects of authoritarian and permissive discipline apply to families from working-class or ethnic-minority backgrounds? Many studies have indeed documented that families from lower socioeconomic backgrounds are more likely to be strict with their children than are those from the middle class. But researchers disagree as to why there is a social class difference and whether or not the effects of authoritarian parenting are the same for lower income children as they are for middle-class children.

Baumrind cautions against applying her findings indiscriminately to families outside the white middle class. She argues that the effects of a parenting style depend upon cultural values of the community. For example, Japanese mothers tend to be more permissive than middle-class American mothers. Their behavior, however, is unlikely to have the same negative effects that permissiveness has in the United States, because it serves an important cultural function: maintaining an intense, conflict-free relationship that forms the prototype of other close relations.[3]

Baumrind also argues that the effectiveness of a particular style depends upon the contextual realities of the community. What is adaptive in a quiet suburban community may not be adaptive in a low-income urban neighborhood. For example, the authoritarian parenting she found among the small group of African-Americans in her own study may be appropriately protective of children whose communities are dangerous. Parents in dangerous communities try to maintain social order in their own households, promoting a feeling of discipline and structure that contrasts with the softer, more romantic images of childhood prevalent within the middle class. Thus the very meaning of the authoritarian behavior depends on the community. In middle-class white families it may stem from emotional coldness or detachment, but within African-American families in low-income communities it may reflect—and signal to the child—nurturance and protectiveness.

Baumrind's sensitivity to the varying meanings of her constructs has sometimes been lost on researchers attempting to show that authoritarian behavior has undesirable consequences for all children regardless of their social class or cultural background. These researchers have made little effort to examine parents' understandings of children's misbehavior. Our approach was to examine in detail the values and the strategic reasoning that motivate and guide parents as they socialize their children.

Other researchers analyzing social class differences have looked at the workplace to see how conditions there infiltrate parenting strategies. Melvin Kohn and his colleagues have shown that working-class parents are more authoritarian because hierarchical forms of power characterize their own work.[4] In low-status jobs, initiative and self-direction are rarely rewarded; rather, it is conformity to authority that characterizes a good worker. Kohn reasons that these parenting practices may perpetuate and reproduce social class differences—prohibiting lower-income families from instilling the attitudes and skills that will catapult their children into the middle class.

But many contend that authoritarian parenting is not functional in any community, even those in which adults hold highly routinized jobs and possess few material resources. The cause of authoritarian parenting, these authors argue, is the stress of living with economic uncertainty—and frequently with racism as well—on a daily basis. Vonnie McLoyd chronicles the environmental and psychological stressors encountered by low-income African-American families, including domestic and community violence, poor schools, inadequate job opportunities, unsafe housing, and environmental pollutants.[5] In her view, poor parents do not act primarily from a conscious philosophy of child rearing. They exert overly harsh discipline not to help their children deal with a harsh environment but because they are out of control—overwhelmed by hostility and hopelessness.

These explanations for the origins of harsh discipline are not mutually exclusive. But by attributing parenting styles solely to environmental stressors, one risks losing sight of the philosophy and moral values underpinning the views of the working poor. By listening to women's own explanations of how they discipline their children, we looked for the guiding precepts that interact with the challenges (and opportunities) in their communities. The respect theme emerged from the women's discussions of discipline and child rearing. In this chapter we paint a detailed portrait of their views, setting aside the oversimplified constructs that researchers have imposed upon the notion of discipline. We want to see how these mothers describe and understand discipline—not whether or not they fall into the pattern of authoritative or authoritarian parents. We sought to find out more broadly how these low-income mothers conceptualize child discipline and what discipline strategies they use. In addition, the in-depth interviews allowed us to learn how they understand authority and the values underlying proper social behavior.

Respect as a Fundamental Principle

In general, these women explained and justified their discipline practices by referring to the need for *respect*. All of the women felt it was essential that children learn to respect adults. As Helena put it, "I don't like a smart mouth. I think adults should just be respected and you don't stand and argue and back-talk and be fresh. I just won't stand for it." Learning to respect adults was a moral imperative, but it had instrumental value as well. The mothers felt that their children's school success depended on their settling in under the teacher's authority and submitting to the school's rules and routines. They felt that these skills could be learned in preschool.

For some mothers, the principle of respect went beyond the unilateral mandate for children to respect adults. These mothers recognized the need for adults to respect children as well. Thus Helena described her growing awareness that if she was to require respect from her daughter, she would have to show respect for her as well:

She doesn't like to be talked to like she's an idiot . . . I'll take something from her [and she'll say], "Don't grab!" And it makes me stop and think . . . she's right! I don't like her grabbing things out of my hand.

Mothers who viewed respect as a bilateral principle were more likely to see the power of modeling as a discipline technique. When they became aware of their children's intelligence, they saw more clearly the power of reasoning and learned that they could explain things to their children without having to resort to coercion.

A few of the mothers mentioned the importance of boosting children's self-respect. This concept, and its close cousin, self-esteem, are mantras of the middle class. But self-respect was mentioned only briefly by a few of these low-income women. By contrast, several brought up the goal of achieving respectability in the eyes of others. Being respectable takes on a special significance for women with low-income status. Dressing and speaking well, getting a good education, and holding a job are all strategies for earning dignity and higher status. The concept of respectability shifts the focus from the mother-child relationship to the status of the child in the wider community. Pamela emphasized the connection between respecting adults and being respectable: "I want to raise my son to be respectable . . . It would break my heart if I knew he was in the street, swearing and yelling and disrespecting adults . . . I don't want that to be my son." She dressed him in the latest fashions, complete with silk shirts, because she remembered from her own childhood that "those kids who had the nice clothes got the teacher's attention."

Diverse Models of Discipline

As we explored the topic of discipline with the fourteen women, various models emerged. One model relied heavily on adult coercion, including physical punishment. The mothers who espoused this conception of discipline strongly endorsed the need for children to respect adult authority. They conceptualized the parent-child relationship as a hierarchy whereby children must respond to adults with unquestioning obedience. This model of discipline defined respectful behavior as deference to adults, good manners, and politeness. Respectful behavior was thought to benefit children when pursuing education, another important goal. Two women, Shirl and Kathy, drew heavily upon this cultural model.

SHIRL: "I THANK GOD FOR THE WAY MY MOTHER RAISED ME ROUGH"

Shirl, age twenty-four, believed that her parental responsibilities hinged on inculcating in her children respect for adults. Characterizing her own mother's discipline practices as "rough," Shirl expressed complete gratitude for the structure and supervision her mother gave her:

> I thank God for the way she raised me rough . . . But I thank God for that, because now I'm not a dirty person, I'm a clean person, I got my priorities together . . . I'm not a slob now, I respect my elders . . . I'm not a person that goes from job to job . . . I'm not lazy at work . . . so I do thank God for the way she brought me up.

Shirl felt that the tight control her mother exerted over her had paid off. Accepting responsibility and being accountable and hard working are elements of Shirl's conceptualization of discipline.

To Shirl, problem behavior began when a child no longer respected the distinction between child and adult status, which was fundamental to her views of discipline. Thus Shirl considered "talking back" to adults to be the quintessential form of misbehavior. In one interview, she expanded on her view of misbehavior:

> Talkin' back! It's basically talkin' back. When I say, "Martin, I want you to do that." "But I don't wanna!" I'm like, "It's not what you wanna do, it's what I tell you to do." He's like, "Why do I . . ." I'm like, "'Cause I say so!" [bursts out laughing].

Shirl explained that Martin could get carried away with other adults as well: "The baby-sitter's husband will play with him . . . but he [Martin] goes overboard with the conversation. It gets to a point where he's disrespecting you."

Because she believed that adults should have the prerogative in determining appropriate behavior, Shirl did not encourage Martin to engage in prolonged discussion over disciplinary issues, and she did not feel compelled to explain the reasons for her actions. She told her son to behave in certain ways "because I say so." To Shirl, social relations were premised on respect for elders: "It's not what you wanna do, it's what I tell you to do."

Many of Shirl's friends and relatives appeared to share her model of discipline. As we have seen, Shirl's approach to discipline was the same as that of her own mother, an active and enterprising woman who was still a major presence in Shirl's and Martin's lives. Martin's family day-care provider also held similar views of discipline. Shirl explained how her provider disciplined the children:

> She uses her best judgment. I mean, she'll call me at work and tell me something that he did. And I'm like, "Why are you calling me? Spank him!" You know if it's something that he deserves. If he pees on himself, he'll get a couple of whacks, because he's awake. Now if he pees on himself during nap time, that's a different story. If he pees on himself and he's up, he gets disciplined and I told her that.

Early in our interviews, Shirl showed that she was aware of alternatives to physical punishment, but she didn't think they really worked with her son. For example, Shirl talked about how she handled her son's temper tantrums:

> He takes real bad tantrums. And I have to spank him to calm him down. He will not calm down. I can say, "Martin, please be quiet." That doesn't work.

Shirl felt that when she tried to explain patiently, instead of issuing directives, he took advantage of her, refusing to back down and displaying "an attitude."

By the end of our interviews, in spite of the amount of support Shirl apparently found within her immediate community for her views of discipline, she showed some ambivalence about physical punishment:

> I do more yelling than I do spanking. I should do more spanking, but I don't. He's just so cute. I can't hit him. Even though he deserves it most of the time!

As Martin turned four, Shirl began rethinking her conceptions of appropriate punishment and shifted from spanking to yelling, moving somewhat away from the rigid model of discipline she had described almost two years earlier. Shirl began to see physical punishment as less preferable, but she still believed in power assertion—yelling in this case—as an appropriate way to coerce the child to comply.

KATHY: "HE'S SO SLICK IT ISN'T FUNNY"

Kathy, age twenty-eight, was aware that her conception of discipline flew in the face of some people's standards of how to treat children. In her initial discussion of discipline she noted:

> Nowadays, you give a kid a slap, you're an abusive mother. You know? So it's so weird these days. Everybody'll turn and look. I don't think you should slap a kid in the face, but I definitely think you can give him a couple of good slaps around just to set him straight. These days, you can't do that . . . [takes on mocking, gentle tone] You have to work through the mind.

Like Shirl, Kathy understood discipline primarily in terms of an adult-child hierarchy. The adult has the power and prerogative to control the child and not let the child control her. She reminded her son of her view of the social order: "I'm the boss, and you're the child."

Kathy worried that her son, Darren, would somehow manage to gain power over her and invert the hierarchy. Viewing her child as "slick" and inherently devious, Kathy feared that he would manipulate her. This view justified Kathy's conceptualization of discipline. She believed that directive and coercive adult control was necessary to protect the adult from being manipulated by the child:

> You have to talk to him firmly . . . because he will try to run circles around you . . . He'll run you into the ground! He knows exactly how to use you, use your mind. He's so slick it's not even funny.

Kathy felt that Darren's tendency to dominate others and manipulate adults led him to be willful and wild, as well as physically out of control:

> I have to fix him every Monday when he comes home [from spending a weekend with his father]. I have to, because he is going to do whatever he wants, and . . . I tell [his father], "Get him and hold him, and tell him he cannot." I go, "He's running you! Understand?! . . . Just don't let him drive everybody nuts!" Like he [child] almost ruined his father's sister's wedding! He threw himself down, he wouldn't do this . . . I'm like, "What do you

mean, 'He wouldn't'? You stand him up, you give him a nice swift slap on his ass, and he's gonna do what you say!"

Darren's Head Start teachers perceived that he had emotional problems, and they tried to work with Kathy to change certain aspects of her lifestyle and her way of treating Darren. They helped her realize that her hectic work schedule was taking a toll on Darren, who would see her for only a few minutes between the end of his preschool day and the beginning of her shift as a cocktail waitress. For the first time, she began to discuss how the stress of dealing with a number of different baby-sitters and relatives every week was leading to his unhappiness and misbehavior in the classroom. She also perceived that the teachers had an approach to discipline that was very different from hers. The following comment illustrates how carefully she observed the teachers' strategies for handling Darren:

What I say is, "Look, you're going to do what you're told." 'Cause that's the way I am. He does what I say then. But with them [Head Start teachers], that's not their—his—mother. He's not going to listen to them all the time. So they play this game where they make him choose and choose and choose. He always has three choices. No matter what. Three situations that you can deal with, and if you don't like any of them, we'll go back to: you can't have any, and they'll just leave him alone.

In spite of her clear understanding of how the teachers approached Darren, she was very ambivalent about using their techniques. She alternated among scornful rejection of their ideas, grudging acceptance that they provided a reasonable alternative, and uncertainty about whether she would be able to incorporate their techniques:

I have a loud, aggressive way of dealing with him. But they [Head Start staff] can't be like that. And they have to talk to him real nice. But I'll just take his hand and put him straight down, and look him in the eye, and he will stop, believe me! . . . [In a parodying, singsong voice, she mimics the Head Start teachers] "You have to use your mind; you have to work through the mind," and I'm like, "Hah! A nice sock on the butt will work!" you know?

After Darren had been in Head Start for six months, Kathy admitted, "I'm trying to do it more like them because that is working too. It probably is true that if you get into some psychological aspect of it the child understands better." Kathy now talked about the child's "understanding," not just obeying.

Through personal experience interacting with their own children, and by working with educators who promoted different standards of treating and interacting with children, Shirl and Kathy became aware of the limitations of their basic premise of discipline: children should respect adults. They came to see that the issue of discipline was far more complex. Yet they never fully bought into the alternative discipline techniques, preferring to stick with the power-assertive methods that reflected their deep conviction that their adult prerogative consisted of using power to control their children and coerce them into complying with the social norms that they, the mothers, valued.

Discipline Designed to Foster Understanding

Many of the fourteen women had ideas about child discipline and child rearing that were different from those of Shirl and Kathy. When some mothers referred to respect they implied that children needed to understand that their behaviors had consequences, and thus learn to take responsibility for their actions. In this sense, respect means justice: if children failed to show respect for adults, there were consequences to pay. If children got the message that their actions had no consequences, they would have nothing to fear or to be accountable for. To inculcate this important lesson in their children, the mothers relied on a range of discipline practices—including physical discipline, taking away pleasures or privileges, and explaining why certain behaviors are harmful or inappropriate. Punishment sent the message that these standards of behavior represent what parents hold as sacred principles to live by and let children know they could not violate them without consequences.

DELMY: "YOU HAVE TO EXPLAIN IT TO THEM"

Unlike Shirl and Kathy, Delmy did not see discipline as merely a matter of preventing a child from manipulating an adult. Whereas they believed that misbehavior stemmed from the child's personality traits, Delmy implied that it resulted from the child's failure to comprehend the situation and his or her lack of knowledge about appropriate ways to behave. When misbehavior is attributed to lack of knowledge, discipline revolves around educating and explaining the situation. Delmy felt that discussion should be accompanied by punishment to drive home the moral imperative. In the following passage, Delmy delineated several types of misbehavior as well as the various strategies—including both reasoning and punishment—with which she would respond:

> If a child is doing what she shouldn't be doing, what you can do is . . . tell her that what she's doing is wrong. Or if she hit another child, or pushed her, let them know what they have done and what the consequences are . . . let's say a child hits another child. Sometimes it happens. Sometimes in a violent manner . . . Explain to them what they've done, that they shouldn't do it. Or you don't involve them in something they like to do, then they would feel bad.

Delmy repeatedly emphasized two discipline strategies: communication and punishment. She acknowledged and respected her child's developing capacity and intelligence, and believed that discipline involves reasoning and explanation. Most important to her was communication: "You have to explain it to them, because the child doesn't understand . . . It's very important that parents communicate well with children, and explain what they should and should not do." Delmy also understood the importance of teaching her child that behaviors have consequences. She used punishment to drive home the point that misbehavior was more than just an intellectual mistake. She reported using forms of punishment ranging from physical chastisement to the removal of privileges: "What I use most is sending her to her room, and that's how I 'kill' her—and [taking away] the TV. That's her punishment."

Delmy contrasted discipline in El Salvador with what she observed in the United States:

> In Latin America, people use strong punishments a lot. I know many people who, with these strong straps, or these belts, hit very hard. That's not good. Over there, you're accustomed to punishing very hard.

Most of the women in the sample shared Delmy's feeling that the current generation of parents was relying less on physical punishment than their own parents had. To Delmy, strong physical punishment was ineffective because "it just results in one's rebelling more against them [one's parents]." Delmy characterized her own upbringing as "very disciplined," involving formal interaction between children and their parents, as well as rules, schedules, and tight parental supervision. But Delmy also recalled that her mother "respected our opinions very much and would take them into consideration within certain limits." These experiences led Delmy to appreciate the importance of validating and respecting her own child's opinions.

Discipline Founded on Respect for the Child

Mothers like Delmy who recognized and respected the child's capacity to understand explanations conceived of discipline as a reasoning process. They thought of alternative ways to discipline, to explain and teach what children had not yet understood. Yet Delmy did not strongly articulate the individuality of her child's point of view. For other women, a primary component of the respect theme was acting in a way that demonstrated respect for the child. Jackie was one mother who elaborated a child-focused view of discipline.

From her experiences as a child, Jackie learned how adults used and sometimes abused their power over children. Her mother abused her emotionally, burdened her with household and child-care chores, and failed to protect her from being sexually abused by her stepfather. Jackie felt that because no one respected her as a child, she developed little self-respect and as a young adolescent began engaging in substance abuse and promiscuous sexual activity. While she was involved in such self-destructive behavior she kept hoping for a "white knight" to come and rescue her from the degrading circumstances of her life. It took more than a year of counseling in a residential drug rehabilitation program for her to understand how the dynamics of power and abuse had shaped her life. In her treatment program she learned the power of communication with words rather than by coercion and physical force. Jackie articulated her conviction that adults have to respect children's rights, feelings, and ideas:

And another thing that I don't like, is that say if, like if a kid has something? Um, and they're not supposed to and you just come and take it away from 'em? I don't like that, I feel that because— number one, because both of my kids are so sensitive. And I've seen people just come and snatch something away from a kid, or just make them sit down or whatever. It's important for me to explain to the kid why I'm taking it from them. Because, it's you—you're hurting their feelings. And I don't like to see that, you know, for an adult, because I just look at it as a misuse of power! That's how I look at it. It's like, OK, because you're bigger than me, you just gonna come and take my toys.

In describing situations that called for discipline, women like Jackie tended to focus on the reasons a child had misbehaved. Jackie acknowledged that her older son was having problems in school, and she identified his attraction to the "negatives" in his environment—the boys hanging around on the street with boom boxes and low-slung pants. But her emotional energy went into investigating the causes of this behavior. She acknowledged his continuing resentment and anger that her drug involvement had led to the children's placement in foster care, his embarrassment when she openly talked about her struggle, his fear that she would backslide and lose her grip on the family she had reconstructed. For her, misbehavior was a sensitive and thoughtful child's response to many painful events.

Jackie's response to misbehavior involved, first of all, listening to the child's explanation for what happened. When we asked Jackie whether she had learned anything from the numerous professionals with whom she had been involved, she responded, "One is to listen to the kids. You have to like, take the time and find out what happened. And listen to them." Her willingness to listen to her children highlights her respect for their ability to reason and understand. She considered four-year-old Tiffany's conversation to be on "an adult level." Jackie also thought that it was her responsibility to help her children think strategically—to evaluate what they did, then think about alternatives. Asked how she taught her children not to fight with each other, she replied:

Well, I try to, like, say if Tiffany asks her brother for something, and you know, he snaps at her, like, "No!" You know? Then my thing is, "Look, wait a minute." I come in and I intervene and I play the referee, ask him, "How could you have done that differently?" I have him look at himself. And then I ask Tiffany, I say, "Well, didn't you see your brother doing something and so forth?" "Yes." And I'll say, "Well you know, what should you have done?" "I should have waited," or what have you. I try to do it like that.

She saw herself as a "referee," acknowledging that it was the children's responsibility to resolve the problem, and conveying to them her conviction that they had the skills to do so.

Jackie's focus on respecting the child led her to question the authoritarian style of one of her daughter's teachers. After a series of incidents in which she observed a teacher intimidating or denigrating the children, she happened to hear her yelling at a child who had been caught swearing at another child. She entered the classroom and asked the teacher why she was yelling:

And the teacher says, "Oh well, do you think that I could stay in this classroom a whole day without yelling at any of these children?" I said, "Excuse me. There's a thin line between verbal abuse and getting a child's attention. What I experienced is verbal abuse."

Fed up with this teacher's rudeness and insensitivity to the children, Jackie demanded that her child be transferred to a different classroom. Jackie later summarized what was wrong with the staff at her child's day-care center: "They just don't have any respect."

In talking about discipline, these women displayed patterns of conscious thought and evaluation. They assessed the beliefs and strategies of their own parents and considered their effectiveness. They observed the effects of certain strategies on their children and made changes. They listened to advice from social workers and child-care providers, evaluated its usefulness, and incorporated it according to their needs. They articulated their views to their own children and to their children's providers. The consciousness that permeates these processes of co-construction led us to the conclusion that the mothers were not simply reproducing cultural norms or patterns of behavior learned from their families; nor were they merely responding reflexively to structural conditions of employment.

By focusing exclusively on the research-generated dimensions of affect and control, developmental psychologists miss the central organizing rubric of respect, the salient principle that organized these women's responses to children's misbehavior. However, a few scholars whose work is informed by an anthropological perspective, and particularly those concentrating on Latino families, have come to the same conclusions as we have. Robin Harwood, for example, in her work on Puerto Rican mothers and their infants, has noted that mothers expect their children to learn to respect adults and comport themselves in an appropriate manner in their company.[6]

Also missing from many discussions of child discipline is a sense of how the immediate context—family and community—gives meaning to particular discipline approaches. Our data indicate that features of their impoverished communities figured into women's views of how to discipline their children. In particular, they worried about the dangers of peer groups, community violence, and the drug culture. They analyzed these dangers in terms of the principle of respect. Harriet, for example, attributed violence on the street to children's lack of respect for themselves and for others. Thus our data call attention to the women's active role in attending to certain features of the environment, interpreting the meanings of those features, and strategizing about how to deal most effectively with them.

Writers pressing for social action call attention to the violence, the degradation, and the racism that constitute part of each low-income parent's experience. Indeed, we saw in our study the crushing effects of these problems on the women and their children. But the oppression created by these conditions does not constitute the sole, nor even the primary, driving force behind the child-rearing practices of these women. To argue that it does is to strip away their humanity and sense of dignity—defining them as another species whose feelings and actions toward their own children are motivated by factors different from those motivating the rest of us. Our data call attention to the constant dynamic process in which they are trying to make sense of their world and that of their children, and trying to adapt their behavior in a way that, according to Harriet, "paves the way for the child." Respect emerges as one principle, or value, that inspires and guides how these mothers make sense of discipline.[7]

CHAPTER SEVEN

Cultural Models of Education

❦

I think his education is going to be the key that makes him
or breaks him. —*Pamela*

Americans' ambivalence about education is evident in our myths.
On one hand we have the myth of the self-made man, the Horatio
Alger who makes it with no more than an eighth-grade education. On
the other hand we have the traditional view of education as the key to
social mobility, even for those who live within communities that are
virulently racist or sexist. In fact, in current times, the Horatios of
America are not likely to be successful. As the gap between the wealthi-
est and the poorest members of society grows larger than ever before,
those without at least a high school education have little chance of
maintaining a middle-class lifestyle. Between 1973 and 1993 the hourly
wages of high school dropouts fell by 22.5 percent.[1]

Do impoverished parents recognize the strong link between education level and income? And, more important, do they feel that their
own children have a chance to pursue the American dream of educational attainment and financial security? The anthropologist John
Ogbu has suggested that minority groups such as Native Americans
and African-Americans, who did not migrate voluntarily to the United
States, have given up on education—developing a deep mistrust of the
public schools because for them academic performance has not always
been rewarded commensurately by employment opportunities. He
dubs the attitude of some African-Americans "an oppositional frame"

in which they preserve their own identity by defining themselves in opposition to dominant institutions such as schools.[2]

Research findings provide partial support for this theory. Interviewing working-class men and women in the Midwest and Northeast, Lois Weis found few individuals—black or white—who had faith that persevering in school would improve their economic prospects.[3] Yet many voluntary immigrants, particularly Asians, have successfully moved through the educational system, attaining university degrees and eventually higher social status.[4]

But these blanket assertions about the coping strategies of a particular ethnic group may mask important variation within the group. Certainly there are many African-American youths, for instance, who have succeeded in school rather than acting in opposition to it. Low-income parents who have very young children may be more optimistic about their children's education than they were about their own. Doris Entwisle and Karl Alexander have extensively studied parental expectations among low-income families and typically find that both black and white parents have high expectations for their children.[5] Furthermore, most parents feel that preschool is the place to begin preparing children for school; indeed, 73 percent voiced this opinion in one recent national survey.[6]

In this chapter we explore the fourteen mothers' views on the purpose of schooling in their children's lives. Do they see school as a ticket to the middle class? Or have they lost faith that public schools—plagued by violence and lack of funding—can prepare their children for a successful future? We will see that the answer lies in between these extremes. Indeed, mothers are suspicious and fearful of sending their children to public schools. But their faith in education remains strong—and they have developed a variety of strategies for providing their children with a good education outside mainstream public classrooms.

Role of Parents

Americans seem to feel that many parents are reneging on their duty to support children's school efforts. In his 1996 State of the Union address, President Clinton told Americans to "turn off the TV and help your kids with their homework." Low-income parents are often criticized for failing to become involved with their children's schooling. The sociologist Annette Lareau conducted a careful qualitative investigation of parental involvement in one working-class and one middle-class school.[7] She found that lower-income parents were interested in participating, especially if their children were having difficulty. Frequently they were not aware of problems their children were having, however, and when they did try to become involved they often had trouble establishing effective communication with the school staff. She emphasizes the joint responsibility of parents and school personnel to learn how to communicate with each other.

Low-income parents are also criticized for not providing enough educational experiences in the home, or for providing experiences that may be intended to be educational but are actually counterproductive. For example, Deborah Stipek and her colleagues found that "poorly educated" parents are more likely than educated parents to engage in structured learning activities such as flash cards, which many early childhood educators consider an inappropriate method for teaching young children.[8] Ethnic differences in family literacy practices have also been noted. A national survey of parenting practices found that Hispanic and African-American parents do not report spending as much time reading to their young children as do Anglo parents—only 29 percent of Latino parents and 27 percent of African-American parents reported doing so compared with 52 percent of Anglo parents. Among Anglo mothers, 95 percent reported that their children owned more than ten books, compared with 71 percent of African-Americans and 66 percent of Latinos.[9]

Other scholars chronicle the many competing demands upon the time and resources of single parents, demands that multiply when money is tight. Proponents of theories emphasizing inadequacies in the surrounding contexts of poor families ask how mothers can be expected to come to school conferences, for example, when their attendance would require leaving the house after a long day of work, when household chores are waiting, and when costs are involved for a baby-sitter and transportation. They question the presumption that impoverished parents lack the motivation to read to their children, but suggest that parents may themselves lack sufficient education to read, or may feel uncertain about how they can help with homework or select educational toys.

What is missing is a sense of how mothers themselves perceive the role they play in their children's education. What do they think about the importance of flash cards or of reading to their children? What gets them to do these things or prevents them from doing them? We look at how these mothers see their role and examine how successful they feel they are in meeting their own goals and expectations.

Role of Child Care

If preschools are perceived by most parents as the first step on the way to educational achievement and financial prosperity, what do mothers want preschools to look like? Many early childhood educators feel that there is a large discrepancy between mothers' views about how preschools should educate young children and the views of professionals. Didactic, teacher-centered instruction is anathema to members of America's early childhood establishment, who endorse the Piagetian notion that for preschool children cognitive development occurs within the context of play. The National Association for the Education of Young Children (NAEYC) has been the most influential advocate of early childhood practices that are "developmentally appropriate," that is, those that allow children to follow their own interests, that provide a variety of stimulating toys and other materials for them to explore freely, and that do not involve paper-and-pencil activities found in elementary school.[10]

In spite of NAEYC's efforts to stamp out "academic" preschools, many parents—particularly those outside the white middle class—want their children to begin academic training in preschool and are dissatisfied if their children are not being taught to recognize letters and numbers, or even to read and perform addition and subtraction. In exploring this issue of how and what child-care providers should "teach," we will see not only what these mothers' preferences are, but also how their views are affected by the examples set by the providers themselves.

Although parents may focus their attention on the educational benefits of preschool, they may be less explicitly aware of the "hidden curriculum" in each program. The Piagetian approach endorsed by most early childhood educators aims to create a child who is verbal, self-confident, curious, assertive, and intrinsically motivated to achieve in school. Teachers are encouraged to create a democratic atmosphere in which children can develop strong opinions and articulate them forcefully. Is this the type of behavior that most parents wish to encourage? As we learned in Chapter 5, the mothers in our study were often just as focused on instilling in their children a sense of responsibility to family and community as they were on promoting individualistic goals like self-esteem. They also expect their children to respect authority, not to challenge it. In fact, teachers may also attempt to control and constrain children's autonomy and self-expression far more than the ideal might suggest. Joseph Tobin, for example, has pointed out how children's opportunities for verbal expression are carefully channeled by teachers during traditional "self-expression" activities such as sharing time.[11]

Harriet and Pamela: Two Contrasting Views

We begin with the views and practices of Harriet and Pamela, two African-American women with quite different agendas for how to raise and "educate" their children. They were selected for this chapter because they exemplify the common emphasis on teacher-structured learning, and they differ in their sense of how they, as mothers, can help their children attain the goal of school success.

Harriet

At the time of our first interview, Harriet was thirty-three, the mother of two sons ages thirteen and eight, and a daughter age three. Over the course of the study, we learned about her one-woman battle to create a stable and loving environment for her family. Rebounding resiliently from a difficult childhood, she projected an image of determination and resourcefulness in providing for her children.

Harriet's mother was from Mississippi and her father was from Alabama. When Harriet and her twin brother were born, her mother was already coping with five children and was chronically ill with heart disease. Her father and mother eventually separated, and her father moved "in and out of the picture." One of Harriet's older sisters was charged with caring for her, but Harriet always felt "unwanted" within her family.

Harriet graduated from high school and went to a secretarial school for a year, and from there landed her first job. At age twenty she became pregnant with her first son. Five years later, she had a second son. When she was thirty, she became pregnant with her daughter, Shondra. The pregnancy was very difficult because, like her mother, she had a chronic heart condition. Yet she was determined to have the child:

> I had open-heart surgery when I was six months pregnant . . . Thank Jesus I'm still here, and she's here . . . We call her "Special Girl" you know, because she's like, when I look at her sleeping sometimes, my heart melts, because I know what I went through with her.

For a time, Shondra's father lived with Harriet and the children. During the data-collection period, Harriet and her partner separated, and she moved from an inner-city apartment to her own small house in a working-class community south of the city.

Pamela

In many ways, Pamela's background is similar to that of Harriet. Like Harriet, Pamela grew up with six brothers and sisters. Pamela's mother struggled by herself to raise the children, while their father drifted in and out of their lives, providing little emotional and no financial support. At the time of the first interview, Pamela was twenty-six years old and had a four-year-old son, Cedric. She was employed as an administrative assistant.

Pamela's mother was a social worker for DSS. At the time of the interviews, she also owned a business and worked in an outreach program in which she "goes in people's houses, and teaches them how to play with their kids, and how to relate to their kids." Pamela remembered her mother as "one of those people who work, work, work." As children, Pamela and her siblings were enrolled in after-school and summer programs to keep them occupied.

Pamela was an excellent student in high school, but she was severely shaken by her initial experiences in junior college, where she felt unprepared to take on the work. She soon dropped out and began working two jobs. She became pregnant with Cedric at age twenty-two.

When Cedric was a year old, she ended her relationship with his father, who was physically abusive and addicted to drugs.

Pamela returned to work within three months of giving birth. She found a family day care where Cedric stayed until he was three and a half. At that point, the agency providing child-care funds encouraged Pamela to move him to a center, where he remained until he was six.

The Importance of a Good Education

There is no question that helping their children get a good education was a very high priority for these mothers. Pamela's expectations for Cedric's preschool years were multifaceted. She wanted him to develop excellent language skills, learn appropriate ways to resolve conflicts, and develop cognitive skills that would lead to success in school. Pamela felt that ensuring Cedric's school success was crucial: "I think his education is going to be the key that makes him or breaks him. And I need to do all I can do to make sure he gets that." When he was still an infant, she put him on a waiting list for Metco. Harriet shared Pamela's faith in education; she was determined that her two younger children would attend college: "I can see [my son] going ahead into college and you know really making me proud that he's my son, and Shondra, she wants to be a doctor already, you know."

The women in our study expressed various reasons why education was crucial to their children's future. Most, like Pamela, saw schooling as essential for social mobility. Beatriz felt that if she hadn't pursued her education she "would still be cleaning," so education was very important to her: "Because if you don't study, you can't get a better job." Harriet viewed education as an opportunity for self-actualization as well as preparation for the workplace. She longed for her daughter to have all the opportunities that she herself missed as a child, and she hoped to go back to school herself: "I know it could further me, and what my dreams and goals are in life. I feel like if I have no dreams and goals then my kids won't." Only one other mother, Helena, defined school-related learning purely as a source of pleasure or fulfillment. Helena was excited about her daughter's learning to read because she enjoyed reading so much as a child: "I used to live in the library . . . Oh, I loved it, and I hope she likes it as much as I did."

In spite of their optimism about the benefits of getting a good education, few of the women thought the public schools would provide the type of experience they wanted for their children. None of the women described her own schooling in positive terms. Those who were immigrants tended to emphasize the strictness of educators in their home cultures, as well as the limited opportunities for women's advancement. Those born in the United States often described their own school experiences as boring, stifling, or alienating. Pamela told of how ill prepared she was for junior college. In spite of being an honors student, she "didn't learn too much" in high school, and "when I went to college I was the dummy! I was real dumb."

The women were very conscious of violence in the public schools and felt that teachers had lost control of the classrooms. Harriet frequently articulated her preference that her daughter attend Catholic school or enroll in a busing program: "I mean kids that I know who go to Catholic school, they seem to be smarter. Not smarter, but learning more, you know what I mean?" Brenda selected a Catholic school for kindergarten because the teachers were more strict and better organized. According to Brenda, "They were going to start the kids on a phonics book, use an English book, and math book." Above all, these women still had hope that if they could find the right educational environment, their own children would be on the road to financial security.

Preschool Learning: More Than the ABCs?

It was important to all the women in our study that their preschool children begin preparing for formal schooling, and they emphasized the attainment of basic literacy and numeracy skills in meeting this goal. Harriet was satisfied that her daughter's child-care center was providing these experiences:

> But I like the day care, you know. I like the results I'm getting so far. She's singing songs, she's saying "ABCDEF," then she starts messing up after F, you know, she's counting to about five before she starts messing up. And I really feel that, I really feel that, you know, this is a good atmosphere for her.

Aggie was in agreement with Harriet about the role of preschool:

You know, preschool should be getting them ready for kindergarten. They're going to know their letters and know their numbers, and know that stuff. Like see, now if I had gotten him [her son] into Head Start, they learn that stuff in Head Start!

The mothers became dissatisfied with programs if they could not find evidence of teacher-structured activities. Pamela, for example, became disillusioned with her family day-care provider, a close friend and reliable advisor who was very attached to Cedric, because she did not have a structured academic program. When the agency providing Pamela's child-care vouchers told her to move him to a center, she looked forward to the educational opportunities he might have in center care:

As much as I liked her [the provider], I didn't think he was learning, you know, what he needed to know. [Interviewer: "Such as?"] Alphabets, and 'cause he wasn't speaking well. She said she was working with him, but he was really, his speech was bad . . . I felt he needed to be in with other kids his own age because he was baby-talking too much.

The three mothers who remained satisfied with their children's family day-care providers emphasized the "school-like" atmosphere, as in this statement from Sol:

It's as if she [the provider] had a school in her home. She designs, she makes them play games, she puts them to school, she does everything as if it was a school. I think my daughter has learned a lot. And it's a home! She knows the numbers, she knows her colors, she can sing.

Although learning letters, numbers, shapes, and colors was viewed as crucial, the definition of "learning" espoused by most mothers encompassed far more than these rudiments. They believed that their children should also be exposed to books, go on field trips, learn songs, do art activities, and participate in cooking projects. For example, Helena was very satisfied with her daughter's kindergarten because she was learning "her letters, her numbers, just everything! They do everything! They explore the earth, they go on field trips. Music." Jackie voiced her objections to the overemphasis on drill and practice at her daughter's school: "The other teacher . . . would drill them . . . and they would do the ABCs and stuff, which is fine, they need to know that, but they also need to have play time too."

Whether or not the activities were directly related to literacy or numeracy, most women felt that they had to be carefully structured by the teacher. As Kathy said, "The teachers are really good. They have a lot of, a lot of discipline, a lot of structures like, you know, this is what you have to do, and, it's all intense schedule the whole day." Jackie felt that her older son didn't do well if children were "all over the place" or "freestyle."

Given the great value that most of the mothers placed on education, it is not surprising that they emphasized literacy and numeracy more than self-expression or personal fulfillment. Studies of parents' views on elementary schooling suggest that working-class parents see school as the place where learning occurs, whereas home is a place to play and relax.[12] In contrast, middle-class parents may be more likely to see both the home and the school as environments in which adults "make *learning fun* and make fun a form of learning."[13]

Do Mothers Lack Information about How Children Learn?

Early childhood educators argue that parents endorse didactic instruction because they simply do not know how preschool children learn. They suggest that a parent's memory of her own formal schooling biases her image of early education settings in favor of a skill-centered, teacher-directed approach.[14] Indeed, preschool teachers themselves often have difficulty explaining why play-oriented programs offer the best methods for stimulating children's intellectual growth.[15]

We found little evidence that the mothers in our study had acquired information from teachers about the role of play in fostering children's learning. The only overt mention of play-focused learning was from Kathy, whose son attended Head Start:

> I don't think they're teaching Darren alphabet and I don't think they are teaching him like strict, sitting down teacher like at school. Like, it's basically letting the activities that they play teach

them. Whatever toys they're using, it's something that has to do with his mind, that's going to, you know, work in some way.

Kathy's views were also influenced by her former employer; she worked for several years as a nanny for a nurse who held an administrative position in a large hospital. Kathy credits the mother with exposing her to Montessorian philosophy as well as teaching her about "routine, structure, and schedule," which she now views as the keys to raising a child successfully.

Most women were easily able to access preschools and family day-care providers that reinforced their convictions about didactic instruction. Harriet absorbed the child-care teachers' belief that Shondra's performance on traditional academic tasks was a sign of her cognitive ability:

> She's doing good, real good, as far as learning. She's doing wonderful! They got her doing stuff that five- and six-year-olds are learning, and I think they said now they could teach her how to put stuff down on paper, writing her name, you know, writing out sentences, because she knows everything about colors, shapes, sizes, you know, letters. They say, "Oh! She's so smart! She's so smart! Please don't put her in public schools!"

Messages like the one from Shondra's teachers contradict the play-oriented Piagetian philosophy of the early childhood establishment. And they represent the dominant influence on most of these women in shaping their ideas about appropriate learning experiences for a young child.

Who Is Responsible for a Child's Learning?

How might one explain the variation in the degree to which parents *activate* their resources to help a child succeed in an academic setting? Annette Lareau has discussed this issue with respect to middle-class families, who possess the social capital to invest in their children, meaning that they have the educational background and sufficient knowledge of how the "system" works to create learning experiences that lead to school success.[16] But, depending on factors such as their own self-confidence and the degree to which they feel that the goals of the school are attainable and legitimate, parents may or may not put those resources into play. Harriet and Pamela, though similar in educational background and financial status, were quite different in terms of the confidence with which they passed along their "social capital" to their children.

Harriet's model of socialization featured the importance of creating a loving environment rich with communication and interaction of all types on all subjects. The goal of preparing her children for school was embedded within this rich network of shared knowledge. She had little difficulty thinking of activities that would capture their interest and attention. Harriet was aware of limits in her own educational background, but, consistent with her overall philosophy that the family must function as a key support of the child, she plunged into the role of educator:

> I help them count, like I live on the fourth floor, so we would count going up the stairs, you know. And how I got my son to tell time, is that I don't have any digital clocks, I have clocks like that, you have to count by five. 'Cause when you have digital, it makes it too easy for them. So I taught them how to tell time that way.

Harriet often took advantage of learning opportunities that came up in the course of everyday activities. The following is her description of how she taught math to her eight-year-old son:

> I try to think of things to do with them. To get them involved. Even when we're paying bills. I help them. I say, "See? This is a bill, this is the amount." And he'll [eight-year-old son] say, "What happens with this?" And I show him how the balance goes down and stuff. Because he's really into numbers. He's showing me fractions right now, because I could not get fractions in school. It wasn't sinking in. And here I am learning fractions!

For Harriet, learning was inextricably linked with active participation in warm family interaction:

[At the grocery store] I try to get everybody involved in it so they're not standing around going "Oh!" [puffs and pants with mock impatience] you know. So I say, "You take this part." And Thomas [older son], I always give him the milk, the eggs, and stuff like that, and try to teach him how to watch out for dates [that indicate when the product should be used by]. You know, "Make sure the date's like two weeks from now, Thomas. Don't get the one weeks from now, Thomas. Don't get the one that's the next— right around the corner!" And Allen [younger son], I give him the stuff he likes to pick up, the cereal, the cookies, the juice, you know, stuff like that, and then me and Shondra take care of the meats and stuff like that.

Pamela confided that her time with Cedric was often not enjoyable for her, and she frequently left him with relatives while she pursued social activities. Her interactions with him around school preparation were formal and sporadic. It seemed as though she simply did not know much about her son's interests or experiences in settings outside the home. She also didn't know what a child was capable of doing at a particular age. She thus felt at a loss as to how to gauge his level of knowledge, how to engage his attention, and how to make learning experiences rewarding for both of them.

During the first interview, when Cedric had just turned four, she expressed her belief that "learning" would come in kindergarten:

I think [in kindergarten it is] . . . going to be important for him to know, you know, his colors, and his ABCs . . . I think if he doesn't know his colors [now] it's all right. With me, I don't *know* what you're supposed to do, if there's a standard. Maybe when you get in kindergarten, I'll ask them what he'll be learning . . . colors. Maybe he should be knowing that before that, I don't know.

Throughout the interviews, Pamela acknowledged that her lack of involvement with Cedric inspired criticism, primarily from her mother:

My mother told me, "You know, you're supposed to play with your kids!" I said, I was like, I'll buy him anything, you know . . . And then I feel bad, because I don't . . . I won't sit and play you know. If I do, it's only like, maybe a half an hour, and then I'm tired. Or at night, I'll read one book and then he wants me to read another one. I'm like, "I can't! I can't! I can't read this book no more!" You know, so I feel bad because I don't think I'm a mother type, you know.

By our second interview, Pamela had begun managing two bands in the evening, in addition to holding her day job. During this period, she became aware of some delay in Cedric's development. At age five, he was unable to give his address, recite the ABCs, write his name, or state his age. She was furious with the providers at her son's preschool because she felt that they had failed to fulfill their responsibility to prepare him for school:

Everyone in there [the day-care center] is a qualified teacher. They should know more than me. They should be able to get me outside help. I was put in a predicament where he's behind . . . If they tell me my son's not where he should be, I don't know. He's only my first kid! They're the ones that know! They are trained professionals. They're professionals. They could have told me, educated me, to find my son help, to work with him at home.

When Cedric was six months away from entering first grade, she decided it was up to her to help him catch up: "I just never sat down with him to do it. I'm now taking responsibility to teach him, and I've asked the school to support me." She reported on her efforts to help him, but admitted that she was unsure about how to proceed:

Now I do a lot with him. We read a lot now. I joined a book club. I read to him about a half hour or an hour. I tell him, "Listen to me," but he always wants to turn the page. I've got me some flashcards I keep in my pocketbook, when we're in the car, on the train, you name it. I was crazy with him! I take those flashcards everywhere, and we got the book club, so I get books now. He's gotta learn his ABCs. When he's getting it wrong, I get nervous, so I stopped. But I'm not a teacher.

Pamela was not the only mother who found it difficult to incorporate less formal instruction into daily routines with her children. Those who were not accustomed to a daily give-and-take of ideas with their children became frustrated when they tried to teach them literacy skills. As Aggie put it, "[My son's] attention span with me just isn't long enough for him to really learn anything." She felt that the preschool instructors, "with their degrees in teaching," should take the initiative in helping children prepare for school.

If a mother is not confident about her role in preparing her child for school, what does she do? Under what conditions do mothers accept "expert opinion" and when do they reject it? These are crucial issues for parent education, yet often parenting programs are devised with little thought to whether the target population views the received knowledge as valid, helpful, or legitimate. When expert knowledge is perceived as legitimate, cultural models evolve in response to it; this is the active process of *producing* culture.[17]

Indeed, most of the mothers in our study provided evidence that they attended to "expert" opinion on a variety of topics related to child rearing. Pamela in particular tended to be receptive to outside opinion. Her goals for Cedric were affected by a television program on the importance of social competence, as well as by the disparaging views of her own mother. She lamented the fact that the teachers in Cedric's school did not "educate" her about how to teach her son academic skills at home. Pamela also tried to elicit our advice on how to help her son. Other women showed an awareness that there were experts whose insights might provide some legitimate solutions. Kathy articulated clearly her attempts to integrate professional opinions about discipline with her own views: "I have to train myself to be like the teachers a little more."

The women were receptive to advice on issues that were of importance to them. But on the topic of preschools and learning, they were exposed to a rather narrow range of ideas that reinforced their emphasis on didactic instruction. For these mothers, *Sesame Street* had come to epitomize the correct educational approach; many of the fourteen women mentioned it as an important educational experience for their children. Ironically, the program embodies a didactic approach to teaching decontextualized elements of literacy, albeit in a playful and attention-grabbing format.

Interdependence as a Cultural Model for Child Rearing

Ultimately, mothers' views about learning in preschool are connected to other models of child rearing. As we saw in Chapter 6, respect for elders was emphasized by all the mothers as an essential ingredient in children's socialization. This orientation is not embodied in play-oriented programs that portray children as active explorers and philosophers who create their own understandings and shape their own knowledge. In these programs the authority of the adult is often softened or diluted; indeed, many observers of the effects of extended schooling on children from traditional cultures have noted that schooling often undermines the authority of adults in the community.[18]

The women in our study felt that the teacher's authority had to be respected in order for learning to occur. Brenda put this most clearly:

> But they [the preschool teachers] are not really like forcing them to learn. They're showing them pictures, you know, "This is the A." They count blocks and say, "This is ABC." . . . They don't really sit them down and say, "This is the letter A, B," you know. They're not really sitting them down and focusing them on their letters and numbers. And I feel they should.

For mothers to accept a child-focused orientation, they would also have to accept the underlying individualistic cultural model that highlights the contributions and activities of the child without creating a role for a respected adult authority figure.

Another important component of the interdependent orientation of low-income families is the notion that individuals are obligated to contribute to the family's welfare rather than maximizing their own resources.[19] The women in our study were embedded in complex extended families and provided detailed accounts of the services that they provided—and took advantage of—within that network. We have already seen how Pamela made use of her family for child care. Indeed, half the women counted on relatives to care for their children for several days and nights each week. Three women—Helena, Pat, and Shirl—placed an older sibling of the target child with relatives on a permanent basis. In return, these women performed diverse services for family members. They cared for their relatives' children, prepared meals, ran errands for those without transportation, and cleaned houses for those too old to do it themselves.

American preschools tend to emphasize individual rights more than responsibilities.[20] Teachers may inculcate social values like cooperation or nonaggression, but the focus is on respecting the rights of others rather than encouraging children to sacrifice their own self-interest for the good of others. To mothers like Kathy, participation in structured learning activities is a way that children can begin to establish themselves as contributing members of the community. Accordingly, parents may feel that didactic preschools are more likely than child-focused preschools to encourage a child to become a responsible citizen. Kathy, in effect, defined a preschool "work ethic" in which it behooved children to take advantage of their time in preschool by learning "anything" rather than lying around: "So I was just hoping they [the teachers] were going to teach him [son] something and not just let the kid lie around all day . . . You know, it's not just rampant play. I don't like that. What I really want him to learn, anything was better than nothing."

These fourteen mothers strongly believed that education was the ticket to social mobility. Our findings in this respect are strikingly consistent with the results of other qualitative studies on the importance of children's education to low-income parents.[21] The mothers in our study were not disillusioned about the "American dream" of self-betterment through education, but were convinced that the Boston public schools could not deliver the experiences their children needed. They had begun exploring other options, most notably, Catholic schools and the Metco busing program.

Because these women's opinions about teaching strategies were constructed from their personal experiences and interactions with members of their own communities, they did not always match the goals and strategies of middle-class families. In particular, they put an emphasis on didactic school preparation, which is at odds with the recommendations of many early childhood educators. They had not been exposed to developmental theory and its implications for pedagogy. In fact, many of the early childhood programs they had encountered reinforced their beliefs about teacher-structured learning by providing a teacher-structured environment and giving them feedback as to the positive progress of their children in those environments. Even *Sesame Street*, frequently mentioned approvingly by these mothers, hammers in the didactic message with its predominant emphasis on number and letter recognition.

In the course of their daily lives, these women reflected upon their own upbringing, on experiences in other cultures, and on the differing perspectives provided by family and friends. They accepted the possibility that learning was facilitated through participation in a variety of hands-on activities as well as through exposure to numbers, letters, and other decontextualized information. They were willing to incorporate the views of professional "experts" into their child-rearing routines if they perceived that there was a serious problem that their current strategies were not dealing with successfully.

We detected a limit to how fully these women would embrace the "developmentally appropriate" curriculum touted by early childhood professionals. To the extent that a child-focused curriculum contravened the fourteen women's deeply held beliefs about the importance of respecting authority and participating reciprocally in close-knit communities, it was unlikely to gain their full endorsement. To gain the confidence and cooperation of low-income parents—particularly those from traditional cultures—professional organizations must be more thoughtful in examining the underlying cultural views expressed in supposedly "neutral" documents such as the NAEYC guidelines or other prescriptive writings on "appropriate" practices.[22]

CHAPTER EIGHT

Negotiating Child Care and Welfare

❦

Myths and realities surrounding the choices made by single mothers, like old fishing line, remain hopelessly entangled. In this chapter we focus on the important and often difficult decisions that poor mothers make about child care. We explore the fundamental questions that govern their decision-making: Who will care for my child as I struggle to get back into the workforce? What are the dangers if I leave my child in the hands of a child-care provider I don't really know? What can I afford? With whom do I feel comfortable talking about my youngster? As my child grows older, should I move her into a formal preschool to increase her learning?

To grapple with these questions, the fourteen women in our study weighed two morally charged social roles: being a mother and being an economic provider. As we saw in Chapter 3, some women thought about the independence and feeling of self-worth that going back to work entailed for them; others saw work as a necessary act that kept them from spending precious time with their young children. But the necessity of piecing together income—from kin members, low-paying jobs, and welfare—required these women to search out and assess different child-care options. Their decisions in this arena reveal much about how they see child rearing and how they make sense of welfare and child-care organizations.

Motivating Families to Act in the Interests of Their Children

Debates over how to combat poverty in America have sparked an inventive folklore. One popular story, told by those on the political Right, goes something like this: single mothers have grown overly dependent upon welfare and are no longer motivated to work outside the home. They and their toddlers would be better off if they got jobs. Making this story come true requires cutting off welfare checks to reduce the disincentive to work, and expanding child-care options. To empower poor women, in this view, government should provide child-care vouchers or tax credits, which require little bureaucratic control and afford parents a "choice" as to where they place their children. Many conservatives who long opposed formal child care now see it as the linchpin enabling poor women to spend more time in minimum-wage jobs. And by being allowed to *choose* their own child care, are not these single mothers being empowered to find their own pathways out of poverty?[1]

This theory of motivation is largely rooted in neoclassical economics. One early proponent, Harvard's Gary Becker, argues that the house-hold should be viewed as the primary social unit of motivation: a collective organization that seeks to maximize economic returns gained through work, income drawn from public welfare, and (in the long run) investment in the human capital of children, including their preschool development.[2] If parents have sufficient resources to "invest" initially, they will make rational choices for their future work and for the development of their children. This conception of family motivation and action has stimulated a variety of antipoverty initiatives, including housing and child-care vouchers and refundable tax credits for fourteen million families living close to the poverty line but with a working member.[3]

Missing from this idealized model are the cultural and institutional contexts in which these women live. Can low-income families draw upon a network of friends and family who can help them to find and maintain jobs and high-quality child care? What are the cultural and declared models that define the options that they see as legitimate pathways of action? These pivotal questions are not addressed by this framework.

The centrist version of this position focuses on income-support and other welfare programs that encourage the "correct choices." Economic carrots are used to entice mothers to take actions sanctioned by those in charge of the purse strings. Bill Clinton talks often of the return to "personal responsibility." As the poverty scholar Lawrence Mead argues, "The challenge to welfare statesmanship is not so much to change the extent of benefits as to couple them with serious work and other obligations." Low-income families receive benefits, but they are not told "with any authority that they ought to behave differently."[4]

Those on the political Left, including many child advocates, tell a second story. They like the empowerment scene in the conservatives' tale, and they agree that finding child care is pivotal in the struggle to move women from welfare to work. But their story gives stronger roles and many more lines to those players involved in shaping the quality of child care and preschooling: national administrators, particularly those from Head Start, local professionals, and government regulators. If these players do not have a major role, the storytellers claim, poor women will be forced to use cheap, low-quality forms of child care. If government does not step in, this tale will end in a nightmare—as women enter low-paying jobs while their youngsters spend the day in poor-quality day care.

A focus on the social context in which poor families find themselves—the *culture of poverty*—has been a crucial complement to the structural critique advanced by the Left and (until recently) political moderates. The basic argument is that over time economic conditions create social behaviors and personal characteristics that erode the family structure, erase motivation to achieve, and give rise to a sense of helplessness and despair—contexts and psychological states that may be immune to economic incentives. Evidence has accumulated to bolster elements of this portrayal of the poor's motivations and practices.[5]

Cultural Foundations of Motivation and Family Action

This dialectic persists among the polemicists. A third way of thinking about the family's motivated actions and processes of "choice" has recently emerged, rooted in cross-cultural studies of the family and child rearing. Rather than taking an implicitly culture-less conception of families situated in poor communities, this perspective recognizes and explores the *diverse*, even contradictory, nature of the cultural models and behavioral scripts available to them. For many women, tacit pathways give way to novel, declared models of how to find jobs or locate child-care programs that fit their preferences. The range of job, welfare, and child-care options available is without doubt tied to material economic conditions. But alternative cultural models or action pathways are known and assessed by actors within poor families. In a sense, this third framework rests between personal responsibility and structuralist accounts of family action. It suggests that conscious choices are made by parents who are acting rationally. Yet the available cultural models are particular to the setting—they hold utility given the uncertainty and fragility of life in poverty—and they often depart from the pathways observed in middle-class settings.

How Do Parents "Choose" Child Care?

All fourteen women approached the question of child care with trepidation. Leaving one's infant or toddler with another person, often someone about whom one knows very little, is not easy to do. For women in poverty this uncertainty is combined with additional pressures: how to retain welfare benefits, how to find and hold down a minimum-wage job, even how to spend some time each day with friends and family. In short, mothers assess their options within a context replete with constraints and contradictory cultural models pertaining to who can best care for their children. In this chapter we will report on how four women viewed their child-care options, as they struggled to satisfy the competing demands of bringing home a paycheck and raising a young child. But first we will briefly review existing evidence about parents' child-care choices, most of which comes from cursory surveys.

Family-level studies provide several lessons on how poor families make choices. Parents from all social backgrounds typically draw on limited information and shop around only to a limited extent before selecting their child-care arrangements. For low-income and single mothers this selection process most often occurs before the child is a year old, given economic pressures to enter or return to the workforce. The type of child care chosen—be it a baby-sitter, family day care, or a center-based program—depends heavily on endorsements or leads provided by friends and kin members. Some parents are linked to resource and referral agencies, a common source of "market information" in many states. Yet only a portion of parents actually visit and carefully inspect alternative child-care programs. One study of *middle-class* mothers found that two-thirds investigated only the workings of the center they chose.[6]

In recent surveys, parents report concern with program quality, proximity, and price. The last factor is less important for women on welfare, until they re-enter the workforce and their child-care subsidies are reduced.[7] Although some surveys find high levels of satisfaction with the quality of current arrangements, others indicate that if affordable alternatives were available, up to a third of all parents would prefer to move their youngsters from family day care into center-based programs.[8] But some mothers, particularly Latinas, less frequently select formal preschools, relying heavily on kin members and family day care. Families placing greater emphasis on early cognitive stimulation and reading tend to put their youngsters in formal centers or preschools, whereas parents committed to warm, home-like settings report selection of baby-sitters or family day care.[9]

Realistic choices, of course, are constrained by the supply of proximate options. *Organization-level* studies have focused on how inequality in the availability of centers and preschools may constrain the choices of poor families. For example, affluent urban counties have two-thirds more preschool slots per 1,000 resident children than poorer counties populated more heavily by working-class or rural families. Unequal availability may constrain choice even in states like Massachusetts, with relatively high funding levels for child care and preschooling. One recent study found that the per capita supply of child-care spaces in that state was 40 percent higher in affluent suburbs than in inner-city neighborhoods.[10] Another study from Chicago found that some inner-city neighborhoods with many unemployed single mothers had *no* available centers or preschools.[11]

Single mothers often patch together a variety of child-care arrangements, especially if they work full time. And as their toddlers grow older, these women are encouraged by welfare agencies to move from informal types of care into preschools. To the mothers this may seem an organizational maze, with uncertain turns and false starts. We turn next to the sequence of constrained choices made by the fourteen mothers in our sample.

Common Paths Taken

Some similarities are apparent in the routes taken by the fourteen mothers following the birth of a child. Table 8.1 provides an overview of the types of child care they used, the sources of information on which the women relied in finding child care, and economic or social benefits they perceived in particular services. All women stayed home for at least two months following the birth of a child. All but two received AFDC support at that time and set up their child-care arrangement with either a kin member, a baby-sitter, or a family day-care provider. The other two received financial support from DSS or a child-care subsidy during these early months. Under workfare requirements operating at the time of our data collection, AFDC recipients in Massachusetts had to find a job or go back to school after twelve months. Child-care subsidies could be retained after they gained employment. Several women also received housing subsidies, job training, counseling, or drug rehabilitation services. Two women spent time in homeless shelters, even though each had a parent living close by. Although all but one of these women eventually returned to work or entered job training, they were quite familiar with public-assistance agencies.

The mothers mobilized various resources and actors in arranging child care and preschooling during the first five years of their children's lives. Most relied on kin members and family day-care homes until their children were two years old. As the children turned three or four, mothers typically became concerned that they begin to "learn something" or "get ready for real school," and so they would search for formal centers or preschools. The institutional structure of child-care subsidies and organizational practices encouraged mothers on AFDC to select formal centers, even for children under age three, as we detail below. The extent to which kin members were available to help out with child care varied. Four of the mothers reported that as many as three different kin members assisted them, whereas two women had not relied on kin in any way since their children were born.

Two sources of information were consistently cited as important to the fourteen women. First, social workers, primarily working within welfare offices, provided crucial information about where child-care slots were available. Five of the fourteen women believed that the agencies had "checked out" the family day-care providers or centers appearing on listings. Second, resource and referral (R&R) agencies provided useful information in the eyes of all but one of the sampled mothers. Eight of the fourteen women mentioned that their R&Rs helped them find their initial providers or locate preschools as their children approached age three or four.

Reacting to Initial Child-Care Choices

How did these women evaluate the child-care providers or formal organizations that cared for their children? Our findings contradict the frequent assumption, inherent in the culture-of-poverty mythology, that low-income mothers are too overwhelmed with daily problems, too uncertain or uneducated, or too negligent to evaluate child-care settings. Most women had thought a lot about different types of arrangements, reflecting on the advantages and disadvantages of care by kin members, friends, family day-care providers, and child-care centers. Three sets of criteria were expressed over the life of the study: (1) cost, proximity, and material features of the child-care settings; (2) the children's own reactions to the settings; and (3) considerations linked to the quality or character of the child-care providers.

All fourteen women were concerned about the cost of child care. In particular, they worried about whether their subsidies would cover the full cost of care, whether the fees would go up after they went back to work, and what the price of child care would be if they could not find subsidized slots or vouchers. Proximity to home, workplace, and public transportation, and whether adequate meals were provided were common concerns. Five of the mothers mentioned the number of toys and educational materials available at the family day-care homes or preschools as a factor in their decision making. The particulars of financing care also motivated certain "choices." For example, child-care vouchers were viewed as a less stable form of subsidy by several of the women. Some were coached by social-welfare workers to take subsidized slots at preschools when they became available, rather than continuing on

Table 8.1 Pathways through child care, information channels, and economic resources

	HC1	PD2	HA3	SH4	WM5	BM6	PK7	JV8	SL9	KM10	BB11	SM12	AG13	DM14
Age of target child at first interview with mother (years.months)	3.8	4.7	3.1	2.2	2.8	3.10	4.0	3.1	2.6	3.4	1.10	4.10	4.3	4.5
Types of care or preschool utilized since birth of target child														
Mother	■	■	■	■	■	■	■	■	■	■	■	■	■	■
Father	■	■	■		■	■				■		■		■
Other kin member	■ 2	■ 3	■ 3	■ 3	■	■ 2	■ 2	■		■ 3	■			■ 2
Friend	■	■ 2				■								
Baby-sitter	■	■ 2								■ 2				
Family day-care home				■ 2							■	■ 2		
Formal center or preschool	■	■ 2	■ 2		■	■	■	■ 2	■	■			■	■
Kindergarten	■	■	■			■		■	■				■	■
Information sources (for initial and subsequent child-care providers)														
Kin member	■	■	■	■		■			■	■	■	■	■	■
Friend		■ 3	■		■ 2									
Welfare office/social worker		■				■	■	■	■	■	■	■	■	
Child-care organization	■ 2	■ 2	■	■	■ 2	■		■				■	■	
Community or church organization	■ 2	■ 2			■				■	■	■	■	■	
Checked into other providers (not shown)	■ 2	■			■ 2	■			■	■ 2	■ 2	■	■	

Formal sources

Financial support from father

AFDC

Child-care subsidy (slot, voucher, rate)[1]

Department of Social Services (DSS)[2]

Job training or schooling subsidies

Subsidized housing

Informal and in-kind sources

In-kind housing support (extended family)

Church linkages with child care

Community meetings/civic action[3]

Note: ■ signifies one individual or instance; ■ signifies more than one individual or instance (count appears below symbol).

1. Subsidies provided in the form of a fully subsidized "slot" in a family day-care home or center; vouchers that can be used only within approved settings that generally did not differ from locations of slots; and reduced fees were charged when mothers were working and earning above a certain threshold.

2. DSS support provided to women who become "cases" of the agency, usually for drug abuse or reported abuse of a child. Subsidized services include drug rehabilitation treatment, counseling and home visits, transportation subsidies for children.

3. This includes meetings at child-care center as well as civic and political action related to child-care funding or changes in local organizations.

vouchers; as Shirl put it, "With a slot, you are in there for good." Another consideration for ten women was selecting providers and preschools that would help their children avoid eventual enrollment in inner-city public schools. Strategies used by some included enrolling children in preschools affiliated with parochial elementary schools.

These women had concerns about particular sites that do not surface in most household surveys about parental choice of child care. They were attentive to how their children were reacting to the child-care settings, as well as how the children's developmental changes placed new demands on their child-care providers. They thought about physical features of the child-care setting: Did it look clean and well organized? Was the provider licensed or screened by a formal welfare agency? Was there any record or rumors of child abuse? Concerns about abuse were expressed by nine of the fourteen women, and were at times backed by stories of incidents involving the children of their kin members or friends.

Some mothers were suspicious of formal centers and preschools, viewing them as impersonal or cold. Whether the provider seemed warm and loving was important to all the women. Some of these women eventually enrolled their children in formal centers, when the desire to prepare them for school outweighed preferences for seemingly warmer family day-care providers or kin members. Six of the fourteen mothers knew someone else whose child already attended the settings they selected for their children.

The women articulated numerous impressions of what occurred in the settings they eventually selected, usually based upon short observations during drop-off and pick-up times. The number of activities in which the children were engaged was a common proxy for the quality and learning content of the program. All fourteen complained about— or praised—their current providers for the number of learning activities and the literacy content offered. Several women reluctantly gave up their family day-care providers and enrolled their children in preschools to help them "develop an idea of what school would be like" or because they weren't "learning enough" in the less formal settings. In addition, the ways in which providers disciplined children, set rules for behavior, and provided (or restricted) children's freedom was discussed by eleven of the fourteen mothers.

Cultural Models Guiding Family Action

Within the social communities of the fourteen women, clusters of competing pathways and values influenced the important decisions they made about child care. For our discussion of the alternative models or paths of action available to these mothers, we focus primarily on four women: Brenda and Jackie, both African-Americans, and Beatriz and Delmy, both Latinas. When we began to interview her in 1991, Brenda was twenty-three years old and resided in Roxbury, a section of Boston populated mostly by African-Americans. Her boyfriend was in Miami when her daughter Cora was born, although he returned and cared for her occasionally. Brenda's mother worked as a private nurse; her father, an immigrant from Jamaica, "drove a cab for practically twenty-four hours a day." Brenda lived with her parents in a house they owned with her brother and two sisters. Following Cora's birth, Brenda went on AFDC for about a year, then placed Cora with a licensed home provider and entered the local community college.

Jackie is a thirty-year-old African-American who, when she joined the study, had recently left a residential drug rehabilitation program and had been reunited with her two children. As a young girl, Jackie was shuffled back and forth between her alcoholic mother and relations in Boston and Georgia. When she was seven, she was sent to Los Angeles, where her mother had moved with a new husband. Jackie was asked to take on the housework and care of her younger stepbrother and stepsister. Neglected by her mother and sexually abused by her stepfather, she became sexually promiscuous and involved in drugs. At age twenty-one she had a baby, then fled back to Boston to escape her violent, drug-addicted partner. She "got tired of welfare" and began working nights at a bank's data-processing office. At age twenty-seven, Jackie gave birth to her daughter, Tiffany, on whom we focus. Six months later, Jackie, heavily into drugs, was evicted from her apartment. She moved into a homeless shelter with the infant Tiffany and her elder son, then age five. Within the next few months both children were taken from her by DSS and placed in foster care. She entered a drug rehabilitation program. Several months prior to our first interview, Jackie had been reunited with her two children.

At age twenty, Beatriz emigrated from El Salvador to a Latino section of East Boston. We first interviewed her in 1991, when she was twenty-eight. After moving to the United States, she worked nights as a maid in a downtown hotel, earning $200 a week, and attended English classes. Her mother also immigrated to the Boston area and lived with her son in nearby Chelsea. Beatriz's eldest son was six years old and her younger son, Jorge, was two months shy of age two when our interviews began. Beatriz went on welfare for seven months after giving birth to Jorge, then went back to work as a receptionist, putting Jorge in a family day-care home run by a Latina.

Delmy, age twenty-nine, also an émigré from Central America, came from a family of fourteen children. She left El Salvador in the early 1980s, settling in an ethnically mixed, working-class neighborhood northwest of downtown Boston where her mother and three siblings already resided. Delmy was married when her daughter Carla was born, and rather than going on welfare, she relied on her husband's income and child care provided by her mother and sister. During our period of contact with her, she split up with her husband, a move supported by her family: "They never liked my husband. They didn't want me to marry him." She found a job as a classroom aide in a local elementary school. Delmy reported great satisfaction with Carla's preschool and kindergarten. But in the third year of our study, Carla's first-grade teacher recommended that she be held back a year, given her "immaturity" and apparent learning problems.

We selected these four women primarily because their work, welfare, and child-care arrangements are quite varied. This variety illuminates the multiplicity of cultural models that circulate in poor neighborhoods, as well as how ethnicity, in part, patterns salient models and scripts. Ethnic boundaries to a certain extent define which models of action in the child-care domain are tacit and which alternative models are contested.

Cluster 1: Who Should Care for My Baby?

A significant proportion of the fourteen expressed regret over being unable to follow a conventional pathway, wishing that they could stay at home or work part time to spend more time with their children. But to maintain a minimal level of income, these women were pushed to find jobs or training programs. In turn, all but one of the fourteen women wound down their AFDC benefits, although all remained eligible for child-care subsidies. Enacting the stay-at-home model was not materially possible unless they found an employed partner or relied heavily on kin. But this idealized model remained in their minds and became a source of concern for some. Just one of the fourteen (Helena) intentionally changed her work situation to spend more time with her child, quitting her job of four years to find part-time employment closer to home.

Most of the fourteen women expressed a preference for having a family member care for their infants, primarily because they trusted family members more than they did "strangers." Harriet was leery of any form of child care other than that provided by relatives:

I just don't trust day cares for infants. I don't trust baby-sitters. I'm too scared for that, because I think a loving grandma or loving great aunt, or somebody like that, is better than the day care for little babies . . . I figured there would be a lot of neglect going on, you know. I was real scared of that. I trusted my aunt. [Harriet's aunt was already taking care of two grandchildren.] I thought one more [child] wouldn't be too bad, you know, she wasn't doing anything, so she started taking care of [my child] for me. I just don't trust day care for infants.

In addition to a family day-care provider, Brenda relied on her best friend, who had a son Cora's age:

My friend Annette, me and her are real close. She goes, "Oh, just bring her down, I'll watch her." You know, she'll watch her, bring her to the park, feed her, and bring her back, and I do the same for her child. One more kid doesn't make much difference. It's like part of the family. Her son and my daughter gets along real, like sisters and brothers. I knew her for a while, but we really didn't become close since like almost two years ago. So we got real close and started talking, so we like baby-sit each other's child, went to the park together, did a lot of things together.

Brenda talked a lot about her stepfather's beliefs about child rearing, which included the view that children "should be walking and talking" before their mothers returned to work. With exasperation mixed with amusement, she recalled his eagerness to become involved in Cora's care:

> He interferes all the time. [Imitating his voice] "Have you eaten? You sure look hungry." I mean he tries to feed her everything: fruits, fish. When she was first born she was seven pounds, five ounces, and I was feeding her. Then she was gradually losing weight. [Imitating her father's anxious voice] "What's the matter? What are you, you need to give her nutrition!" So he tells her to drink all her milk. He acts like he's the mother. It's hard sometimes, you know. [But] I get a lot of help from my family, so that makes it better.

Providing child care was just one of a variety of favors that these women and their relatives exchanged. Delmy's mother originally cared for her daughter Carla when Delmy returned to work. Three sisters lived close by, each of whom could also take care of Carla if Delmy's mother was unavailable. Delmy often provided reciprocal services to her relatives. In her journal Delmy reported spending one Saturday cleaning her mother's apartment. Shirl, who lived with her brother, his wife, and their four children in a house owned by her mother, reported that Martin "sometimes just falls asleep [at night] downstairs in his cousins' apartment." Shirl paid her mother rent; a second brother was asked to move from the house when he failed to do the same.

Several of the women did not receive the warm and reliable support provided by the families of Delmy, Brenda, and Shirl. When Jackie returned to Boston with her father, she was severely disappointed by his failure to help her with rent money or child-care support. While she was living in the drug rehabilitation center, her aunt was temporarily assigned to provide foster care for her children. But the aunt refused to let Jackie visit after she failed to repay a $100 loan. Helena also experienced uncaring responses from her family during times of crisis. When her husband moved out and she entered a homeless shelter, her mother and sister refused to assist her in any way:

> When Shannon was born we were still in the shelter, and my mother didn't want to be involved in that. She never offered me

a place to stay. My sister Stephanie, the same thing. She was in her own apartment at the time . . . never once got an offer from either of them: "Here's my couch if you want to use it for a night or weekend."

INTO WELFARE AND THE MIXED MARKET OF CHILD CARE

When trustworthy kin members were not available, the women were more apt to apply for AFDC and become reliant on community organizations. Twelve of the fourteen women assumed that applying for welfare benefits was a legitimate way to acquire resources following the birth of a child. Beatriz believed that the system encouraged women to go on AFDC. She applied to enter a job-training program but was deemed ineligible because she was earning $200 a week as a maid. While pregnant with her second son, Jorge, she decided to quit work and go on AFDC: "I was making too much, so I went on welfare. [Now we are both working] but still it's too much. Why are we working if all the money is going in baby-sitting, apartment rent, food?" Beatriz reported feeling "like less than a person" in dealing with the local welfare office: "Everyone has to lie . . . you can't tell them you're married or living with someone, [but] one person alone can't make it." After completing a secretarial training program, she went off AFDC, maintaining her child-care subsidy, and took a job as a receptionist, at which she earned $260 a week.

Pamela was unapologetic about applying for AFDC after becoming pregnant with her son Cedric. Her friends and mother (a social worker) coached her on how to apply and how to speak to her welfare caseworker. But her moral interpretation of being on welfare shifted in the study's second year, after she went back to work and struggled to raise her son single-handedly:

I've always worked since I was in high school. It bothered me because I had to keep going there [welfare office]. I always felt like I was taking something that wasn't mine. I have girlfriends who are on AFDC and have day care, and they don't do nothing but stay at home. I get mad sometimes, you know? I go to work every day and, I mean, she'd sit there and talk to me on the phone most of the time. She runs around with boyfriends and stuff while her kids go to day care.

Pamela illustrated the countermodel when discussing her friend Rachel: "She's amazing. She's got both her kids in day care [and] she goes back to work two weeks [after giving birth]!"

Other women, including Harriet, the mother of three who eventually fled Roxbury for the southern suburbs, reported strong misgivings about growing dependent on AFDC:

> It makes me feel good when people say to me, "How do you do it?" I'm like, I don't know, I just do it. I really enjoy working. On welfare they don't give you the self-respect that you, they should give you. By me working it gives me a lot of self-respect . . . and gives my kids an idea that hey, Mommy's working! You know, they don't have to worry about kids teasing them, saying, "Your mother's on welfare" [in taunting, singsong voice].

Harriet's comment illustrates how these two competing models—the legitimacy of going on AFDC versus the virtue of getting off—circulated within her neighborhood and were linked to moral signals that she wanted her children to understand. They are declared models in the eyes of some women, consciously examined and debated within their communities.

Harriet, an African-American, was one of the few mothers who invoked race-based categories to describe community norms. She regretted her move from a neighborhood that was "mixed . . . blacks, whites, Spanish, a variety of people," to one that was "all black" and beset with "lots of drugs, lots of crime, prostitution." She invoked imagery of black welfare recipients who were making no effort to return to work. Attributions to race or ethnic-based norms, however, were rare throughout the course of the study, except in the case of the Latina mothers, who commented on the individualistic and permissive forms of child rearing favored by Anglo parents.

When it came to obtaining child-care subsidies, the women did not feel as ambivalent. The receipt of child-care support was an accepted script that was not subject to debate over its legitimacy and moral significance. All fourteen women received child-care subsidies throughout the study; not one expressed reservations about receiving this form of public assistance. Their attitudes were likely influenced by institutional signals. Whereas "welfare queens" are derided by politicians and the media, less opprobrium is attached to subsidized child care. Since the 1960s, neighborhood child-care centers and subsidized slots have become expected fixtures in most low-income Boston communities.

What we found most striking was the diversity of preferred pathways into and through the child-care maze. There is little question that welfare checks and work requirements—carrots and sticks—were pushing these women in certain directions, determining when they entered the child-care market and how they maneuvered within it. Their immediate social networks, including the experiences and norms of kin and friends, also guided them down certain pathways. These networks, however, were not always strong and supportive. For some, like Helena, homeless shelters, housing subsidies, and child-care vouchers were essential foundations for the survival of the family. Without a supportive partner or extended family network, their options narrowed and their choices were channeled down pathways set by others.

Cluster 2: What Kind of Formal Child Care Is Best?

For women who did not have relatives available to provide child care, family day care was the preferred alternative for the first two or three years of their children's lives. Nine of the women used a family day-care provider at some point. Several reported that these providers were "grandmotherly" or had become close friends, contrasting these warm relationships with centers that seemed too big and impersonal. Brenda talked glowingly of her first provider, "a Spanish lady" named Josefa who cared for two infants and two toddlers. Brenda preferred this arrangement to a center when Cora was under three:

> The sitter was real nice. Real nice. You know, she used to talk to me about what happened during the day, the things they did. Josefa would read to them, their little letters. Cora got really attached to her . . . she reached her arms right out to Josefa. She remembers her house [and says], "Mommy, look, that's where my friend [Josefa] stays." I think they pay more attention, because they have less kids [than a center], it's like really small.

Beatriz, aided by a community agency that distributed child-care vouchers, found a Honduran family day-care provider named Isabel for Jorge, who was almost two. Beatriz liked the warm atmosphere of the provider's home and the fact that she spoke Spanish to Jorge. She was enthusiastic about what Jorge was learning: "They sing, she records their voices, she has them paint, she has a lot of things to do . . . things that if I cared for him, maybe he wouldn't do." Beatriz gave Isabel's husband gas money to pick up her older son at the end of the school day and take him to their home as well. Beatriz also reported that Isabel had received training that enabled her to enrich the educational content of her program:

> If I search for a person, like a family member or someone who doesn't have a license, they would not care for them in the same way [that] she cares for them. They would just care for them. They would not do activities with them or teach them anything. It would only be baby-sitting.

Jackie was one of the few to express concern over the variable quality of family day-care homes. When she was working nights at a data-processing office, she found a family day-care provider who would keep her son, then age two, overnight and drop him off at her apartment each morning:

> One day he came home, and he just kept drinking water. He was like starting to throw up, and kept drinking water, like he was dehydrated. You know, I took him to the hospital, and we sat there for hours and hours . . . They said he had gotten hold of some rat poison, or some kind of poison. He started foaming at the mouth, that's what scared me.

Jackie went to the director of a church-based center and "begged" her to let her son attend. The director agreed even though she had exceeded the regulated class size.

Jackie had witnessed many substandard facilities when she worked for the city agency charged with supervising licensed family day-care homes:

I don't like family day care. I was a supervisor for family day-care homes. I've seen things happen I don't like. Doing surprise visits, you know, and the TV being going on for like all these hours. There's no type of activities. I could stay home to put my child in front of *Sesame Street.* You know, I can sit there and let them play outside all day long. The child is not getting anything. You need something to have them to be stimulated and stuff. There was times when I would have to close a provider's home. We had to file a 51-A . . . it's like for neglect or something like that, when they're neglecting or abusing a child.

GETTING READY FOR SCHOOL

As their children approached age two or three, several of the mothers decided that center-based care would be more educational than family day care. The distinction between "baby-sitting" and "school" became clearer in the minds of these women as their children grew older and as they spoke with friends who also had young children, with kin members, and with social workers. These individuals suggested that a three- or four-year-old child will benefit more from a formal preschool program than from a baby-sitter or a family day-care home.

When Cora was three, Brenda moved her into a neighborhood preschool when a subsidized slot opened up:

> Going to a preschool, it gives them more activity for when they get to first grade . . . [they learn] that not everybody is going to be your friend . . . you [will] know what to expect when you go to first grade.

Beatriz, at our initial interview, expressed dislike for formal preschools: "I don't like them. I imagine that they have lots of children. They don't have special care like she [Isabel] gives." But one year later, with her son approaching age three, Beatriz shifted her opinion, stating that she would prefer to find a center: "If I could put him in a center, I would . . . to develop [in Jorge] an idea of what school will be like." Delmy "wanted her [Carla] to go to a place where she would learn, so that she would be ready for kindergarten. She needed a place like that."

CULTURAL CONFLICTS AT PRESCHOOL

The professional norms expressed by preschool teachers often came into sharp conflict with Latino models of child rearing. Beatriz defined the advantages of formal preschools in terms of learning social rules: "It's better to be with other children . . . then children develop faster and learn to get along socially." But Beatriz also criticized "kids in this country [who are] very independent, so they don't take studying seriously. In Salvador it is different. There you must obey the teacher, as you obey your father. They have rules."

Delmy expressed a positive view of the American values that were criticized by Beatriz:

Americans are different. They bring them up more independently. They put their coats on alone. You don't want to be carrying them all the time. When they take their first steps, they're being told, "You're walking very well [encouraging tone]." We [Latinos] are a bit harder, stricter. At times they [Latino children] want to be like the other children. But we can't, because we have another way. They leave their children to develop, to explore. They let them do what they want, and we are not like that. Coming to this country, having two cultures is not easy. If those Americans would go to Salvador, they would die [laughs]!

Here we see how Delmy's once tacit models for raising a child were consciously compared with other forms of child rearing. In this way, alternative methods were contained within a set of declared models that are no longer taken for granted.

Learning to speak and read Spanish was an important element of their children's socialization for Delmy and Beatriz. Delmy described how she sent books in Spanish to the preschool aide, who would read to her daughter individually, since none of the head teachers was Latina. Beatriz was delighted that her son was able to enter a bilingual program in first grade, but she worried that "these days he's speaking more English." She felt that it was also the family's responsibility to encourage a child to become bilingual: "I find fault with parents who do not teach their children Spanish, who only talk to them in English."

While children are in family day care, they are likely to be surrounded by other children from similar backgrounds. But in center-based care they are more apt to encounter children from a variety of ethnic groups. Some women in the sample reacted negatively to parents and children who appeared to act in ways they found strange or incomprehensible. Pat, a thirty-five-year-old Anglo, was still living in the working-class community where she had been raised. She complained of the rising number of "Mexicans" moving into her previously white neighborhood, and expressed concern about the "aggressive" Haitian children at three-year-old Joshua's Head Start center. When Joshua's expensive winter coat disappeared from his cubby at school, she implied that it had been taken by a Haitian.

Some of the mothers grew dissatisfied with their child-care providers or centers. Several took action, either expressing their concerns to the provider or exiting and finding another child-care setting. A few even mobilized their resources and left the neighborhood, searching for a better environment for their children.

Most discussions of how parents choose preschools address factors such as cost, proximity, and basic quality. These criteria are of obvious importance to low-income mothers, but they only scratch the surface of how culturally diverse women evaluate their child-care options. As policy makers and scholars lock horns over the rational-choice versus structural interpretations of "opportunity," we are missing the culturally varying criteria employed by women like Beatriz and Delmy. Although they had access to a variety of preschool organizations, their agendas for how to raise their children, including both socialization and pre-*schooling* components, often did not match the views set forth by preschool professionals. Variety in child-development agendas can be found not only *among* ethnic groups but also *within* ethnic enclaves. Crafting general strategies for raising quality while responding adequately to these varied criteria and socialization aims is a major challenge, especially as urban communities become even more pluralistic. Child-care leaders and policy makers should at least begin to listen more carefully to parents when they speak about the values and skills that they are trying to instill in their children.

Cluster 3: How Can I Improve My Child-Care Arrangement?

Debate often turns to the issue of whether low-income parents can efficaciously push for change in local institutions. Policy makers who advocate for more child-care aid in the form of vouchers and tax credits argue that these remedies will "empower" poor families. But how do low-income parents respond when they are dissatisfied with their child-care arrangements? Do they exercise voice by demanding changes within the organizations? Do they exit and search for alternative providers?

Two models appear to predominate in this cluster. Some women were aware of problems in their children's child-care settings but felt unable to change or improve the situation. The first model was to find alternative educational pathways for the future, usually involving Catholic or private schools. A second model was to express concerns to center directors or teachers, fighting for changes within the setting without searching for alternative organizations.

As we have seen, exit behavior was prompted by mothers' assessments either of the preschool staff or of other families served at the setting. Since child-care centers were viewed by most of the fourteen women as "schools," their assessments were linked to a lack of faith in Boston city schools. Brenda believed that things had changed for the worse in her community:

> Now there's more violence . . . the way the school system is now, it seems like they [school authorities] don't care about anything. You know, they don't care for the kids. It just seems harder for them . . . it's more violent. When I was going to school we would get into fistfights, you know, we spit at each other, call each other names. But now there are kids pulling out guns, and they're only eight or nine.

To combat these dangers, Brenda talked often about the importance of being "strict" in raising children. This cultural model of child rearing, and her own experiences attending Catholic schools, provided reference points in assessing how the preschool approached discipline and learning. She could see value in her daughter's preschool teachers' focus on learning social skills: "As far as hitting goes, they tell the children [to] face each other and tell why they hit each other, or talk it over." But she believed that the program's structure often broke down and was "unorganized." During the two years that Cora attended this preschool, Brenda tried to take an active role in school issues but did not feel that she was able to improve the quality of teaching. She moved

Cora to a Catholic preschool, where "discipline is more enforced. If there are any discipline problems, the nuns tell the kids they will call their parents, if time-out doesn't work." Brenda's girlfriend had earlier followed this path, pulling her son from the neighborhood center and putting him in "a Christian day care." Mothers who adopted this model of avoiding the public schools believed they should act when their children were still preschool age, because securing a space in a parochial preschool or kindergarten guaranteed a smooth transition to the first grade of a like-minded elementary school.

Jackie practiced both strategies, intervening forcefully when she felt she could have an impact and finding alternatives when a bad situation could not be improved. As a result of having been sexually abused herself, Jackie was adamant that Tiffany learn "values of her body . . . that she doesn't have to give her body to anybody. I want her to be happy, but I also want her to be careful." When three-year-old Tiffany came home singing suggestive lyrics, Jackie spoke to the teacher about whether she could prevent this from occurring. Jackie also planned to use Catholic schools as a strategy for helping her son to avoid unde-sirable peer influences: "I was really afraid of the Boston schools, I wanted him to get a good education. I really wanted to protect him, [so I] put him into private school." She placed Tiffany in the preschool attached to this private school while she was on AFDC, but when she lost her voucher Tiffany had to move to another preschool. At the new center, Jackie remarked, "The children are predominantly Haitian, and they [the staff] feel they can say anything to those parents and they just say, 'ah, ah.'" At one point, Jackie lobbied the preschool director and had Tiffany moved to another class: the children were supposed to "cut up little tiny pieces of colored tissue paper and roll it up into a ball. I dropped her off one morning, and the kids were doing that. When I picked her up in the afternoon, she was still at the table doing it, and I had a fit!" In this case, Jackie successfully exercised voice, working within the same preschool because her child-care subsidy did not readily allow movement to another preschool.

As we saw in Chapter 7, Pamela left her son, Cedric, in an apparently low-quality preschool throughout the three-year period. She made a few attempts to "work with" the teachers when she realized that he was seriously behind his peers in the development of cognitive skills. But she was waiting for the day when he would enter kindergarten because she had signed him up for Boston's Metco busing program, which would allow him to attend a kindergarten in a more affluent town outside Boston. She explicitly interpreted this program as an alternative script to follow, a pathway for her son's upward mobility. She recalled her own childhood:

> The Metco kids got up at 5:00 A.M. and took the bus and came home late. We were teasing them because they just came home and we'd be out playing. But then I met a guy that had been in Metco. He come in, looks sharp and looks, you know, making money. I'm thinking, you know, maybe that Metco did help him. They were [more] motivated than we were. So, Metco's the route.

In describing this "route," Pamela was thinking in terms of scripted pathways. In this case, Metco provided an institutionally structured model for avoiding the typical script: entry into the Boston city schools.

Two of the women moved from the impoverished Roxbury and Dorchester areas during the course of the study. Harriet complained in 1991 that her new apartment was located in a particularly bad section of Roxbury. In year two of the study, Harriet and her daughter were waiting for the bus when gun shots rang out and they had to flee for cover. By year three she had moved to an urban community just south of the city, keeping her job downtown. Aggie, after receiving a portable housing voucher, also moved from Dorchester to a suburban town, because, as she put it, "I don't want him [her son Fred] going to Boston public schools. I want him to get a decent education, which I know he's not gonna get in the Boston schools."

The passivity pictured so vividly in the culture-of-poverty framework was not to be found, at least not when we watched Brenda or Harriet strategize and act to put their children on better pathways. When it came to challenging how the preschool was run or exiting a bad situation, these women were decisive. Some raised their voices, aiming to improve the organization and classroom quality of their preschools. Others, such as Harriet, became fed up with the uncertainty and violence of their neighborhoods and fled for the more tranquil towns at the city's edge. Exit requires resources, initiative, and social support. Here again, social welfare institutions can offer the women some help in fleeing from distasteful circumstances. Initiatives that cue the legitimacy of choice, such as housing or child-care vouchers that may be used in more than one neighborhood, benefited some women. The Metco program is another example of attempts to define new pathways and broaden constrained cultural models for action. When these options were facilitated by assistance from family and social service workers, the women's sense of agency and ability to choose new futures began to blossom.

❧ The pure market paradigm of choice and empowerment seems unrealistic when one considers how these cultural models and institutional constraints serve to channel mothers' maneuverings through the world of child care. The women were rationally trying to boost their income and find affordable child-care arrangements of the highest possible quality. Yet tidy notions of context-free choice do not provide an adequate framework for explaining the ways in which these goals are translated into action. If the women tacitly accepted welfare as a legitimate way to augment their budgets, or had no other options, they applied for AFDC. Once within this institutional realm, they were channeled into certain alternatives. They were encouraged to use family day care for infants and toddlers because it was cheaper and more plentiful than child-care centers. Indeed, family day care was favored by some of the mothers, while others preferred family members for child care. But as we saw quite vividly, kin members could be unreliable or uninterested in helping. As the children grew older, the welfare bureaucracy pushed the idea that center-based programs and preschools offered high-quality alternatives to family day care. The result of this dynamic system of opportunities and barriers constructed by social service agencies and family networks was a channeling of women's child-care choices.

Those mothers who preferred center-based programs had conceptions of "quality" that were often quite different from those of the professional community. The market model recognizes that consumers have differing conceptions of quality and expects that they will shop around and find services that better match their preferences. But this is unlikely when it is the social worker who cues when a shift is advisable and when alternative child-care providers are scarce and inconsistent in quality. Scarce preschool spaces are rationed by the welfare bureaucracy and children are routed into slots as they open up.

Yet not all of the fourteen mothers conformed to the system when they discovered that their children were being subjected to dreary classrooms or teachers who sat them in front of the television for hours each day. Some women fought back, either pushing for improvements or exiting bad situations. But costs were significant whenever the women attempted to change their child-care arrangements. They often had to negotiate with their social workers, wait for slots elsewhere to open up, and rearrange transportation and work schedules. For some it was easier to let things be, even if it meant leaving their children in a low-quality program.

The idea of empowerment is appealing. Opening up more options for poor families is a reform that cannot be opposed. But it must be recognized that these families will always have limits on their ability to make choices about work and family matters. They now are subjected to carrots and sticks by a welfare bureaucracy that is becoming more like a police force and less like a source of support. This institution pushes them back to work and into predetermined sequences of child-care settings. Cultural models about how children should be raised also come into play: their tacit expectation that an aunt will care for their infant, or their aversion to formal centers that seem cold and impersonal. These mothers may yearn for a greater sense of agency and control over when they work and where their young children spend forty hours a week. But the range of possible choices is quickly reduced as only a few narrow pathways become visible on the horizon. If ample and high-quality child-care organizations appeared throughout the inner city, this tale of market magic would have a better ending. But in the absence of these contextual transformations, the myth of the market may remain just that—a fanciful portrayal falling far short of the reality single mothers face each day.

CHAPTER NINE

Teachers' Views of Preschool

BRUCE JOHNSON-BEYKONT

As we have seen from conversations with the fourteen women in this study, child-care providers and preschools are pivotal institutions. They allow single mothers to return to work, and they also influence the quality and character of children's development. Preschoolers in full-day programs commonly spend more waking hours at child care than at home. Indeed, child care is the dominant setting outside the home where the mother's own hopes for child rearing and socialization are played out. We have seen that the fourteen women have definite conceptions about the type of upbringing and learning that should occur in preschool settings, agendas that may conflict with teachers' and child-care providers' beliefs about how children develop.

What are the tacit beliefs and models that guide preschool teachers? Do they resemble low-income mothers' own socialization agendas or diverge from them? How do teachers introduce and respond to novel, declared models of how to organize children's play and work?

To inform these questions, I spent many months inside several child-care centers and preschools that serve families in Boston. The purpose of the project was to observe the "other half" of the child's social environment, settings that may complement or contradict the home setting. I conducted interviews with thirty-seven teachers over a two-year period. Four teachers are highlighted in this chapter; their words, panoramas, and models for how children should learn and "develop" proved especially illuminating. Like the fourteen mothers, these teachers operate from varied models and interpretive frameworks that they may adjust when exposed to alternative novel pathways advanced by fellow teachers, parents, and professional associations.

Prior Research

Few researchers have sat and asked preschool teachers about their own conceptions of how youngsters should be raised and schooled. Several studies provide important exceptions to this scarcity of evidence, and three are particularly relevant to the research presented in this chapter.[1] In the early 1980s Sally Lubeck compared a low-income Head Start program staffed by working-class African-American teachers with a middle-class, private preschool staffed by middle-class Anglo teachers. She illuminated differences in use of time and space, selection and utilization of materials and activities, and styles of teacher-child interaction. The teachers with whom Lubeck worked revealed their perceptions of what children should learn, how children learn, and how teachers should teach.[2] After spending a year with teachers in both settings, Lubeck concluded that the variation across classrooms was reflective of culturally based child-rearing strategies and goals that served to transmit the values of the respective communities to the next generation.

William Ayers worked closely with six preschool teachers to explore the effects of their experiences from childhood onward on their teaching beliefs and classroom practices. Ayers utilized ethnographic observation, interpretive activities such as working with clay or paint, and informal interviewing and written communication to elicit their active engagement in a collaborative process that led to written portrayals of each teacher's practice and life. Ayers found that the teachers were self-critical and self-reflective concerning their teaching, and that each was engaged in "some sense of struggle against officialdom and a defining of oneself in opposition."[3] Ayers noted the missing voices of preschool teachers from public policy debate around educational reform, and argued that they are valuable sources of knowledge and expertise for policy makers who may be too quick to look for universal, "quick fix" solutions to apply to the complex world of the early child-hood classroom.

Janice Jipson's study injected teachers' voices into the debate over how to define "developmentally appropriate" classroom practices. Jipson asked an ethnically diverse sample of preschool teachers to keep a daily diary to comment on the NAEYC's official definition of developmentally appropriate learning in preschool classrooms. They expressed sharp reservations about the NAEYC's guidelines, reporting that they ignored ethnic variations in child-rearing goals and strategies. Jipson argued that early childhood teachers should emphasize *culturally appropriate* practices, taking into account non–middle-class, non-Anglo cultural tenets.[4] The fourteen mothers in this study have exemplified some of these tenets: expecting respect and deference to adult authority, using languages other than English, and emphasizing structured lessons in early literacy and numbers rather than learning through play.

As discussed in Chapter 1, a number of cross-cultural studies of childhood and child care have been conducted in societies throughout the world. But professional associations in the United States, and many developmental psychologists, often assume that North American parents are culturally homogenous, and that theories emphasizing universal aspects of development are optimal for all preschools. They frequently ignore variability in the cultural models that guide parents' values and child-rearing practices.

The Teachers

The urban preschool teachers interviewed for this project were attentive to cultural and individual variability in the social rules that youngsters brought from home. The teachers themselves came from different ethnic backgrounds, and they often vocalized two or more alternative ways in which children could be encouraged and socialized. Although a teacher may have settled on a script that guided her teaching, she was usually aware that these views were not universally accepted.

Conversations with the thirty-seven teachers were focused around broad questions: What do you most want the children to learn from their preschool experience? How do your beliefs and practices compare with the practices of other teachers you know and with the practices recommended by professional organizations? What conflicts arise between the preschool director's preferred practices and those that you favor? The four teachers on which this chapter focuses reflect the diversity of models—tacit and declared—invoked in their classrooms, as they attempt to nurture children within the low-income neighborhoods served by these preschools.

The teachers were employed in four preschools in the Boston area. Most of the teachers and classroom aides in each school were interviewed; many were also observed in their classrooms. The full sample represents the ethnic rainbow of child-care staff found in many American cities: fourteen teachers grew up in Spanish-speaking environments (nine of these were Puerto Rican and five were of non–Puerto Rican Latino descent); seven were African-Americans; six were of Anglo descent; and the remainder were from countries outside the United States. They ranged in age from eighteen to sixty. All but two were women. Several had taught for more than twenty years at the preschool level. A few had earned college degrees; several had completed just one course in early childhood education.

The teachers' stories revealed a dynamic process whereby their early tacit models of classroom learning and child socialization came under self-scrutiny. Many reported that they entered their jobs with certain taken-for-granted models for how to care for young children. Many adjusted their assumptions and daily classroom practices as a result of their experiences with children and interactions with colleagues and parents. Several experienced conflicts with their directors or fellow teachers over how to discipline youngsters, organize their classrooms, or relate to parents. Four of the teachers, Krista, Martha, Karen, and Rosa, represented the diversity of beliefs among the thirty-seven teachers interviewed. Let's turn now to how they crafted their particular ways of caring for children.

Krista: Children Must Learn Their Letters and Numbers

I've seen big changes in day care. When I first started I was teaching the basics, you know, writing, ABCs, numbers, colors, shapes. We had three tables in the whole classroom, they sat at the tables and they did work. But now it's like we teach 'em through play. That's how we're teaching now. So there's no more pencils and paper . . . [for] teaching the basics. I'd rather have them. I'm a pencil and paper person.

Krista, a thirty-one-year-old African-American teacher at the Little World Day Care Center, had changed her ideas about children greatly during her career. She started out at a preschool that taught her to emphasize academics and teacher-directed approaches to learning. After eight years she left and started to work at other centers, where she began to see that there were other ways to teach. Krista reported that she was strongly influenced by these novel ideas. She moved away from teaching letters and numbers in her classroom, but continued to emphasize academics and teacher-directed activities more than her directors or mainstream early childhood education discourse would support. Krista had integrated child-development models and practices with her original ideas about teaching, and she was comfortable with the mix. She had chosen to deemphasize academics, but she still listed them as among her three most important learning goals for children. Learning letters and numbers had been deemphasized, but only slightly.

Born and raised in Boston, Krista had attended Head Start as a child and later enrolled her daughter in the same program, even to be taught by the same teacher. She had enrolled her second child, a boy, at the center where she now worked. At the time of the first interview, Krista had nine years of experience in child-care classrooms and had completed four courses in early childhood education. She had taught for eight years at a large day-care agency in the city, worked as a substitute for a while, and had come to Little World only a few months before the interviews began.[5]

Little World Day Care Center is located within a short walk of several low-income housing developments. Almost all its students are from low-income working families or families receiving federal or state income supplements. Little World is housed in a new building along with other human service organizations. In the entryway are a colorful bulletin board for parents, a staff sign-in sheet, a receptionist's desk, and a long wall that during one visit featured children's art work and later displayed a montage of photos, magazines, and news clippings featuring prominent African-Americans. The long hallways leading to the five classrooms are bare of any decoration.

Krista's classroom was lined with windows through which the sun could stream in. Krista explained that she was still "putting her room together." She had been in the classroom for only four months, and for the most part she had worked alone, because the enrollment of only eight to ten preschoolers did not legally require a second adult in the classroom. Teacher-cut paper letters hung from the ceiling, children's art work was displayed in several locations on the walls, and the furniture was arranged so that a relatively large open space was available for group activities. Books, puzzles, Legos and other pint-sized building materials, and play kitchen equipment were all being used by children during one observation. The furniture and many of the toys and educational materials were brand new.

When explaining her goals for learning and her definition of appropriate practice, Krista often referred to her own experiences as a parent. She was critical of her eldest daughter's preschool program because it did not teach academic skills and concepts. Her experience as a parent shaped her views of what and how young children should be taught:

> [Children should] know those basics, the things that they are supposed to be able to do. The reading, the writing . . . [My] daughter wasn't taught like that. She was behind. Yeah. And I had to teach her. Yeah. Somebody had to teach her, teach directed activities so she could be at her level in kindergarten. And [now] she is.
>
> If you're at that age level where it's time to write, okay, let's do this work paper, then we can go play whatever, whatever . . . I feel they should do the teacher-directed activities . . . They don't have to sit there and write for hours and hours . . . Give them a couple of minutes a day. Teach them something. Letters in their names. At least the letters of their names.

Krista was concerned that children would fall behind in kindergarten and elementary school if they failed to begin learning their letters in preschool. She expressed the same concern regarding the learning of numbers; young children should be able to recognize numerals and begin to write them. Accordingly, she emphasized the learning of letters and numbers in her classroom. This priority, however, brought Krista into conflict with supervisors and those whom she saw as purveyors of the prevailing ideology. She had witnessed an ideological shift in the early education world over her years of teaching. Krista grasped the debate between those who advocated "learning through play" and those who supported "learning through teacher-directed activities." And she had thought through the effects of these differing approaches:

> You can see . . . the differences between the two kids. There's a big difference. If you give one "teach 'em through play" and you give [another] one "teacher-directed" all the time you can see the difference. Maybe that child who's teacher-directed may not be . . . able to go over here and there and make his own choices. But, then again, that teacher-directed is going to come in handy in the future as far as educational-wise . . . They're going to know those basics, the things that they are supposed to be able to do. The reading, the writing . . .

Krista had observed that a classroom in which children chose what they should be doing produced different effects than did a classroom in which activities were primarily teacher-directed. These two sequences touched children in quite different ways. It was her opinion that children learned to make choices in a curriculum that was child-initiated, yet such a curriculum did not teach them the academic basics that would prepare them well for future schooling. Although Krista understood the benefits of having children make choices, she did not simply accept the new and rid herself of the old; rather, she chose to integrate some of the new with some of the old. She emphasized teacher-directed time as well as time spent learning through play:

> Kids . . . should learn to experience their own things on their own and then I can teach 'em what I want 'em to learn . . . So it's both ways. They're having their freedom of choice and they're also getting that little bit of teacher-directed activities . . . Let them have their time, and just give me about fifteen minutes . . . It works out fine.

When Krista began to encounter criticism and prohibition of teacher-directed activities focused on the learning of letters and numbers, she did not comfortably accept the restrictions. She covertly resisted "developmentally appropriate" ideology:

Seeing as how I'm the Head Teacher, I do most of what I want
to do anyway. Once that door shuts this is my class. This is my
classroom, that is how I look at it . . . So like I said, if a child asks
me I'm gonna teach him . . . If it's just one out of five wants to
sit there and learn how to write, I'm gonna teach that child . . .
What else am I supposed to say, "Oh no, I can't teach it to you?"
No, I'm gonna teach it to him.

Krista, like other teachers who emphasized academics, presented a
complex set of beliefs. At first glance it may appear that she held views
far removed from those promulgated by the mainstream early childhood community. Yet her beliefs and practices did not remain static
through her nine years of teaching. Her beliefs had changed, and she
had moved closer to mainstream ideological positions. She had gone
from sitting children at tables with paper and pencils for eight hours a
day to believing that a balance of child-initiated play and teacher-
directed time was a more effective method to spur development. Still,
she felt the pressure; devoting even a small amount of teacher-directed
time to learning letters and numbers was viewed negatively by her
supervisor and some colleagues.

Whereas Krista had constructed a set of beliefs and practices that
made sense for her, other teachers had chosen different priorities for
preschool children's learning and emphasized different teaching practices. One such teacher was Martha, who said, "Before you can do the
. . . academic aspect . . . you need to do the social piece . . . because if
they can't get along with people, they won't be able to sit down and
learn among people." Martha placed academics lower on her list of the
most important things for preschool children to learn. She prioritized
the goal of learning to get along, which for her meant children's
learning to solve problems independent of adults, and in particular to
resolve conflicts without physical violence. She believed that using
child-initiated activities in the classroom helped to achieve these goals.

Martha: Emphasizing the Importance of Social Skills

Martha, a twenty-nine-year-old African-American teacher at the ABC
Child Care Center, was born and raised in the Boston area. She was
the fourth of five children and the youngest girl in her family. During

Martha's childhood, her mother sometimes worked as a day-care assistant and baby-sitter. Her father was described as "not in the picture." Whereas Krista referenced her experience as a parent in explaining her ideas about teaching and learning, Martha spoke about her own childhood:

> My mother was a single parent and very dominating and very controlling. There were five of us and she had to maintain control to get things done, and so it was pretty much, you did as you were told, when you were told, and how you were told. I had two brothers that challenged my mother constantly on doing it their way . . . [and] she used the discipline method of hitting as a way of getting you to obey. Watching them I learned very quickly . . . I didn't get hit a lot because I figured out you just must do what you were told despite what you were feeling or thinking. You just did what you were told. I've made a big leap . . . I don't want to be that way. As a teacher it's like I'm totally different from what my upbringing was.

Looking back, Martha thinks that she grew up as someone who "couldn't advocate" or speak up for herself. While she was attending high school, her chosen program of study was unexpectedly discontinued. Apparently without being asked, she was assigned to the early childhood teacher-preparation program. She stood out as "knowing this stuff" even though she had not studied child development. Her teacher encouraged her to apply for college scholarships. Several years later she graduated with a two-year degree in early childhood education and quickly found employment. Her college training had primarily focused on "activities . . . [where a teacher's role was to] provide the kids with activities and . . . set goals for the activities." But staff at the child-care center where she went to work placed more emphasis on child-initiated play and training teachers in "these developmentally appropriate techniques." Comfortable with this new focus, Martha remained at ABC Child Care Center for ten years.

ABC Child Care Center is situated in an urban, low-income housing development. Serving residents of the apartment complex and the surrounding community, it houses four classrooms, each with sixteen to twenty preschool-age children. Like Little World, the ABC center serves children from low-income families. Located in the basement of a residential building, the center lacks natural light and ventilation. Yet the hallway walls are freshly painted and decorated with children's art work, notices to parents and staff, and the like. Signs containing information about developmentally appropriate practices are posted in the entryway. Martha's classroom is small, with little open space, but it is arranged to clearly define learning centers, for example, an art area, library, block area, and make-believe playhouse area. The equipment and materials are old, but appear to be well maintained. Educational materials are placed where children can reach them, and children are allowed to choose activities from shelves. Written signs and symbols inform them about the daily schedule as well as where to store play materials and how many can play in a particular area. Children's colorful art work is prominently displayed, as are posters and photos of people of many races and nationalities, all at a height so that young children can examine them. Much of the furniture and some equipment and materials are labeled in both English and Spanish.

Martha had completed eleven courses in early childhood education. She had worked with infants, toddlers, and preschoolers, and during the course of the study took over teaching five- and six-year-olds in the combination prekindergarten-kindergarten classroom. She had been working full time as a teacher for nine years. The extent of her formal training and her experience in preschools set her far above the average teacher in the sample.

Whereas Krista emphasized learning letters and numbers, Martha placed high priority on children's learning to be problem solvers, planners, and thoughtful decision makers. It was important to Martha that her children learn to resolve problems without fighting and to get along with peers. Martha thought that learning to be a planner and decision maker was much more critical for subsequent school success than learning letters and numbers. She mentioned that being able to search for resources when writing papers required planning and decision-making skills. Martha spoke of how the children would often come to her with an idea, "then I say, let's make a list . . . what do we need to do?" She encouraged them to figure out where and how to get the things they needed. Martha explained, "It teaches them initiative." Looking past school to life in general, Martha believed that the skills of planning and decision making were crucial: "You always got to go out and ask for things whether . . . you're going to get your heat turned on or [pay] medical bills."

Also important in preschool and throughout life was the ability to resolve conflicts without physical violence:

> We're in a big world. You're going to be with people. Shouting and pushing and fighting . . . doesn't solve things in our world today. It just gets you in a lot of trouble. We teach the kids now that we need to talk it out. Don't yell. Talk. You stop, you listen, you talk, you listen. Try to compromise . . . we bring the two children together and we say, "What is it about what he just did that you don't like?"
>
> We teach children to communicate without always being physical and without always being angry. We teach the children to help other children to do that . . . Those are skills that I focus more on for them, because those are skills you're going to need as adults, as you go on up in life to get what you want. If they don't learn it, it's going to be a struggle. They're going to learn it the hard way . . . You're going to jail or there's going to be some heavy consequences.

Nonviolent conflict resolution was viewed as a skill that would help children throughout life. Many of the thirty-seven teachers in the study emphasized the learning of this skill, with some calling it "learning to get along," others "not fighting," and others "learning to use your words." In each case teachers spoke of a similar method—having children talk through problems in face-to-face discussions, expressing their feelings verbally. This verbal expression of feelings was viewed as a key part of the process of solving problems peacefully.

Martha's beliefs and practices had changed considerably over the years. In the beginning she had organized most of the activities for the children, but over time she had become a strong proponent of a child-initiated curriculum in preschool classrooms:

> I was . . . [using] more the book style . . . In school they just focused on activities . . . you provide the kids with activities and you set goals from the activities . . . When I started teaching I found that the kids have their own agenda. We would say I want

you to learn colors out of this activity, but they would take it off
in a different direction . . . [I came to believe that] open-ended
activities are the best . . . [and that] kids will pick up what they
need to know as they address the activities. I start it off teacher-
directed and then I let them branch off, if some kids want to go
in a different direction, then I let them go off in that direction.
Most of it just came from practicing and here, when I did start,
they were getting into this child-initiated play . . . Everybody plays
a role: the kids, the teacher. I have a role in not being controlling
of their learning but to be supportive and have my ears and eyes
open . . . to just keep expanding on what they're doing.

Martha had considered different practices. But as a result of the
influences of training, directors, and fellow teachers, she had embraced
the child-initiated approach. Rather than integrating a few new elements into an established repertoire, as Krista did, Martha seemed to
have adopted a complete package of new ideas:

> I had bits and pieces of it, but when we went through accreditation
> three years ago it brought it to me. There's books out there, the
> agency has standards too, and then the center . . . produced our
> own [plan for] quality that went along with the agency's quality
> [standards]. We put it into practice and I saw it work. This is what
> quality is all about.

Though Krista and Martha both used the word "balance" to describe
the appropriate mix of teacher-directed and child-initiated activities in
their classrooms, they differed in the relative emphasis placed on each
and on the learning goals that were paramount. Martha was a strong
proponent of teaching through child-initiated activities, but she saw
decision making as a skill that would be developed over time. As she
and her students progressed through a school year, she would turn over
more and more of the responsibility for choosing the curriculum to
them:

> It has to be a balance. I don't think you can do one and [not] the
> other. Some kids need to have a model . . . in order for them . . .
> to get it started. At the beginning of the year I do initiating,

mid-year it's really a balance where I'm adding and they're adding. At the end of the year they pretty much [are in charge] of what we do. I'm just there to make sure they start it out and that it can happen and that it's a safe thing.

Martha's goal was for children to take increasing responsibility for controlling the flow of the classroom. She was trusting the children to choose the curriculum, to decide in effect what would be emphasized and what would be learned, within the limits of safety and practicality. This strategy was different from that of Krista, who permitted children to make choices but also believed that they may not choose everything they needed to know. Krista insisted on a period of teacher-directed time every day so that she could "teach them what I want to teach them."

Martha's ideas matched closely those of the director and official center policies. She was outspoken in proclaiming the center's goals and comparing this philosophy of teaching with that of other preschools:

What the center's about is child-initiated activities and child-initiated play. A lot of our ideas are generated from what the kids are thinking, what the kids are acting out in their play. If the interaction between the teacher and the child is on a plane that is dominant, like you're dominating the child, then I don't see it [as] quality.

Karen: Returning to a More Teacher-Oriented Curriculum

The sentiments of Karen, a twenty-three-year-old European-American assistant teacher at the Porter Street Children's Center, were different from those of Martha. Working about ten miles away, Karen thought that a child-initiated curriculum and the "too-liberal guidelines regarding teaching from the NAEYC" had gone too far. She strongly believed in a return to greater teacher control in certain aspects of the preschool curriculum, a return to "some traditional limit setting and teaching":

At first I bought into the new notion of child-initiated activities, allowing [a] child to make decisions for him/herself. I feel these are appropriate sometimes and with certain skills, such as motor skills, play, art. At other times I feel we need to get back to more teacher-oriented styles of teaching. Today's preschoolers are given too much power to do for themselves. At this age, children need the safety of limit setting, they need to be taught by a teacher certain skills (colors, numbers, behaviors, rules). If these skills are not acquired young, I feel the child has a more difficult time in later years.

The youngest of two daughters born to a schoolteacher and an architect, Karen grew up in a middle-class home near Boston:

I would say [my parents] were both fairly mainstream, but a little more to the conservative side. And so I had . . . a lot of . . . things I was told I had to do . . . I had curfews, I had chores . . . a lot of little rules . . . [that] . . . at the time I may not have agreed with.

Karen attended public schools in a "very liberal city." She earned a B.A. with a double major in sociology and early childhood education from a state university in New England.

Karen's worksite, the Porter Street Children's Center, is located in a new building. Porter Street predominantly draws children from the surrounding community and serves families of socioeconomic status similar to that of families at the ABC and Little World programs. Unlike the classrooms in the older ABC center, the four classrooms at Porter Street are large and sunny. All the furniture and equipment are new, and are arranged to delineate activity areas.

Karen was aware of the mainstream, professionally endorsed view of what constitutes "appropriate" teaching. But many of her views diverged from that mainstream professional culture:

I know I tend to have . . . more of a traditional view on this. I don't necessarily agree with a lot of the newer early childhood philosophies of really having everything be child-directed and everything brought from the child, because I think there are some traditional values that should try to be instilled in children.

Respect was a key value that Karen found lacking in the preschoolers she taught. She was troubled that many children were no longer learning to respect adults. Karen was in her first year of full-time preschool teaching when we met her. She was shocked by what she encountered:

> I think there's a real lack of respect from when I was a child . . . toward other children but also really toward adult figures and teachers. In my day, which isn't that long ago, we never spoke back or spit or hit at a teacher. And kids are doing that and I'm just floored sometimes at how these kids treat me as an adult. It's kind of dumbfounding once in a while to think that these kids really have no respect for anyone else, you know?

Karen believed that showing respect for adults was essential. Because adults "have more experience," children should learn "that an adult should be listened to and respected," and that adults can teach children "things that are right and things that are wrong." She went on to explain why she was so exasperated:

> [I] want [children] to question me if they don't think what I'm doing is right, but question me with respect. And [ask me] why [what they did was] wrong, rather than hitting me or running away from me or spitting at me. It kind of worries me. What's going to happen to this child if they don't learn that they can't go around just hitting when they want to? It scares me to think of what it can turn into. It could turn into somebody very violent, somebody who feels that the only way they can have their needs met is to be aggressive. At this age it may be hitting and pushing. Older it may be guns and everything.

Neither Krista nor Martha mentioned this strong concern over respect. It is clear, though, that there were areas of agreement between Karen and Martha. Both were worried about the consequences for children of not learning to resolve problems peacefully. If children did not learn to "use their words" at a young age, they might very well find problems further down the road. Karen was also concerned about preparing children to live with the routines and strictures of public-school kindergarten. In contrast to Martha, who spoke about the need for children to develop into planners and decision makers to succeed in school, Karen emphasized her belief that children needed new social skills to fit into the social structure of public-school classrooms:

> Having done student teaching in the kindergarten and now working here, I see the importance of being in a preschool: learning how to play with each other appropriately, to follow a routine and be in a classroom with twenty other kids, to be able to speak up for themselves but also be able to play and share. In kindergarten the teacher ratio is usually not as good as it is here on the preschool level. So I think kids need to be able to sort of take care of themselves somewhat by the time they get to kindergarten.

Karen wanted to help children learn to respect adults, was concerned about children who fight and hit, and was displeased with the notions of "child-choice" and "positive discipline" that she felt had gone too far. She was irked by workplace rules that eroded the autonomy that she felt she needed to be an effective teacher. Whereas Martha was in sync with center policies and professional guidelines, Karen felt quite constrained. She complained about being told what she "could and could not do" in her classroom:

> A lot of decisions are made at a higher level by people that I'm not certain have ever worked in a classroom. I don't know the résumés of all the people [but] it's almost like they have so much information coming into them—the latest early childhood development [theories and research]—and will sometimes impose regulations on things that we can and can't say. I just feel like sometimes they don't work. Why am I being told by a man in a suit in the office [that] I can't [use words like] "no," [or] "don't"—basic words that I feel are clear words to a child. If a child is absolutely hurting another child, I just say "no." And maybe they'll stop right away. Maybe they won't and of course, then I'll go over and talk with them. These sort of hierarchical things are just said: "This is the way that we practice; our agency follows these guidelines," and they don't always work. Every center and every teacher should

have the ability to interpret those philosophies, with their own philosophy. And I don't find there's a lot of room for that.

Karen understood that teaching the way she wanted to teach and instilling the values she wanted to instill would mean contradicting the professional mainstream. Her way of organizing classroom activities and disciplining children represented an internal logical sequence leading (among other goals) to respect for adult authority. But it was the wrong model in the eyes of her director and some colleagues.

Other teachers, such as Martha, were more convinced of the effectiveness of teaching through a child-directed curriculum. Rosa, a thirty-year-old teacher at the New Day Children's Garden, comfortably integrated old and new models. She felt that she could instill in her students the values that she believed important while only occasionally running up against workplace rules or edicts from the professional early childhood culture.

Rosa: Limited Choice for Children

When I first started to work with preschool children, I thought that you have to give all the information to them so they learn. I used to tell [them] what to do and how to do it. [But now I] create children who are confident and able to think, create, and solve situations by themselves.

Rosa had changed her beliefs over time and now found child-choice to be central to her teaching. She reflected a lot on her own childhood and parenting experiences, as well as on her formal training in early childhood education. These forces significantly changed her definitions of appropriate and effective teaching. She was aware of alternative models of learning and child development. Her original, taken-for-granted model was no longer tacitly accepted. These contrasting models for teaching had become quite conscious, the subject of debate. She now emphasized child-choice and did not push academics. But she still maintained a crucial belief that she had brought to teaching: it is "appropriate" for children to respect their elders and their elders' authority to set limits.

Rosa grew up in Puerto Rico, where she was raised with six siblings by a single mother and grandmother. This experience shaped the way she wanted to teach in her classroom *and* raise her children at home:

It was not easy, with just a mother it was hard. And like I say, poor . . . having what I needed but not what I wanted to have. My mother had to work [to support] seven children. She didn't have time to be with them. We were with many people while she worked. I didn't like it at all. There were a lot of rules: "This has to be this way and that's it, no matter." [My mother could not] be with us so much. My grandmother was the one who raised us and she kind of thought like, "Whatever I say that's the way it [is] and I'm the only one [who is] right. You [children] don't have the right to be right."

Rosa believed that her teachers in school had not been interested in her or whether she learned. They were interested in the best students, which she wasn't, and they gave good grades to students whose families could afford to buy fancy project folders and insert expensive photos into their reports. Married and with two children before the age of twenty, Rosa and her husband brought their family to Boston. She felt that she had made a big mistake in raising her first child; she learned a lesson when her son was "turned off to school" by her insistence during his preschool years that he practice letters and numbers. She now believed that her emphasis on academics had a negative impact on her son's interest in education:

I would tell him, it's sad but it's true, I would tell him, [at] three years old, "When you finish writing your name then you can play." You know what I mean? "Practice your name. Do your home-work!" He wasn't even in school. When I did that I was so excited, I thought I was doing something good because he was learning. But what I did was that then he started hating school. My kid was burned out. And now with my children in the classroom . . . I would never do that again.

Rosa's first job in child care was as a cook's assistant at the New Day Children's Garden. When she offered to fill in as a substitute in a preschool classroom, the teachers recognized her as someone who was "good with kids." The director offered her a teaching assistant job and said the preschool would help pay for a state-sponsored course in child development. Rosa continued to pursue training opportunities and eventually earned a lead teaching position. At the time of the interview, after four years of working with children, she had completed six courses in early childhood education. She credited both her teaching experience and her training with reshaping her conceptions of teaching and learning in preschools.

The New Day Children's Garden is situated in a building with other community service agencies. The center enrolls children from the surrounding ethnically diverse, predominantly low-income community. Rosa's classroom received little sunlight. Many materials and pieces of furniture were old, but everything was well maintained and orderly. Signs in Spanish and English labeled most materials and areas of the room.

Reflecting on her childhood, Rosa had decided, "I'm not raising my child the same way I was [raised]." She didn't believe she had "the right" as a teacher or a mother to insist that her way was the only way that "things are [or] should be." Rosa felt strongly that misbehavior could be explained and discussed. But she believed just as strongly that she had the right and responsibility to make certain decisions and set certain limits. She tacitly expected that her students and her own children would respect her authority and her decisions:

> They take the toys, right? I'm not going to clean for them. I say, "I could help you but I'm not the one to put it [all] away and I don't think it's fair either for you to leave it there and [then] somebody has to come and pick up for you. You could do everything you want but you have to do this too for everything to work for everybody, for you, for everybody." So, it's okay to have the choice but it's okay to have limits. The children [are] free to do whatever they think it's good for them to do but there's a limit. You [are] still a child. You still need to grow, and [there are] people that have to be listened to, respected.

Like Martha, Rosa emphasized the importance of children's learning to be planners and decision makers. She believed that children learned by practicing, so they were often allowed to make choices in her classroom. But Rosa was quick to point out that she set limits to their decision making and taught them that with choices came responsibilities. Rosa found that a child-initiated curriculum model allowed her to nurture children's independence. It was one of her goals that children learn to be independent:

> [But not] independent to think they could do everything by themselves. Like they don't need nobody to tell them nothing, but to learn in case they needed it to survive. Because we have many children here that have parents that don't really care about them so much. If the children don't have a person to be there for them most of the time, then what [are] the children going to do? The children learn here, "I can pour my own cereal, I can put the milk out. I'm not going to die, I'm going to eat something. If mommy doesn't put [out] the clothes, I could do it myself."

Rosa felt that the youngsters needed to acquire knowledge and self-help skills relating to health and hygiene. Her priorities in the preschool classroom were shaped by her perceptions of what was not learned at home. If she taught independence and self-help skills, then the child would be better equipped to survive and get ahead.

Whereas Rosa's emphasis on child-choice and independence fit well with mainstream ideology, she encountered some conflict with her supervisors over her discipline techniques. She occasionally utilized a teaching strategy of denying outside play privileges as a consequence of children's repeated misbehavior. Her belief was that children would stop misbehaving if faced with the denial of a favorite play activity. Rosa reported that she only had to do this a few times before children changed their behavior. But Rosa was told by her director that this was inappropriate, that children need outside play time to develop motor skills:

> And I understand that. That [is] why we have the free play time. But the children also need to understand that there are some limits. If I know that this is the only way he can change his behavior, I can't understand why they will tell me that [my method] is not okay. I won't be doing it with every child or [in

every] situation. But if this works for a particular child, why shouldn't [I] do it?

Here Rosa was voicing frustration with directors who did not view children and the context as she did. The supervisor seemed to be reciting a regulation more than seeking to understand the situation Rosa faced and the behavior to which she was responding. Two models of discipline were in direct conflict. Like Karen earlier, Rosa was frustrated by directors who took away teachers' authority to push their own models of child discipline and learning.

Rosa did not believe that learning letters and numbers was among the three top priorities for children in preschool. But many of the children in Rosa's classroom were, in fact, developing these early literacy and numeracy skills. She reported that they chose to work on letters and numbers and that, if they were interested, there were always pencils and papers and examples of writing all around the room for them to emulate:

If you come here, you will see that they do learn everything. They learn shapes, numbers, they learn letters, colors. They even learn parts of the body. They listen to us telling them. We play games, most of the time they're playing. That's the way they learn better, playing. So we do games or fingerplays or we use music. We sing songs with numbers, with letters, with different words. We teach them both singing Spanish and English so when we do the calendar they know how to say it in Spanish [and] they know how to say it in English.

Rosa's students were learning about letters and numbers within a child-choice environment. They were learning these concepts through play, through games, and through singing songs.

Implications: What Is Appropriate Child Rearing?

The views expressed by these teachers have much in common with those of the fourteen mothers. The themes of preparing for school, learning to be independent, and learning to respect one's elders were ranked of highest importance, both to the mothers and to many of the thirty-seven teachers in the full sample. Within each topic, however, distinctive issues arose as a result of both the training and supervision that teachers had received and their experiences in the classroom and as parents of their own children.

Like the fourteen mothers, many of these teachers felt that it was important for them to prepare children for elementary school. And like the mothers, many believed that this preparation could be accomplished through the teaching of basic concepts, including letters and numbers. Many of the teachers believed in the efficacy of teacher-initiated activities much more than in the normative guidelines advanced by the NAEYC. Yet a number also endorsed child-choice and play as major aspects of a preschool curriculum. Compared with the mothers, the teachers were more enthusiastic about the benefits of play. Whereas the mothers saw play primarily as providing enjoyment, teachers saw it as a way of learning. The debate for these teachers emerged around where one finds a balance, that is, how much time one should allocate to teacher- versus child-initiated activities. Each of the four teachers spoke about the need for limits on choice.

Preparation for later schooling was an area in which teachers actively considered and attempted to reconcile conflicting models. Although no teacher was ignorant of what the NAEYC had to say about developmentally appropriate practice, few accepted all of its premises. For many of the teachers, beliefs about teaching were grounded in their personal experiences as children and, later, as parents. Certainly, some reported that they were greatly influenced by formal training in early childhood education, as we saw in the case of Martha and Rosa. Karen and others culled ideas from colleagues at their centers, and sometimes found these "tried and true" techniques more effective, particularly in the areas of child guidance and discipline, than their preservice or inservice training. Their adopted models represented a conversion, a movement away from the mainstream early childhood ideology found in college textbooks and the NAEYC's developmentally appropriate practice guidelines.

The fact that teachers consciously debate these competing models has important theoretical implications. In preschool settings, these contested models have become explicit and declared, even politicized, since a teacher's own performance is judged on which script she follows. The fact that alternative child-rearing models are discussed among teachers means that mothers' own cultural models are more likely to be subjected to scrutiny and debate.

The mothers in the study were likely to change their beliefs and practices only when the source of the new ideas was highly credible and was showing mothers a way to achieve goals that they themselves believed were important. They did not respond to dictates that were sprung on them by "experts" who had not bothered to ask for their perspectives. The teachers expressed similar reluctance to take suggestions that conflicted with their own sense of what the children needed in a given situation. The feeling that they were being handed a formulaic remedy appeared to occur more frequently in the area of academic preparation than anywhere else. What seemed to rankle teachers most were prohibitions that were so stringent as to disallow flexibility and discretion on their part. As Karen explained, "I feel like at the time that's what's going to get through to the child, that's what the child is going to respond to. I mean, I use my best judgment in what would work with this child, at this time, you know?"

Part of this conflict in child-rearing models results from differing interpretations of the developmentally appropriate practices promoted by the professional culture. The basic guidelines—those most closely adhered to in making accreditation decisions—provide rather detailed suggestions for what is appropriate, but they say little about how to introduce early literacy experiences into the classroom. Although the guidelines do not strictly prohibit the use of teacher-initiated, academic activities, they do forcefully stipulate that developmentally appropriate practice should avoid "frequent" use of such activities. In other words, some of it is okay, maybe. Because of this confusion and hedging, as well as the difficulty that many experts in the field have in describing what the teacher's role is in "play-oriented" programs, supervisors and teachers vary in their interpretation of what goes on in a developmentally appropriate classroom. Some supervisors appear to believe that nothing resembling a letter or a number should make an appearance in the classroom. One teacher reported that her supervisor required her to remove an alphabet chart from the classroom wall, even though children appeared to be interested in identifying and writing letters and numbers! Such inaccurate interpretations of developmentally appropriate practices were a source of great frustration for these teachers.[6]

Teaching children to respect adults and authority was another social goal that some teachers set for the children. This goal was quite important to the fourteen mothers as well. Although mainstream early childhood educators frequently discuss the need for children to respect the rights of others, this point is usually made in reference to peers. The notion of respecting one's elders fits less well with mainstream early childhood professional norms and values. Among the four profiled teachers, Karen emphasized the importance of learning to respect adults most emphatically. Fiona, a preschool teacher with more than twenty-five years of experience, related how "respect for adults" was central in her own childhood in the Azores and commented on the changes she witnessed in children's respect for adults and authority:

> When I first came to teaching, when I first came to this country, I brought my culture with me. I was brought up with nuns in the school. They spoke and I listened. That was true of every child in the school. There was none of this "I won't listen to you." If I came home and said I was spanked, my mother would say, "Good. You must not have been listening." I was raised with respect and love and discipline. I was never hit [by my parents]. My sisters and siblings were never hit. We didn't need to be. My parents spoke and we listened. When I first started here in the day care I expected children to listen and respect, like I had. The children's behavior then was excellent. Now . . . behavior is unbelievable. These children are asking for attention with negative behavior.

In sum, it is apparent that the active debate among academics in the early childhood field concerning the best way to prepare children for school and life is often paralleled in teachers' own consideration and integration of competing models for appropriate child rearing. The NAEYC guidelines and professional debates—in conferences, worksite training, and journals—gave the teachers in our study a vocabulary for debating teacher- versus child-initiated activities. Teachers mulled over these suggestions, integrating them with experiences and knowledge from other sources. The result was a philosophy tailored to the values and beliefs of the individual teacher.

A weak link in the chain appears to have been the way in which some administrators used the NAEYC guidelines as a sacred code that had to be implemented without discussion or tailoring to fit the teacher, the center, the community, and individual children. The teachers we listened to in this chapter expressed a sophisticated view of teaching that said, "We can and must prioritize several things," whereas some center directors and teacher-educators appeared to worry about keeping teaching guidelines simple and clear. The four teachers on whom we focused were saying that the development of children is not simple but complex and multifaceted, and that one can determine "best practice" only by sitting in a teacher's classroom and getting to know her students individually.

In the eyes of these preschool teachers, the dominant professional culture's ideology constitutes one particular model of appropriate child rearing and teaching, in many respects a middle-class Anglo model. Leaders in the early childhood world, as well as local preschool directors and agency-level supervisors, would do well to recognize, listen to, and learn from the varied voices of classroom teachers. It may be that teachers' alternative models fit with some parental models and social norms better than do models described by professional educators.

At the very least, family policy makers and local early childhood leaders must be aware of their own taken-for-granted beliefs—models of child rearing that have come to dominate the "professional" culture. These cultural models are better viewed as *one* set of child-rearing goals and practices rather than being promoted as the only way to do things or the best way to teach preschool children. Low-income mothers will not accept child-rearing models that seem foreign. Nor will preschool directors and teachers hold much credibility when they display little curiosity about parents' own models for how best to bring up a young child.

CHAPTER TEN

Lessons from Listening:
Strengthening Family Policy

❦

A friend is someone who may be considered . . . a suitable mate for one's child or a suitable candidate for political office; a stranger is someone who is not. —*Alan Peshkin (1991)*

When people are no longer strangers, Alan Peshkin reminds us, we stop defining them in terms of their "otherness" and feel compelled to "accept the burdens (and joys!) of compassion, support, and caring."[1] By viewing life through the eyes of fourteen impoverished women, we have gained a deeper appreciation of their goals for themselves and their children, of the obstacles and opportunities they encounter in their daily lives, of the way in which, to echo Selma's words, they "do the best with what they have."

They have revealed much about their lives, from their daily worries to their long-term goals. The desire to get ahead is unmistakable in most of the fourteen. Their efforts to lay down stepping stones for their children's advancement are equally evident. As with many middle-class women, their own identities and feelings of self-worth are wrapped up in their jobs. Work is necessary for the family's survival; heading out to a job each day is also evidence of their success in making it on their own, against stiff odds.

When a baby is born, mothers' priorities must shift. One need not be poor or single to realize this. But these fourteen women—poor and ngle—live on the razor's edge. They must devise a strategy both for iving economically and for being good mothers. Impoverished en are often quite alone with their young children as they maneuver through this minefield, experiencing varying levels of support from mothers, aunts, sisters, boyfriends, or social workers.

Poor women control few of the events that shake their economic security or shrink the time available for being an attentive mother. Helena did not expect to be raising her infant in a homeless shelter after her husband disappeared with the car, the furniture, and rent payments. Delmy could not foresee that her marriage would collapse, forcing her into a minimum-wage job that stole precious time with her three-year-old daughter. Nor did Shirl anticipate that she would have to flee from a husband who attacked her friend with a baseball bat. These mothers wanted to spend more time with their young children, and they struggled with whether or not they were doing what was best for their children. But the exigencies of poverty meant that these women faced a constant, daily challenge simply to maintain a minimal income.

The toughening of welfare rules means that mothers may have to go back to work or job training when their infants are as young as six to twelve months old. Once again, these women feel little control over the fundamental conflict between mothering or working for wages—an either/or choice that many middle-class parents do not have to make. Enabling single mothers to stay with their young children is no longer the state's priority—working is. For all the rhetoric around "empowering" the poor, these women constantly face forces that are thoroughly disempowering.

The essential lesson we have gleaned from our study comes in two parts. First, the immediate economic context and social networks encircling one woman vary significantly from those surrounding the next woman. Shirl received a good deal of support, financial and emotional, from her mother, who had worked at the post office for thirty years, tacitly modeling the assumption that women could work and live independent of men. Jackie, in contrast, had no avenue out of her drug addiction; with no shoulder to lean on, no kin to help out, her children were taken by the state when she entered the drug rehab center. Such stark variation in immediate contexts is marked in part by economic elements. But the key differences in these women's settings are *social* in character, distinguished by whether kin members and close friends are present and reliable, and whether cohesive obligations for support are operating.

Second, the *resources* available in these immediate contexts—both economic and cultural—indicate possible pathways out of poverty. When forks in the road become apparent, the individual woman's knowledge and wherewithal often make the difference between action and passivity. The presence of kin, friends, welfare workers, and pre-school staff defines the range of concrete options available, as well as the normative ways in which single mothers react to these "choices." These immediate, human-scale contexts also vary in the cultural and declared models that are most credible, such as the tacit commitment to work and maternal independence, the related aversion to welfare dependence, or the expectation that kin must pull together to ensure that the young child grows up closely supervised and warmly nurtured. These cultural models and pathways were variably present in the daily social settings in which these fourteen women lived out their lives.

If we are to improve the odds that these women will rise out of poverty, we must find ways of enriching their small-scale contexts; once a fork in the road appears, we must devise more effective ways to guide them along preferred paths. Rhetorically offering "empowerment" in contexts that possess few economic choices or culturally recognizable pathways is a false promise. And when policy makers or local practitioners offer highly constrained alternatives, or options that fail to flow from women's own indigenous pathways, wrong turns may be made. These women must paste together cultural models that flow from *their conceptions* of how they define parenting, how they want to see their children grow up. Ignoring these prior assumptions simply ensures that novel behavior driven by policy "interventions" will fail to stick over the long haul.

Creating More Forks in the Road

The diverse routes taken by the fourteen women as they fell into poverty are matched by the equally different methods they employed for climbing out. Yes, there are familiar scripts and tacit pathways for surviving when a newborn arrives and a male partner leaves. Heading to the welfare office to sign up for AFDC, even before the baby is born, is a common script. Obtaining assistance in paying for child care, through parental vouchers or subsidized slots in centers, is another path that these inner-city women feel entitled to travel, without any moral stigma attached. However, staying on AFDC for more than a year *is* a morally contentious issue in their communities. For some women, the salient cultural expectation is that one's own mother or other close kin will lend a hand.

Novel pathways also appear in their lives. The fourteen women suggest in their conversations that these new turns must meet two essential criteria to move them out of familiar, well-worn tracks: a credible actor must show *support and resources*, be they economic or cultural; and the fork in the road must aid the woman's journey toward *her* self-defined destination. When these criteria are met, models for action are no longer taken for granted. Alternative pathways and behaviors are consciously discussed and debated. The women are now operating from more contested, declared models.

Stories abound of opportunities that opened up when the women found new resources. Shirl, landing a job even before her first AFDC check arrived, also discovered a family day-care provider who proved to be ideal. Selma found a church close to her family's housing project that provided warm support and proper social values for her three girls. Kathy encountered Head Start teachers who crafted a rich, play-based curriculum for her son and helped her find new ways to discipline. Even neglectful Aggie, after receiving a portable housing voucher, realized that there was an important choice she could make. She boldly departed inner-city Boston for a suburb with less crime and better schools.

In each case, when these women approached a fork in the road, they turned onto a new pathway. But equally important, the novel pathway flowed from prior travels. Continuity from their old, tacit pathway, and a modest departure from it, were both apparent when new choices were made. Supportive actors were visible in the immediate contexts—Head Start teachers, social workers, close kin—and they helped to construct choices that invited women to build from their own cultural models and tacit beliefs. These stories tell of success—of how government services can host enormously helpful human beings who bolster women's ability to take new turns.

In this final chapter we pursue the question, What are the major lessons learned from three years of listening carefully? How can these fourteen voices help to strengthen family policy and local practice, from the work of political leaders to the craft of preschool teachers? What's working well in how family policies are implemented and community practices are organized? In short, how can these success stories be repeated with greater frequency?

We speak most directly to three sets of readers. *Policy makers* play a key role in providing resources to poor families. The level of economic security felt by poor families stems from their policy decisions. Policy also drives the work of supportive people—working from community agencies, child-care centers, churches, and schools—who are available to aid single parents. These *community practitioners* have much to learn from the tales and experiences of the fourteen women. We have heard many instances of how one individual in a human-scale neighborhood organization provided crucial assistance or novel information. Yet we have also seen how community workers can ignore, even belittle, these women's tacit beliefs about mothering, child rearing, and work. We hope that *scholars and analysts* reading this book will reflect upon their own assumptions about the motivations, contexts, and real choices available to impoverished women.

Memo to Policy Makers: Recognize the Cultural Pillars to Which Resources Adhere

Our cultural approach to understanding the paths taken by poor women should not divert attention from the fact that minimal income and the close presence of supportive human beings are essential ingredients for creating more choices. In addition, the fourteen women reveal that they actively assimilated the sprinkling of income supplements and human advice offered by community workers into the dominant cultural models that ordered their daily lives. Income assistance and social workers necessarily operate at the edges of these women's lives and in rather blunt ways, contrasting with the rational and surgically incisive intentions expressed by policy makers. Policy advocates argue that their specific "intervention" is engineered with neat precision, yielding crisp effects for poor families: tax credits encourage the poor to keep working, and vouchers allegedly encourage the active choice of better housing or better preschools. Conversations with the fourteen women do reveal that such positive effects are felt at the grassroots in some cases. Yet the cornerstones of their lives, and the tacit pathways being followed, often are unaffected. To be felt, policy remedies must allow parents to pursue their self-crafted goals, or be in synchrony with credible and clear objectives—shared widely within particular contexts—such as ensuring a steady income, finding reliable child care, or teaching respect for adults.

One lesson for policy makers is that poverty programs should strengthen (or at a minimum, understand) the indigenous social foundations of women's lives rather than "intervene" from the periphery. We can better aim assistance not only at the individual parent but at the family collective and via grassroots organizations that help open up routes out of poverty.

Income support—channeled to which social unit? Many Americans, adhering to the myth of rugged individualism, habitually locate the poverty problem within the impoverished *individual.* But low-income mothers who survive and climb out of poverty rarely act alone; they are situated in social networks composed of kin and friends who are variably trusting and supportive. Such culturally defined pillars of support—enacting obligations shared by kin members and close friends— are rarely rewarded by policies and income supports. Instead, cash assistance goes to an individual parent, or the working-poor couple who files a joint tax return and receives a refundable tax credit.

Two novel policy ideas illustrate how we could better aid the household, rather than allocating cash supports into a social vacuum. First-generation taxpayers could be rewarded when they provide a home to a second-generation child who has given birth or when they care for a grandchild. Half of all black mothers and a third of Hispanic mothers with preschool-age children live in households with their own mother or another adult present (excluding husbands).[2] In fact, one strategy aimed at making the family more cohesive is incorporated in recent welfare reforms: the requirement that teenage mothers remain in their parents' household in order to be eligible for AFDC. But this forces some teenage mothers to remain in abusive households and provides no economic incentive to the first-generation member. Tax incentives could be devised to aid supportive families while giving the second-generation mother the freedom to decide whether this arrangement is her best option.

A second way to build on positive cultural pillars addresses the working poor, those low-income parents who are employed and living just above the poverty line. Sardonically dubbed the "deserving poor" by the historian Michael Katz, they can receive an unrestricted credit or cash refund under the earned income tax credit program (EITC). The EITC initiative—an income-support program with little bureaucratic overhead—has shown robust political popularity. A brainchild of Richard Nixon's domestic policy advisors, including Daniel P. Moynihan, the "negative income tax" provides refunds to poor families with a working member. Originally enacted under Gerald Ford's watch, the EITC now provides $20 billion in tax credits or checks to 14 million families with children, averaging about $1,400 annually. Eligible families earn under $25,000 a year. Many are struggling close to the poverty line, but one household member must be employed for a family to qualify. The program provides a crisp and sizable incentive to stay off welfare. Importantly, the tax benefit is allocated to the household, which must consist of at least one parent and her child. The majority of beneficiaries are intact two-parent families filing joint returns.

If a parent becomes unemployed and falls below the poverty line, her options are quickly curtailed and she is channeled into the welfare maze. Rather than receiving EITC cash to spend as she chooses, she receives vouchers earmarked by the state for housing, transportation, food, and child care. She must follow government dictates of when to return to work and what form of child care to use. Mothers who are living within extended families might benefit from being allowed more discretion in how vouchers can be spent. Consolidating these disparate benefits into a single voucher would be an obvious improvement. We see no harm in providing an incentive to return to work, provided that a steady job and high-quality child care can be found. But employment status should not be a consequential line in the sand: on one side, jobless women's benefits and options are strictly controlled, while on the other side, the working low-income woman's tax benefits are totally unregulated. Current policy overemphasizes the moral message sent to the individual, rather than providing long-term assistance to households that support single mothers.

In 1990 President Bush quietly pushed forward a policy change aimed at bolstering not only the individual but also the family unit: the White House successfully moved the Congress to create vouchers that could be redeemed by grandparents and kin members who assist low-income parents with child-care responsibilities. Questions can be raised about how to ensure that such informal arrangements are consistently safe and stimulating for young children. For example, we know that youngsters often spend more hours sitting in front of the TV with informal day-care providers than when they are in center-based care.[3] But the overall goal of directing incentives at the broader family network—thus strengthening social bonds—is worth pursuing and evaluating. Efforts to exempt grandmothers from new welfare time limits when they are raising their grandchildren is another important case of focusing on the family and not simply the individual.

A related program is the federal child-care tax credit for families incurring preschool costs, a targeted income-support program. This $3.5 billion program mainly aids middle-class and affluent households, not the poor. As models of innovative public policy, however, both programs demonstrate how income-support can be focused on strengthening the household, especially families with young children. Whether these programs boost the long-term cohesion of families or raise the employability of single mothers remains to be seen. Regrettably, the popularity of these programs has outpaced attempts to assess their actual effects on families.

Incentives to encourage social linkages and cultural cohesion. In recent years political conservatives have become the dominant social engineers, optimistic about their ability to dismantle disincentives and to construct moralistic incentives emphasizing work, not motherhood. Our point is that the social engineering as it is currently being implemented is really not *social* in character. When it comes to fighting poverty, policy engineers in America in fact hold highly *individualistic* images of both the problem and the mechanical remedies. The poor parent is to be pulled out of her immediate context, injected with new job skills, new cash, new services. The cultural character of her daily life—how she sees work and how she hopes to raise her young child— are immaterial to these neo-architects of poverty policy.

Policy makers too often envision "opportunity" as a window through which the poor or working-class individual gazes—looking out into the promised land of good job, a spot in college, or ascending social status, the middle-class American Dream. The struggling aspirant is supposed to leap out that window, leaving behind her indigenous, now stigmatized origins. According to this view, getting ahead in America requires a determined exit from one's "backward" roots. But our conversations suggest that the modest steps taken often depend upon a boost from a neighbor, a grandmother, or an attentive social worker. The resources and social supports necessary for lifting these women and their young children out of poverty are embedded in, not divorced from, their indigenous social contexts. As the sociologist Judith Blau argues, it is better to see "opportunity" as a small space freed up by a splash of fresh economic or social resources situated within one's immediate social network than as a window through which one must jump, leaving behind the familiar.[4] We know that social linkages among kin and close friends offer resources, labor, and shared income for millions of low-income and working-poor families. Black and Hispanic adults, unlike Anglo parents, commonly pool their income with other household members. Members of these networks share the burdens of maintaining the household, doing errands, and preparing meals.[5]

More difficult is the task of constructing discrete policies that strengthen these resourceful linkages and thus free women to spend more time with their youngsters or to look for a better job. Part of the difficulty is that policy makers are uncertain how to evaluate parents' tacit views of work and child rearing, and how they might differ across ethnic groups. We still suffer from the sometimes racist generalities inherent in the old "culture-of-poverty" imagery, and from liberals' nervousness about sketching ethnic differences. Indeed, even thoughtful poverty analysts continue to advance gross generalizations about "the culture of black America," or counterpose the allegedly seamless family values of an entire racial group against "Western traditions."[6]

Policy crafters also have been humbled by the modest effects on household behavior of decades of welfare reforms, creation of tax incentives, and broader provision of child care. Effects on women's employment rates, reproductive behavior, and parenting practices are either minor or difficult to demonstrate empirically.[7] No policy strategy seems to alter substantially the actions of fathers in low-income communities, relative to economic forces and broad demographic trends. Policy levers represent not surgically incisive instruments that yield clear results but rather crude tools.

Another stumbling block in crafting policies that reinforce the household and not just an individual recipient is that family issues straddle the boundary between public and private domains. The ongoing moral attack on impoverished teenage mothers is a case in point.

Even though the problem of teenage pregnancy has been growing in many poor communities since the 1940s, backers of welfare programs refused to confront the issue. Under classical nineteenth-century notions of liberalism, this behavior was considered to be within the private domain. Ironically, it is now conservatives—those who try to delimit areas of economic life that fall within the public arena—who want to regulate private behavior. Similarly, right-wing policy makers have long resisted expansion of child-care and preschool programs, arguing that they usurp traditional gender roles and home life by interjecting the state into the private sphere. At the same time, liberals remain averse to setting moral norms or community standards. This leads to the heated debate over family values—and whether central policies will make a difference in the behavior of parents.

But if we go back to our elemental building block—the cultural models and social linkages that allow poor women to get ahead—new policy possibilities come into focus. The EITC model could be extended, for instance, to reward cohesive households that help offset significant costs linked to single mothers' employability. As we have seen, the fourteen women often received aid in the form of low rent in a dwelling owned by a parent or kin member, free child care when working night shifts, and shared transportation costs. When family members refuse to lend a hand, the single mother is much less able to search for work. These collective obligations and the expectation of social support will continue to erode if we aim policy only at the individual parent and not at her entire household and nearby friends and community organizations.

The most fundamental social bond—discounted by backers of the 1996 welfare reforms—is between mother and child. About two-thirds of all welfare recipients are single mothers with preschool-age children. Under strict time limits on cash benefits, impoverished mothers are to get back to work, handing their infants and toddlers over to child-care providers. Issues that used to be private, such as how much time mothers can spend with their very young children, have now been placed under the bright lights of public regulation. California's Republican governor, Pete Wilson, recently introduced legislation requiring mothers who receive welfare benefits to re-enter the workforce after a child turns twelve *weeks* old. This reengineering of motherhood is even more strange when one considers the 1996 reforms approved by President Clinton allowing states to define as "work" child-care services provided by grandmothers or aunts within impoverished neighborhoods, even as mothers are prevented from providing care.

Another example is linked to the fourteen women's varied experiences with home-based child care, whereby a woman takes in a few youngsters. Some women, such as Shirl, were extremely lucky to find a husband-wife team who not only had an orderly and warm "preschool" in their home but also delivered Martin home if Shirl missed her bus, or took him for a haircut. Several mothers drew on more emotional support and information about child-rearing from family day-care providers than from center-based teachers. Beatriz felt that Isabel, her child-care-provider, helped her to understand mischievous Eduardo. Wilma's provider was able sensitively to balance Wilma's desire for Janis to look like a princess with Janis's desire to play in the dirt. The Latina mothers, in general, preferred care providers who spoke their language and understood their norms of discourse and child behavior. This match more consistently occurred with family day-care providers than with centers and formal preschools. Yet government support of family day care, in the form of per-child subsidies, can be half or two-thirds less than grants to center-based programs. This represents a disincentive to improve the quality of home-based child care, now a common type of care for infants and toddlers, particularly among non–English-speaking families. Here policy implicitly erodes natural social linkages found within many poor neighborhoods.

Finally, we have seen how community workers—case workers, Head Start teachers, and drug counselors—offer new information and alternative models for poor women to consider. Unfortunately, these resourceful helpers often work out of fragile and transient organizations. Head Start teachers disappear during the summer months, child-care programs shut down, case workers burn out, community-action agencies rise and fall. Policy makers must find ways of making this outside help more consistent and more credible, building stronger links with single mothers' natural nets of social support.

Will civil society and employers encourage positive cultural models? Government cannot solve the family poverty problem alone. Employers and volunteer groups in local communities could play important roles in aiding single mothers who are trying to move back into the workforce. Many corporate leaders and their political allies have exerted relentless pressure to cut spending on antipoverty programs. If the business community redirected this energy to figuring out how to provide incentives for women to leave welfare and to creating jobs with decent pay, the poverty problem would diminish significantly. Business has invested significant resources in trying to improve public schools, in part because of its need for low-wage workers with literacy and basic job skills. Many single mothers have strong skills. What they need are jobs with adequate wages and some flexibility to deal with the uncertainties that come with being a parent of a young child. Inner-city poverty directly affects us all by raising welfare costs, health-care costs, and crime rates. The corporate world should not assume that government is solely responsible for addressing the fate of impoverished women.

Some business leaders have shown signs of real commitment, participating in tax-credit programs that subsidize first-year wages of jobless adults, developing on-site child care for their employees, making the work week more flexible to accommodate family demands, and even carving out new part-time jobs without reducing worker benefits. But if America's broad civil society were more deeply committed to the old Christian virtue of helping the poor, tax incentives would not be necessary. To the extent that training programs in companies do what the schools should have done, or provide skills that the worker may take to another job, government should help cover costs. This is in the broad public interest. But it is plainly hypocritical when business leaders oppose tax credits to the working poor or increases in the minimum wage, both of which provide incentives to work. Then, they urge government to raise tax credits that subsidize wages, cutting employers' labor costs. And we have already seen some employers laying off workers and hiring wage-subsidized welfare recipients in the wake of the 1996 reforms.

Welfare reform will be an empty promise unless the private sector creates more jobs and offers more inviting workplaces for single mothers, many of whom do not have extensive work experience. Working conditions for many women coming off welfare are dismal. In their thorough study of why poor women in four cities failed to hold down entry-level jobs, the sociologists Kathryn Edin and Laura Lein found that employers rarely offered full-time jobs, job security, or even minimal health insurance. Sick days or vacation time went unpaid. Some bosses required women to use pay phones outside the workplace if they wanted to call and make sure their children had arrived home from school safely.[8]

Many moderate politicians, such as former Massachusetts governor William Weld, have reaped much political hay by pushing get-tough welfare legislation while expanding child care and other enabling services. But Mr. Weld's reforms have foundered because few new jobs have been created. Less than a fourth of all AFDC recipients have been successfully placed in part- or full-time jobs. Corporate leaders should share part of the burden.

The Congress's decision in 1996 to raise the minimum wage is an important step forward, for until entry-level salaries in basic service industries move higher, the incentive for leaving welfare to work nights at Burger King or Dairy Queen will remain slight. The mis-organization of work, the scarcity of jobs available in central cities, and the lack of basic human caring expressed by employers—who need to provide long-term training and jobs, not just symbolic charity—will undercut the economic security and integrity of women trying to raise children alone. The American public has expressed strong support for the post-1996 round of welfare reforms enacted in Washington and state capitals, policies that Mr. Clinton and other moderates claim advance "tough love."[9] But after punitive measures are implemented and sink in, will key elements of civil society pull together to lend a warmer hand?

Work, motherhood, and high-quality child care. The most recent attack on poor families and programs serving them has been startling in a number of ways. The most surprising is the value that conservatives now place on getting mothers away from their young children and into the workforce. It's as if the old Calvinists had forgotten about their own virtuous mothers. Long opposed to opening job opportunities for middle-class women, or funding child care to enable maternal employment, many politicians now stigmatize motherhood for poor women and sing praise for the virtues of full-time work.

Civic debate over single parenthood and welfare has become so focused on how to move women out of the home and into a job that we have forgotten a simple fact that remains salient in these women's minds: they are mothers. Imagine that a welfare official shows up at *your* door and tells the woman of the house, who gave birth twelve weeks ago, that she must return to work at a job paying the minimum wage. "Wait!" the mother might protest. "I am now first and foremost a mother. Give me time. I am not sure how I will balance raising my child and working." The smiling social worker replies, "Sorry, the government says your time has run out. You must work." This is the politically imposed mandate that an increasing number of women now face—under welfare reforms approved in California, Florida, Massachusetts, and Texas.

This scenario may seem preposterous for a middle-class or more affluent family, where mothers are able to make their own decisions about whether or not to return to work after giving birth. But it is real for the four million single parents whose benefits now depend on their conforming to harsh new rules from the state. For government, motherhood is second to work. Being a mother is no longer as American as apple pie.

We are not arguing—nor have the fourteen women—that working is antithetical to being a good mother. As we have seen, a steady job provided women such as Harriet and Delmy with strong feelings of independence and efficacy, as well as with economic resources to make a wider range of choices about where to live or where to send their youngsters to preschool. At work these women talked with friends about men, about child-care and school options, about how to find a safer, affordable neighborhood in which to live. Research also suggests that working may introduce new declared models for how to listen to one's child more carefully, relax authoritarian or harsh forms of discipline, or place stronger emphasis on preschooling and education in general.[10]

The policy implication that stems from our conversations with the fourteen women is that we risk a great deal when we think about maternal employment in isolation from the cultural habits and practices that constitute good parenting. Jackie talked a lot about how she did not have enough time to keep tabs on her older son, especially once he entered an inner-city middle school and began hanging with "the boom-box crowd." She was consumed by going to work, looking for a new job that would pay above the minimum wage, and fearing the loss of her child-care voucher after pulling her daughter from a stultifying center. When these mothers are *at home with their children,* they are the principal adults encouraging education, teaching their own daughters to be independent, and searching for ways to avoid bad and dangerous public school settings.

We hear much about intergenerational welfare dependency, a legacy passed from mother to daughter. But the fourteen women in our study illustrated a different legacy: mothers are the conduit for positive cultural pathways, from starting preschool early to learning to be resilient and efficacious as a youngster. As the sociologists Katherine Rosier and William Corsaro emphasize, much of this positive upbringing occurs among grandmother, mother, and third-generation child—living either in the same household or close by.[11] But the ability to engage in close and effective parenting requires ample and calm time at home. Single parents who work, not surprisingly, report having less time than their counterparts in two-parent households to supervise their children's school work, regulate television viewing, and simply talk with their children at dinner time.[12] The push on poor women to get to work results in costs at home.

Child care is the linchpin that allows young mothers to return to work. Unreliable or low-quality child care is a source of considerable uncertainty and stress. Jackie was shocked by the cold harshness of her center's classroom staff, as well as by the amount of time that her daughter Tiffany spent watching TV. Pat pulled her son out of the Head Start center down the street after a few unruly children began to attend. Selma complained of home-based providers who couldn't speak Spanish and failed to display warm *(cariñosa)* attributes, so necessary in caring for infants and toddlers. And Brenda, fed up with an unresponsive center director and seemingly unorganized classrooms, moved her child to a Catholic preschool, providing a pathway around the dreaded Boston public schools. Each mother talked about the amount of time, stress, and consternation sparked by such episodes. The underfunding, uneven staffing, and indecisive management that marked these child-care settings were troubling to these women. If state and federal policy makers are serious about meeting the job-placement goals mandated by the 1996 welfare reforms, they must attend to boosting the supply and quality of child care.

As policy makers address the issue of child care, we should listen carefully to these single mothers. When their youngsters approached age three or four, most of the fourteen mothers were eager to find a formal preschool—to help get them ready for "real school." Liberal policy makers have long placed trust in Head Start or preschools situated in public schools or community-action agencies. But we should learn more about how parents weigh the relative benefits of different types of child care and early schooling, given the uneven mixed-market arrangement of providers. If many Latina mothers, for instance, prefer home-based or kin forms of child care, then policy should aim to equalize subsidies and improve the quality of these options.

Initial policy research suggests that the current $6 billion patchwork of public subsidies for child care and preschooling—tax credits, vouchers, and direct contracts with grassroots organizations—leads to a wide array of organized options for diverse parents, but that access to high-quality care is not equal across family income levels.[13] Improving the quality of noninstitutional forms of child care—kin arrangements, home-based group care, and paid baby-sitters—should be the top priority.[14] Governors bent on "efficiency" are directing new child-care dollars into these cheap, informal options, with little regard for the quality of the settings. In addition, school districts around the country are trying to finance full-day kindergartens. In Massachusetts, for instance, 80 percent of all local schools offer only half-day programs, an anachronism that does not serve the needs of working parents.

Shelter from the rain. We would be remiss not to emphasize the importance of essential services for poor families, those on which simple survival depends and which are threatened by the recurring War on Welfare. When Jackie threw in the towel, addicted to drugs, her only option was to give up her two children and enter a residential treatment center. When Helena's husband took the furniture, locked up their apartment, and drove off in their only car, she had no choice but to enter a homeless shelter with her months-old infant. If some budget cutters had their way, these women would have nowhere to go. Policy makers and budget moguls apparently do not understand that many people in our affluent society end up literally with no shelter from the rain, no shoulder on which to lean. The number of mothers and children living on the streets, forced into hostile kin settings, or enduring abusive boyfriends and husbands will likely increase as cash support is reduced or eliminated entirely. This may well happen as the recent spate of welfare reforms kicks in across the states. Washington has been steadily cutting back support for these immediate community services, or creating block grants for state governments that may be even less supportive.

Memo to Community Workers: Listen Carefully, Interpret Options Respectfully

Listening and learning. One simple lesson for community workers kept emerging throughout our three-year conversation: Those who take the time to listen carefully and get to know their "clients" are seen as more credible and helpful than those who do not. This simple point may be lost in social-welfare bureaucracies, because of a community worker's excessive case load or thinly stretched staff in underfunded child-care centers. The Latina mothers often took a strong liking to their home-based care providers. As Sol reported: "She is like a mother to each of the children. She treats them as if . . . they were her own." Some mothers sat and talked with their providers about problems with their youngsters, even about their own personal difficulties. These grandmotherly women often became adult counselors as well as child minders. Pat had come to know the Head Start director well over the years, since the center was just down the street. These are humble and human-scale organizations. But when they are sufficiently financed, and retain a stable staff, the conditions are right for building closer relationships.

We also heard of instances in which community workers were mistrusted, even disdained by some of the fourteen mothers. Several confronted child-care staff and preschool directors who seemed cold, incompetent, or inattentive to young children. Our own observations in many of the child-care arrangements generally confirmed their perceptions. For example, one large and well-known Boston center went through a succession of directors during the life of our project, and many of the classroom staff did not seem capable of connecting with the parents or children. At another center, we saw staff who humiliated and harangued the children to such a degree that we felt relieved when the kids were plopped down to watch cartoons peacefully on the VCR.

With some important exceptions, most center teachers felt that there was not much to learn from their parent-clients. They expressed little curiosity or respect for the cultural models that parents employ in raising their children. Many child-care directors and teachers—bolstered by their professional associations—follow scripted ways for interacting with parents. Getting parents' "feedback" about the child-care program is obviously a useful first step. But rarely do they take the time to *listen* more thoroughly and *learn* from parents about their child-rearing goals, parenting strategies, and tacit expectations.

Some of these conflicts are far from subtle. Delmy had to send books in Spanish to her daughter's preschool so that a classroom aide could read to her. The preschool had no Spanish-speaking teacher. Pamela felt that constant turnover in the staff at her son's child-care center had prevented the providers from ever getting to know her or her son; as a result, serious developmental delays went unnoticed until he was due to enter first grade. Our point is not that the fourteen mothers have the optimal answers for how child-care and early learning programs should be structured. But women adjusted their child-rearing practices more effectively when they felt respected by Head Start teachers and child-care staff. When child-care staff unconsciously acted from their own cultural models about how to guide children, or mimicked dictates of their professional associations in knee-jerk fashion, they signaled disrespect and disinterest in how their clients understood the process of child rearing.

Institutional habits and the illusion of choice. Policy makers and many community activists believe that empowerment and a spirit of choice have been injected into welfare programs. Tax credits and voucher forms of finance have grown rapidly. The fourteen women, depending upon their employment status, commonly received housing vouchers, child-care vouchers, and chits for public transportation. But the bureaucratic context in which social workers live often leads to narrow and channeled forms of "choice." In the child-care arena, for instance, we have seen how certain institutional habits are followed by case workers: infants and toddlers go into home-based settings for child care because it's cheap. Then, as slots open up in formal preschools, three- and four-year-olds are moved. Often when the case worker comes to the door to take the mother around to different child-care providers, the list contains simply one or two places. This is not real choice. It does not invite dialogue with the client. The preferences of the mothers themselves are rarely factored in.

The one exception pertains to child-care resource and referral agencies, commonly known as R&Rs. These human-scale organizations collect information on a variety of child-care alternatives and now administer the voucher program in many states. Because the *raison d'être* of these human-scale organizations is to figure out mothers' preferences and match them to appropriate providers, a more engaging process of choice seems to occur. Yet cuts in R&R agencies and staff are unraveling this progress, channeling parents into child-care settings that simply meet spending ceilings and have a rare open slot. Many states, such as Texas, still provide no state funding for these essential, market-oriented R&R agencies. The process of "rational choice" is not cost free. Staff time is required to learn about parents' surface-level and more subtle preferences. Unless real spending on child care rises, choice will be limited to selecting from among a shrinking number of low-quality providers.[15]

Whose version of family values and parenting? People still joke about— or revere—Dan Quayle's attack on Murphy Brown, the fictional woman who quickly became the most visible single mother in America. The pointed and visceral reaction to Quayle's moral attack on single parenthood, and the claim that this path was "a lifestyle choice," has been instructive. To claim that there is only one way of defining parenthood is naive at best, disrespectful at worst. Yet many liberal professional organizations express similarly monolithic, culture-less conceptions of how children should be socialized and what they should learn. Following Piaget and Dewey, the middle-class leaders who shape family and early childhood policies have struggled to define teaching practices that are "developmentally appropriate" for all children. Yet there is very little evidence showing that such practices are either appropriate for the contexts in which many poor children grow up or well suited to the socialization preferences that we heard expressed by the fourteen mothers. Nor is it clear that the developmental outcomes intended by mainstream preschool practices are actually realized by children in non–middle-class populations.

Some professional organizations are struggling with the slow recognition that there may not be one best way to raise a child. Recently, for instance, the NAEYC issued "cultural diversity guidelines," acknowledging that it is preferable for preschool teachers to speak to students in their home language, even if it is not English.

This is a step in the right direction. The NAEYC guidelines defining developmentally appropriate practices were revised in 1997 to provide a more accurate picture of the ways in which early socialization is profoundly cultural. Yet many educators have missed the point that classrooms modeled on professional guidelines are teeming with cultural models—but, as in a visual illusion, these models are considered the "ground," whereas the values and practices of the "multicultural" masses are the "figure" that stands out and attracts notice.

We need to assess critically the prescriptive recommendations and guidelines for good practice advanced by early childhood experts, taking care to identify the culturally based values that are embedded therein. It would be an excellent first step simply to make explicit the human qualities that are valued by the experts, then ask whether these values are shared by the diversity of parents and children being served. Only then will parents be empowered to enter into a dialogue about whether those qualities are ones that they value as well. Family policy makers and professionals may disagree with the tacit assumptions about parenting and learning that many parents express, but they should respect the fact that there is often room for legitimate disagreement. And unless they are brought into the light of day and discussed, indigenous socialization practices will resiliently persist, precisely because they are beneath the surface, cultural in character. Assaulting parents' own values and models will limit early childhood educators' own effectiveness. Clothing their own myths and models of socialization in scientific garb is short-sighted and will continue to distance parents from preschool organizations.

Memo to Scholars: Recognize Cultural Models That Open Up or Constrain Choices

In Chapter 1 we emphasized that "cultural elements" of low-income parents and their communities have received ample attention from poverty scholars since the 1950s. The more recent representational invention of "the underclass" reinforces gross distinctions between us and them, and among racial groups. According to Ken Auletta, the impoverished individual "feels excluded from society, rejects commonly accepted values, suffers from *behavioral* as well as *income* deficiencies . . . to most Americans their [poor people's] behavior seems aberrant."[16] But as the fourteen women richly illustrate, low-income parents often act in ways that probably feel quite familiar to their counterparts in the middle class. Other times, faced with economic exigencies, they behave or express beliefs that may seem unfamiliar.

By listening carefully to the women, we came to see how they turned over in their minds explanations for their present fate and alternative pathways for getting ahead. The cultural-model building block, we believe, offers an important breakthrough in how we understand the interaction between the *individual* woman's motivation to act and the *pathways* or *scripts* that circulate within her immediate social and economic environment. This framework offers four fundamental departures from prior theoretical explanations.

First, it moves our thinking away from gross generalizations about a global culture of poverty that surrounds every family unlucky enough to live in a ghetto or *barrio*. It also avoids the mistake of saying that every parent or adult will psychologically respond to an economically depressed setting in the same passive or pathological way. The global use of the term "culture of poverty" implies that all sorts of values are mixed together in the impoverished parent's mind. All bad values go together in this indiscriminate characterization of the "culture" of poverty. In contrast, the fourteen women in our study debated *alternative* models for moving ahead or staying behind. Economic incentives and rewards certainly follow certain pathways, such as going on AFDC, finding a better-paying job, selling drugs. But these alternative models and scripts also carry social and human rewards, as well as morally charged meanings. For the fourteen women, getting off welfare, going back to work, and contributing to the household income yielded affection and respect from kin members, membership in the extended family, and admiration for fighting the odds. We are not arguing that some positive incentives do not yield individual-level outcomes: a personal feeling of efficacy or independence. But the sequences of action and belief—the tacit cultural models from which one chooses—are lodged in the parent's wider and immediate social context.

Second, the cultural-model framework avoids the empirical weaknesses of rational-choice models of human action, which often dominate economists' representations of the impoverished family. This textbook explanation argues that the individual comes to a problem or situation with predetermined preferences, then chooses among alternatives based on an economic calculus. Parents will invest in preschooling rather than rely on relatives or friends for child care when they calculate the human capital returns accruing to this alternative. Or, as David Ellwood convincingly argues, single mothers are unlikely to try to move off welfare unless job earnings exceed benefit levels—which requires finding a job that pays above the minimum wage and finding low-cost child care.[17] But preferences often are formed or acquired from the immediate or broader social context. In our parlance, *declared models* must appear in the context and hold sufficient credibility and economic resources to move women onto a new, seemingly feasible pathway.

As Ellwood emphasizes, the entire discussion of "family values" and "welfare dependency" reveals broad moral preferences in civil society. We see this debate play out at the grassroots in the fourteen women's own settings as well. When Brenda complained of friends who stayed on AFDC and "just sat at home with their kids," she expressed an exogenous moral stance. Similarly, Shirl's uncle invoked a clear cultural model or pathway when he said that Shirl and her young son could live with him only if she got a job and stayed off welfare. AFDC as a source of income should go into their economic calculus, if rational-choice theory were a complete explanation. What's dominant in this picture is contention over cultural models—is staying on AFDC a credible path of action or not? After an individual or a household seizes on a particular cultural model, or moral foundation, then decision making may be influenced by some rough calculus of relative benefits. But both the endogenous flow of economic incentives and the very meaning of those incentives (for example, negative associations linked to AFDC) are conditioned by the cultural models and scripts that come to dominate in particular social networks. The tacit model will not erode or be adjusted until a rival, declared model enters the scene and is experienced as an alternative way to go. The sprinkling of incentives from above will not change behavior until the competing cultures of poverty contain a wider range of declared models that yield tangible social and economic rewards.

Third, the cultural-model framework helps to sketch a dynamic social process by which innovative pathways and actions are introduced and at times taken up, allowing individual women to combat the structural odds that work against them. There is little doubt that structural remedies, including creating more jobs or more affordable child-care slots, would open up fresh opportunities. Clearer economic incentives for getting back to work and staying employed (rational-choice remedies, such as the EITC) also aid single mothers. But we repeatedly saw how having a caring local actor who demonstrated a novel pathway, and offered modest economic or social resources, can make a huge difference. These turns in the road happen when an alternative path or tacit cultural model gains credibility in the young mother's eyes. And the legitimacy of these new pathways depends upon the resourcefulness and support of the human bearers of the novel model.

Fourth, the framework allows us to detail variability among ethnic groups and to capture differences among families within particular ethnic neighborhoods. In recent years, policy makers and analysts alike have come to realize that Latino families, even when similarly impoverished economically, are different from Anglo and black households in some respects. These differences can be identified at an empirical level: among Latino families, two-parent households are more common, mothers have much lower education levels, extended kin reside in households more frequently, and parents' propensity to enroll their youngsters in preschool programs is much lower.[18] The four single Latina mothers that we came to know revealed some of these distinctive qualities: some had broad and strong social networks that could provide child care; they worried about how to raise their youngsters according to the social rules and language demands they faced in their immediate Hispanic context; they often stressed children's obligations to the group and inculcated in them respect for adult authority. These prevalent norms and cultural models, on average, may be more consistently reproduced within Latino communities than within predominantly low-income Anglo or black neighborhoods. This is a major empirical question on which more generalizable data are very scarce.

Other cultural models and scripts circulate without regard to racial or ethnic boundaries. Throughout this study we have asked ourselves whether there is more variability among individual women within black or Latino communities than exists between groups. We saw several black mothers who similarly pushed for inviolable respect for adults. Women such as Brenda or Kathy had highly interdependent and cooperative relations with their children's maternal or paternal grandparents, relations that were necessary for acquiring child care, shared meals, and even access to pooled income. The cultural-model framework allows us to see such communalities across ethnic groups. Certain models and pathways may be more frequently observed in particular communities. But we can also keep an eye on the alternative models circulating within and across ethnic communities, rather than continue to claim that values and beliefs are static and particular to one certain group. Racial and ethnic boundaries are clear in some ways, but highly permeable and shifting in others.

There is little doubt that the recurring War on Welfare is motivated by racist and ethnocentric biases, as well as by prejudices against women who have become, often through no fault of their own, single parents. Did the fourteen women feel that they were being victimized by racism or sexist attacks? We have seen that the Latina mothers, depending on how recently their families had immigrated, did see themselves and their child-rearing practices as somehow diverging from mainstream American values. They still saw themselves and their children as outsiders in a sense. The fact that one member of our research team is Latina allowed us to delve into these cultural questions and explore them in Spanish.

In contrast, the black women talked little of racism. Shirl and others did criticize politicians for not knowing enough about poor families, and Shirl also criticized the governor for cutting back on child-care support. More research needs to be done on how women view the links among their race, ethnicity, and impoverished situation. They may have a critical and politicized view of the welfare-reform debate, or they may be internalizing all the denigrating messages transmitted by some political leaders and some in the mass media. We have much more to learn in this area.

Today we are surrounded by portraits of poor parents that scream with pathology. The very real problems of the most troubled are mistakenly assumed to apply to the rest. Horror stories of abused and neglected children lead to a view of poor parents as monsters, a species different from our own. An entire class is vilified as having departed from any sense of morality. Social services are on the chopping block because they are seen as rewarding the poor for their failure to better themselves economically. Yet once we got to know these fourteen women, our overwhelming conclusion was that most of them were the very embodiment of traditional American values. They wanted to work, they *expected* to work, having grown up with mothers who toiled long and hard hours. They were fervent supporters of the status quo, not interested in undermining or subverting it, even though it had not served them particularly well. They raised their children not to question authority and poured their energy into getting them ready for school by learning their numbers and ABCs. They took their children to church and spent their free time with extended family. With one or two exceptions, these women had their noses to the grindstone from dawn to dusk—single-handedly performing a ceaseless cycle of housework, child care, work, and family responsibilities. These women, in the words of Helena, "did not ask for much." At worst they just tried to survive from day to day, at best they tried and succeeded in making a change for the better in their troubled communities. If you ignore the fact that they were living in virtual battle zones, the lives of some could be the subject of a Norman Rockwell painting or a homily on the traditional virtues of humility, thrift, hard work, charity, and piety.

But one cannot and should not forget that they were surrounded by a minefield of dangers. They were not perfect, and when they made mistakes, the effects were often disastrous, magnified by the fact that there was no one around to pick up the pieces. The consequences of "blowing it" could be life-threatening for them or their children. Helena could not get along with her family; the result was months of living in a homeless shelter. Jackie could not stop herself from taking drugs—and paid the price of losing her children. In dire circumstances, they did rely on social programs to pull them back on track. When partners or jobs failed, most knew the well-worn script of applying for welfare and a variety of other subsidies. Across generations, these normative models had often worked in situations in which few alternatives existed, and these pathways for how to behave and believe were reproduced, scripted in a very real sense.

But norms do shift, community programs introduce new models, and tax credits and income-support programs offer a bit more economic stability.[19] Immigration and occasional movement out of the inner city, as Aggie and Harriet showed, alter the mix of salient cultural models and pathways pertaining to the pursuit of a job, being independent, and raising a child.

In a sense, these fourteen women are searching for those pathways—advanced by resourceful friends, kin members, social workers, Head Start teachers—that offer economic security and moral, contextually sensible ways of raising their young children. This is a search that holds enormous human consequences for mother and child alike. If as a society we fail to aid this search with every effective means possible, it is our own virtue and civility that should be questioned.

Notes

1. Empowering Strangers

1. Data sources: Terry Lugaila, *Households, Families, and Children: A Thirty-Year Perspective* (Washington, D.C.: Bureau of the Census, 1992); Bruce Fuller, Costanza Eggers-Piérola, Susan D. Holloway, Xiaoyan Liang, and Marylee F. Rambaud, "Rich Culture, Poor Markets: Why Do Latino Families Forgo Preschool?" *Teachers College Record* 97 (1996):400–418; Sandra Hofferth, Jerry West, Robin Henke, and Phillip Kaufman, *Access to Early Childhood Programs for Children at Risk* (Washington, D.C.: National Center for Educational Statistics, 1994); Sara McLanahan and Gary Sandefur, *Growing Up with a Single Parent: What Hurts, What Helps* (Cambridge, Mass.: Harvard University Press, 1994); Reference Press, Inc., *Statistical Abstract of the United States 1994* (New York, 1994).

2. The politically constructed aims of family assistance programs, particularly the shift from seeing aid as a means of helping young children to a means of pushing mothers to leave home and go back to work, are discussed in Linda Gordon, *Pitied but Not Entitled: Single Mothers and the History of Welfare, 1890–1935* (New York: The Free Press, 1994).

3. Quoted by the social historian Michael Katz (p. 20), who provides a detailed account of how this earlier academic work came to influence the assumptions underlying Operation Head Start, the funding of community action agencies, and other key elements of the 1960s War on Poverty. Michael Katz, *The Undeserving Poor: From the War on Poverty to the War on Welfare* (New York: Pantheon, 1989).

4. William J. Wilson, *The Declining Significance of Race* (Chicago: University of Chicago Press, 1978).

5. For reviews of evidence on how Great Society initiatives have yielded some concrete and positive effects, see "Is Black Progress Set to Stall?" *Business Week*,

November 6, 1996, pp. 68–76, and David Grissner, Sheila Nataraj Kirby, Mark Berends, and Stephanie Williamson, *Student Achievement and the Changing American Family* (Santa Monica: RAND Corporation, 1994).

6. Aaron Wildavsky, "Is Culture the Culprit?" *Public Interest* (Fall 1993):110–118.

7. Rational-choice theorists assume that parents act from exogenously determined preferences, as constrained by the household budget, to express demand for a variety of consumption goods and investments in their children. Neoclassical scholars are not terribly concerned with the sources of these *a priori* preferences regarding the types of investments and behaviors that shape the child's future propensity to attain a higher-quality life. This idealized rational-choice model assumes that the family operates with intentionality, searching out information (for example, about preschools or child-rearing practices), and adjusts its internal behavior in response to costs and anticipated benefits for the family and for the child. Parents, in this theoretical light, are active, optimizing agents, bounded only by the cost of information, the range of service suppliers, and the family's budget constraints. The application of this neoclassical model to the family has long been debated. For example, see Gary Becker, *A Treatise on the Family* (Cambridge, Mass.: Harvard University Press, 1981); Kenneth Arrow, *Social Choice and Individual Values* (New Haven: Yale University Press, 1951); and Herbert Simon, "Rational Decision-making in Business Organizations," *American Economic Review* 69 (1979):493–519.

8. Naomi Quinn and Dorothy Holland, "Culture and Cognition," in *Cultural Models in Language and Thought*, ed. D. Holland and N. Quinn (Cambridge, England: Cambridge University Press, 1987), pp. 3–40.

9. Quinn and Holland, "Culture and Cognition"; Ward Goodenough, "Cultural Anthropology and Linguistics," in *Language and Linguistics Monographs*, no. 9, ed. P. Garvin (Washington, D.C.: Georgetown University, 1957), pp. 167–173.

10. Clifford Geertz, *Local Knowledge* (New York: Basic Books, 1983).

11. This distinction between cultural and declared models is informed by the work of Shinobu Kitayama and Hazel Rose Markus, who discuss how certain knowledge and beliefs, even in ethnically homogenous societies, are declarative and conscious in character. See, for example, Hazel Rose Markus and Shinobu Kitayama, "Culture and the Self: Implications for Cognition, Emotion, and Motivation," *Psychological Review* 98 (1991):224–253. The broad study of the individual's consciousness of surrounding cultural norms and tacitly held social rules, of course, constitutes an old line of inquiry in sociology and social psychology. See, for instance, Randall Collins, *Four Sociological Theories* (New York: Oxford University Press, 1994).

12. Benjamin Bloom, Allison Davis, and Robert D. Hess, *Compensatory Education for Cultural Deprivation*, Working Paper from the Conference on Education and Cultural Deprivation (Chicago: University of Chicago Press, 1965).

13. Beatrice and John Whiting were pioneers in the cross-cultural study of family practices. See, for example, Beatrice Whiting and Carolyn Edwards, *Children of Different Worlds: The Formation of Social Behavior* (Cambridge, Mass.: Harvard University Press, 1988). Sarah and Robert LeVine have continued and elaborated on this work in Robert LeVine, Suzanne Dixon, Sarah LeVine, Amy Richman,

P. Herbert Leiderman, Constance Keefer, and Barry Brazelton, *Child Care and Culture: Lessons from Africa* (New York: Cambridge University Press, 1994).

14. Barbara Rogoff, Jayanthi Mistry, Artin Goncu, and Christine Mosier, *Guided Participation in Cultural Activity by Toddlers and Caregivers*, Monographs of the Society for Research in Child Development, vol. 58, no. 236 (Chicago: University of Chicago Press, 1993).

15. William Corsaro, "Discussion, Debate, and Friendship Processes: Peer Discourse in U.S. and Italian Nursery Schools," *Sociology of Education* 67 (1994):1–26.

16. Robert Hess and Hiroshi Azuma, "Cultural Support for Schooling: Contrasts between Japan and the United States," *Educational Researcher* 20 (1991):2–8, 14; Lois Peak, *Learning to Go to School in Japan* (Berkeley: University of California Press, 1991).

17. Elijah Anderson, *Streetwise: Race, Class, and Change in an Urban Community* (Chicago: University of Chicago Press, 1990).

18. Hugh Mehan, "Understanding Inequality in Schools: The Contribution of Interpretive Studies," *Sociology of Education* 65 (1992):1–20.

19. Carole Joffe, *Friendly Intruders: Childcare Professionals and Family Life* (Berkeley: University of California Press, 1977).

20. Caroline Zinsser, *Raised in East Urban: Child Care Changes in a Working-Class Community* (New York: Teachers College Press, 1991).

21. Class-based or Marxist theorists of local culture assume congruity between material conditions and social norms, as well as functional integration of cultural models enacted by actors within vertically arranged groups; for review, see Randall Collins, *Four Sociological Traditions* (New York: Oxford University Press, 1994), pp. 232–234. Anthropologists have emphasized, however, that as the local context is penetrated by novel cultural models, largely through the modernization process, the stock of available cultural routines and scripts becomes more pluralistic. The appropriation of cultural models from the immediate context involves not only scripted mimicry but also the individual's active interpretation of the practice (practical consciousness), which results in adaptations of the original model. In this way, the "reproduction of situated practices" is interrupted and the individual is no longer simply reproducing the "structure" of accepted practice or belief. On this last point, see Anthony Giddens, *The Constitution of Society* (Berkeley: University of California Press, 1984), pp. 25, 171.

2. Fourteen Poor Women, Fourteen Rich Lives

1. Demographic data are from U.S. Department of Commerce, *City and County Data Book, 1994* (Washington, D.C.: Bureau of the Census, 1994). Bruce Fuller and Xiaoyan Liang, "Market Failure? Estimating Inequality in Preschool Availability," *Educational Evaluation and Policy Analysis* 18 (1996):31–49.

2. Bruce Fuller, Susan D. Holloway, Marylee F. Rambaud, and Costanza Eggers-Piérola, "How Do Mothers Choose Child Care?: Alternative Cultural Models in Poor Neighborhoods," *Sociology of Education* 69 (1996):83–104. Susan D. Holloway, Marylee F. Rambaud, Bruce Fuller, and Costanza Eggers-Piérola, "What Is 'Appropriate Practice' at Home and Child Care?: Low-Income Mothers' Views on

Preparing Their Children for School," *Early Childhood Research Quarterly* 10 (1995):451–473.

3. The one exception was Sol [SL9], with whom only two interviews were conducted. She moved during the second year of the study, and we were unable to find her. The remaining thirteen women participated for the full three-year period.

4. Yvonne Lincoln and Egon Guba, *Naturalistic Inquiry* (Beverly Hills, Calif.: Sage, 1985); James Spradley, *The Ethnographic Interview* (New York: Holt, Rinehart and Winston, 1979).

5. Richard Shweder, ed., *Fallible Judgment in Behavioral Research* (San Francisco: Jossey-Bass, 1980).

6. Anselm Strauss, *Qualitative Analysis for Social Scientists* (Cambridge, England: Cambridge University Press, 1987).

7. For guidance on these issues of validity with qualitative evidence, see Charles Ragin and Howard Becker, eds., *What's in a Case? Exploring the Foundations of Social Inquiry* (New York: Cambridge University Press, 1992); Joseph Maxwell, *Qualitative Research Design: An Interactive Approach* (Thousand Oaks, Calif.: Sage, 1995).

3. Motherhood in Poverty

1. Susan Kontos, Helen Raikes, and Alice Woods, "Early Childhood Staff Attitudes toward Their Parent Clientele," *Child Care Quarterly* 12 (1983):45–58. Also, Susan Kontos and Wilma Wells, "Attitudes of Caregivers and the Day Care Experience of Families," *Early Childhood Research Quarterly* 1 (1986):47–67.

2. Ellen Hock, D. De Meis, and Susan McBride, "Maternal Separation Anxiety: Its Role in the Balance of Employment and Motherhood in Mothers of Infants," in A. Gottfried and A. Gottfried, eds., *Maternal Employment and Children's Development* (New York: Plenum, 1988), pp. 191–230.

3. Robin Harwood, Joan G. Miller, and Nydia L. Irizarry, *Culture and Attachment: Perceptions of the Child in Context* (New York: Guilford Press, 1995).

4. Karen Slade, "Maternal Separation Anxiety: Views of Mormon Mothers," unpublished paper, Harvard University, 1996.

5. Dorinne Kondo, *Crafting Selves: Power, Gender, and Discourses of Identity in a Japanese Workplace* (Chicago: University of Chicago Press, 1990).

6. Charles M. Super and Sarah Harkness, "The Developmental Niche: A Conceptualization at the Interface of Child and Culture," *International Journal of Behavioral Development* 9 (1986):545–569.

4. Conceptions of Children's Behavior

1. John Cleverley and Dennis C. Phillips, *Visions of Childhood: Influential Models from Locke to Spock* (New York: Teachers College Press, 1993).

2. William Corsaro and Kathleen Brown Rosier, "Documenting Productive-Reproductive Processes in Children's Lives: Transition Narratives of a Black Family Living in Poverty," in William A. Corsaro and Peggy J. Miller, eds., *Interpretive Approaches to Children's Socialization*, New Directions for Child Development 58 (San Francisco: Jossey-Bass, 1992), pp. 67–91.

3. The research program of Daphne Blunt Bugental illustrates this approach. See, for example, Daphne Blunt Bugental, "Affective and Cognitive Processes

within Threat-Oriented Family Systems," in Irving E. Sigel, Ann V. McGillicuddy-DeLisi, and Jacqueline J. Goodnow, eds., *Parental Belief Systems: The Psychological Consequences for Children,* second ed. (Hillsdale, N.J.: Lawrence Erlbaum, 1992), pp. 219–248.

5. Cultural Models of Child Rearing

1. Cynthia T. Garcia Coll, Elaine C. Meyer, and Lisa Brillon, "Ethnic and Minority Parenting," in Marc H. Bornstein, ed., *Handbook of Parenting,* vol. 2, *Biology and Ecology of Parenting* (Hillsdale, N.J.: Lawrence Erlbaum, 1995), pp. 189–209.

2. The dichotomy between collectivist vs. individualistic values stemmed originally from nineteenth-century comparisons between "traditional" social groups and "modernizing" populations within industrializing settings. Early sociologists spent considerable effort trying to characterize individual-level values and attitudes that appeared to differ within these two settings. For example, see Ferdinand Tönnies, *Community and Society,* trans. C. P. Loomis (East Lansing: Michigan State University Press, 1957); Randall Collins, *Four Sociological Traditions* (New York: Oxford University Press, 1994); and Alexis de Tocqueville, *Democracy in America* (New York: Vintage Books, 1961). From the 1960s forward, a version of this dichotomy arose in social psychology related to the individual's locus of control or the level of influence a person was believed to have over his or her own destiny. This long line of research continues to be based on the dichotomous representation that people in more traditional cultures (or autocratic work settings) will be focused more on the collective's interests and be less individualistic, relative to modernizing or middle-class social groups. See, for instance, Susan D. Holloway and Bruce Fuller, "Situational Determinants of Causal Attributions: The Case of Working Mothers," *Social Psychology Quarterly* 46 (1983):131–140. Melvin Kohn et al., "Class Position in the Class Structure and Psychological Functioning in the United States, Japan, and Poland," *American Journal of Sociology* 95 (1990):964–1008.

3. Patricia M. Greenfield, "Independence and Interdependence as Developmental Scripts: Implications for Theory, Research, and Practice," in Patricia M. Greenfield and Rodney R. Cocking, eds., *Cross-Cultural Roots of Minority Development* (Hillsdale, N.J.: Lawrence Erlbaum Associates, 1994), pp. 1–37.

4. Robert Hess and Hiroshi Azuma, "Cultural Support for Schooling: Contrasts between Japan and the United States," *Educational Researcher* 20 (1991):2–8, 12. Susan D. Holloway, "Concepts of Ability and Effort in Japan and the United States," *Review of Educational Research* 58 (1988):327–345. Harold Stevenson and James Stigler, *The Learning Gap* (New York: Summit, 1992).

5. James Coleman, *Foundations of Social Theory* (Cambridge: The Belknap Press of Harvard University Press, 1990); Francis Fukuyama, *Trust: The Social Virtues and the Creation of Prosperity* (New York: Free Press, 1995).

6. Concha Delgado-Gaitan, "School Matters in the Mexican-American Home: Socializing Children to Education," *American Educational Research Journal* 29 (1992):495–513.

7. Çidem Kagitçibaşi, "Individual and Group Loyalties: Are They Compatible?" in Çidem Kagitçibaşi, ed., *Growth and Progress in Cross-Cultural Psychology* (Lisse: Swets and Zeitlinger, 1987), pp. 94–104.

8. Anthony Bryk, Valerie Lee, and Peter Holland, *Catholic Schools and the Common Good* (Cambridge, Mass.: Harvard University Press).

6. Discipline and Obedience

1. Geraldine Youcha, *Minding the Children: Child Care in America from Colonial Times to the Present* (New York: Scribner, 1995).
2. Diana Baumrind, "Rearing Competent Children," in W. Damon, ed., *Child Development Today and Tomorrow* (San Francisco: Jossey-Bass, 1998), pp. 349–378.
3. Ibid.
4. Melvin Kohn, Atsushi Naoi, Carrie Schoenbach, Carmi Schooler, and Kazimierz Slomczynski, "Position in the Class Structure and Psychological Functioning in the United States, Japan, and Poland," *American Journal of Sociology* 95 (1990):964–1008.
5. Vonnie C. McLoyd, "The Impact of Economic Hardship on Black Families and Children: Psychological Distress, Parenting, and Socioeconomic Development," *Child Development* 61 (1990):311–346.
6. Robin Harwood, Joan G. Miller, and Nydia L. Irizarry, *Culture and Attachment: Perceptions of the Child in Context* (New York: Guilford Press, 1995).
7. For a more detailed examination of respect and its association with discipline, see Marylee F. Rambaud, Susan D. Holloway, Bruce Fuller, and Costanza Eggers-Piérola, "'I Put Up a Good Battle before I Get the Butt': Low-Income Mothers Speak on Discipline and Respect." Paper presented at the Annual Meeting of the American Educational Research Association, New York City, April 1996; Marylee F. Rambaud, "Respect and Child Discipline: Low-Income Mothers Speak," Ed.D. diss., Harvard University Graduate School of Education, 1996.

7. Cultural Models of Education

1. Richard J. Murnane and Frank Levy, "Why Today's High-School-Educated Males Earn Less Than Their Fathers Did: The Problem and an Assessment of Responses," *Harvard Educational Review* 63 (1993):1–19.
2. John Ogbu, "From Cultural Differences to Differences in Cultural Frame of Reference," in P. M. Greenfield and R. R. Cocking, eds., *Cross-Cultural Roots of Minority Child Development* (Hillsdale, N.J.: Lawrence Erlbaum Associates, 1994), pp. 365–391.
3. Lois Weis, "Narrating the 1980s and 1990s: Poor and Working-Class Men and Women Speak about Social Critique." Paper presented at the Fifteenth Annual Ethnography in Education Forum, University of Pennsylvania, Philadelphia, Pennsylvania, February 1994.
4. Stanley Sue and Sumie Okazaki, "Asian-American Educational Achievement: A Phenomenon in Search of an Explanation," *American Psychologist* 45 (1990):913–920.
5. Karl Alexander and Doris Entwisle, *Achievement in the First Two Years of School: Patterns and Processes*, Monographs of the Society for Research in Child Development, vol. 53, no. 2 (Chicago: University of Chicago Press, 1988).
6. Barbara Willer, Sandra L. Hofferth, Ellen E. Kisker, Patricia Divine-

Hawkins, Elizabeth Farquhar, and Frederic B. Glantz, *The Demand and Supply of Child Care in 1990.* Joint findings from the National Child Care Survey 1990 and A Profile of Child Care Settings (Washington, D.C.: National Association for the Education of Young Children, 1991).

7. Annette Lareau, *Home Advantage: Social Class and Parental Intervention in Elementary Education* (London: The Falmer Press, 1989).

8. Deborah Stipek, "Characterizing Early Childhood Education Programs," in Leslie Rescorla, Marion C. Hyson, and Kathy Hirsh-Pasek, eds., *Academic Instruction in Early Childhood: Challenge or Pressure?* New Directions for Child Development 53 (San Francisco: Jossey-Bass, 1991), pp. 47–55; Deborah Stipek, Sharon Milburn, Darlene Clements, and Denise H. Daniels, "Parents' Beliefs about Appropriate Education for Young Children," *Journal of Applied Developmental Psychology* 13 (1992):293–310.

9. Bruce Fuller, Susan D. Holloway, and Xiaoyan Liang, "Family Selection of Child-Care Centers: The Influence of Household Support, Ethnicity, and Parental Practices," *Child Development* 67 (1996):3320–3337.

10. Sue Bredekamp and Carol Copple, eds., *Developmentally Appropriate Practice in Early Childhood Programs*, revised ed. (Washington, D.C.: National Association for the Education of Young Children, 1997).

11. Joseph J. Tobin, "The Irony of Self-Expression," *American Journal of Education* 103 (1995):233–258.

12. Melvin L. Kohn and Carmi Schooler, "Occupational Experience and Psychological Functioning: An Assessment of Reciprocal Effects," in Melvin L. Kohn and Carmi Schooler, eds., *Work and Personality* (Norwood, N.J.: Ablex, 1983), pp. 5–33.

13. Lareau, *Home Advantage*, p. 67.

14. National Association for the Education of Young Children, *Developmentally Appropriate Practices: Birth through Age Five* (Washington, D.C.: NAEYC, 1991).

15. Dale C. Farran, Beverly Silveri, and Anne Culp, "Public School Preschools and the Disadvantaged," in *Academic Instruction in Early Childhood*, pp. 65–73; Daniel J. Walsh, "Extending the Discourse on Developmental Appropriateness: A Developmental Perspective," *Early Education and Development* 2 (1991):109–119.

16. Lareau, *Home Advantage*.

17. Robert A. LeVine, Suzanne Dixon, Sarah LeVine, Amy Richman, P. Herbert Leiderman, Constance H. Keefer, and T. Berry Brazelton, *Child Care and Culture: Lessons from Africa* (Cambridge, England: Cambridge University Press, 1994).

18. Patricia M. Greenfield, "Independence and Interdependence as Developmental Scripts: Implications for Theory, Research, and Practice," in Patricia Greenfield and Rodney R. Cocking, eds., *Cross-Cultural Roots of Minority Child Development* (Hillsdale, N.J.: Erlbaum, 1994), pp. 1–37; Algea O. Harrison, Melvin N. Wilson, Charles J. Pine, Samuel Q. Chan, and Raymond Buriel, "Family Ecologies of Ethnic Minority Children," *Child Development* 61 (1990):347–362.

19. Çidem Kagitçibaşi, "Individual and Group Loyalties: Are They Compatible?" in Çidem Kagitçibaşi, ed., *Growth and Progress in Cross-Cultural Psychology* (Lisse: Swets and Zeitlinger, 1987), pp. 94–104.

20. A review of the issue can be found in Susan D. Holloway, Kathleen S.

Gorman, and Bruce Fuller, "Child-Rearing Beliefs within Diverse Social Structures: Mothers and Caregivers in Mexico," *International Journal of Psychology* 23 (1988):303–317.

21. William A. Corsaro and Katherine Brown Rosier, "Documenting Productive-Reproductive Processes in Children's Lives: Transition Narratives of a Black Family Living in Poverty," in William A. Corsaro and Peggy J. Miller, eds., *Interpretive Approaches to Children's Socialization*, New Directions for Child Development 58 (San Francisco: Jossey-Bass, 1992); Katherine Brown Rosier and William A. Corsaro, "Competent Parents, Complex Lives: Managing Parenthood in Poverty," *Journal of Contemporary Ethnography* 22 (1993):171–204; Claude Goldenberg and Ronald Gallimore, "Immigrant Latino Parents' Values and Beliefs about Their Children's Education," in *Advances in Motivation and Achievement* 9 (JAI Press, 1995):183–228.

22. Barbara T. Bowman, "Child Development and Its Implications for Day Care," in Alan Booth, ed., *Child Care in the 1990s: Trends and Consequences* (Hillsdale, N.J.: Erlbaum, 1992), pp. 95–100; Susan D. Holloway and Bruce Fuller, "The Great Child-Care Experiment: What Are the Lessons for School Improvement?" *Educational Researcher* 21 (1992):2–19; Rebecca S. New and Bruce L. Mallory, "Introduction: The Ethic of Inclusion," in Rebecca S. New and Bruce L. Mallory, eds., *Diversity and Developmentally Appropriate Practices* (New York: Teachers College Press, 1994), pp. 1–13.

8. Negotiating Child Care and Welfare

1. Charles Murray, *Losing Ground: American Social Policy, 1950–1980* (New York: Basic Books, 1984).

2. Gary Becker, *A Treatise on the Family* (Cambridge, Mass.: Harvard University Press, 1976).

3. Daniel P. Moynihan, ed., *Understanding Poverty: Perspectives from the Social Sciences* (New York: Basic Books, 1969); Bruce Fuller and Susan D. Holloway, "When the State Innovates: Interests and Institutions Create the Preschool Sector," in *Annual Review of Sociology and Socialization*, ed. Aaron Pallas (Greenwich, Conn.: JAI Press, 1996), pp. 1–42.

4. Lawrence Mead, *Beyond Entitlement* (New York: Basic Books, 1986), pp. 4 and 61.

5. Melvin Kohn, Atsushi Naoi, Carrie Schoenbach, Carmi Schooler, and Kazimierz Slomczynski, "Position in the Class Structure and Psychological Functioning in the United States, Japan, and Poland," *American Journal of Sociology* 95 (1990):964–1008.

6. M. Bradbard, R. Endsley, and C. Readdick, "How and Why Parents Select Profit-Making Day Care Programs," *Child Care Quarterly* 12 (1983):160–169.

7. For detailed reviews of this literature, see Susan D. Holloway and Bruce Fuller, "The Great Child-Care Experiment," *Educational Researcher* 21 (1992):12–19; Bruce Fuller, Susan D. Holloway, and Laurie Bozzi, "Evaluating Child Care and Preschools: Advancing the Interests of Government, Teachers, or Parents?" In *Yearbook of Early Childhood Education*, vol. 7, ed. B. Spodek and O. Saracho (New York: Teachers College Press, 1996), pp. 7–27.

8. Sandra Hofferth and Douglas Wissoker, "Price, Quality, and Income in Child Care Choice," *Journal of Human Resources* 27 (1990):70–111.

9. Deborah Phillips, Sandra Scarr, and Karen McCartney, "Dimensions and Effects of Child Care Quality," in *Quality in Child Care: What Does the Research Tell Us?* (Washington, D.C.: NAEYC, 1987); Bruce Fuller, Costanza Eggers-Piérola, Susan D. Holloway, Xiaoyan Liang, and Marylee F. Rambaud, "Rich Culture, Poor Markets: Why Do Latinos Forgo Preschools?" *Teachers College Record* 97 (1996):400–417.

10. Bruce Fuller and Xiaoyan Liang, "Market Failure? Estimating Inequality in Preschool Availability," *Educational Evaluation and Policy Analysis* 18 (1996):31–49.

11. Gary Siegel and Alan Loman, *Child Care and AFDC Recipients in Illinois: Patterns, Problems, and Needs* (St. Louis: Institute of Applied Research, 1991).

9. Teachers' Views of Preschool

I would like to acknowledge the support of my colleagues on the Harvard Child Care and Family Policy Project for their thoughtful questions and comments during my research, and particularly for helping me draw connections between the mother and teacher data. Special thanks to Susan Holloway and Bruce Fuller for inviting me to join the research team, for their nurturance as mentors and friends, and for their invaluable assistance as editors and critical readers. Finally, I wish to thank my colleague and partner, Zeynep Johnson-Beykont, for her insightful, challenging, and loving support—both intellectual and emotional— throughout this project.

1. Studies that have focused primarily on early childhood educators include the following: William Ayers, *Early Education in Black and White America: A Comparative Ethnography* (New York: Teachers College Press); Janice Jipson, "Developmentally Appropriate Practice: Culture, Curriculum, and Connections," *Early Education and Development* 2 (1991):120–136; Carol Joffe, *Friendly Intruders: Child Care Professionals and Family Life* (Berkeley: University of California Press, 1977); Sally Lubeck, *Sandbox Society: Early Education in Black and White America—A Comparative Ethnography* (Phildelphia: Falmer Press, 1985); Margaret V. Yonemura, *A Teacher at Work: Professional Development and the Early Childhood Educator* (New York: Teachers College Press, 1986); Caroline Zinsser, *Raised in East Urban: Child Care Changes in a Working-Class Community* (New York: Teachers College Press, 1991).

2. Lubeck, *Sandbox Society.*

3. Ayers, *Early Education in Black and White America,* p. 129.

4. Jipson, "Developmentally Appropriate Practice."

5. The number of courses Krista had completed was the minimum required to be designated a "head teacher" in a child-care center. Her four courses set her at the median for the thirty-seven teachers interviewed, but her nine years of teaching preschool put her above the median for experience.

6. The teachers in this study were interviewed in 1994–1995. Two years later, the NAEYC guidelines defining developmentally appropriate practice were substantially revised. The newest version places more emphasis on the role of the teacher in deciding which practices are appropriate in his or her classroom, taking into consideration the ages, cultural background, and individual characteristics of the children. See Sue Bredekamp and Carol Copple, eds., *Developmentally Appro-*

priate Practice in Early Childhood Programs, revised ed. (Washington, D.C.: National Association for the Education of Young Children, 1997).

10. Lessons from Listening: Strengthening Family Policy

1. Alan Peshkin, *Color of Strangers, Color of Friends* (Chicago: University of Chicago Press, 1991).

2. Bruce Fuller, Susan D. Holloway, and Xiaoyan Liang, "Family Selection of Child Care Centers: The Influence of Household Support, Ethnicity, and Parental Practices," *Child Development* 67 (1996):3320–3337.

3. Ellen Galinsky, Carollee Howes, Susan Kontos, and Marybeth Shinn, *The Study of Children in Family Child Care and Relative Care* (New York: Families and Work Institute, 1994).

4. Judith R. Blau, *Social Contracts and Markets* (New York: Plenum, 1993), Chapter 5.

5. Ronald Angel and Marta Tienda, "Determinants of Extended Household Structure: Cultural Pattern or Economic Need?" *American Journal of Sociology* 88 (1982):1376–1392. John R. Logan and Glenna D. Spitze, "Family Neighbors," *American Journal of Sociology* 100 (September 1994):453–476.

6. For example, see Lawrence M. Mead, *The New Politics of Poverty: The Nonworking Poor in America* (New York: Basic Books, 1992), pp. 148, 237.

7. For a candid and thorough review of the evaluation evidence on family-level effects stemming from poverty policies, see Chapter 3 in Mary Jo Bane and David T. Ellwood, *Welfare Realities: From Rhetoric to Reform* (Cambridge, Mass.: Harvard University Press, 1994).

8. Kathryn Edin and Laura Lein, "Work, Welfare, and Single Mothers' Economic Survival Strategies," *American Sociological Review* 61 (1996):253–266.

9. For instance, New York's governor, George Pataki, pushed through proposals in 1995 and 1996 to reduce AFDC checks, to give recipients ninety days to find work before having benefits reduced or cut off, and to eliminate an increment that AFDC grants to women when they give birth to additional children. These proposals were consistently backed by a majority of those polled. See James Dao, "Poll of New Yorkers Backs Curbs on Welfare Payments," *New York Times* (December 8, 1995), p. B10.

10. For an example of work that looks at the interaction of maternal employment and forms of child rearing, see Ellen Greenberger and Wendy A. Goldberg, "Work, Parenting, and the Socialization of Children," *Developmental Psychology* 25 (1989):22–35.

11. Katherine Brown Rosier, "Competent Parents, Complex Lives: Managing Parenthood in Poverty," *Journal of Contemporary Ethnography* 22 (July 1993):171–204; Katherine Brown Rosier, "Like My Grandmother Always Says: Low-Income Black Mothers and the Construction of Ideas about Parenting." Paper presented at the American Sociological Association meeting, Miami, 1993.

12. Nan Marie Astone and Sara McLanahan, "Family Structure, Parental Practices, and High School Completion," *American Sociological Review* 56 (1991):309–320.

13. Bruce Fuller, Stephen Raudenbush, Li-ming Wei, and Susan D. Holloway, "Can Government Raise Child Care Quality?" *Educational Evaluation and Policy Analysis* 15 (1993):255–278; Bruce Fuller, Costanza Eggers-Piérola, Susan D. Hol-

loway, Xiaoyan Liang, and Marylee F. Rambaud, "Rich Culture, Poor Markets: Why Do Latino Parents Forgo Preschooling?" *Teachers College Press* 97 (1996):400–418; William T. Gormley, Jr., *Everybody's Children: Child Care as a Public Problem* (Washington, D.C.: Brookings Institution, 1995).

14. Kin care is not always of high quality. In one interview study many women talked about its disadvantages, including the problems of having relatives who may be neglectful or abusive. See Tamara Perry, Jennifer Harnish, and Kathryn Fitzgerald, "Child Care Preferences, Beliefs, and Past Experiences of Welfare Mothers." Paper presented at the Society for Research in Child Development, Indianapolis, 1995.

15. The bureaucratic demands and dehumanizing quality of welfare case work are well described in Mark R. Rank, *Living on the Edge: The Realities of Welfare in America* (New York: Columbia University Press, 1994); Thomas J. Kane and Mary Jo Bane, "The Context for Welfare Reform," in Bane and Ellwood, *Welfare Realities*, pp. 1–27. Evidence shows that many mothers receiving AFDC prefer to move their children into center-based preschool programs, but they are routed into other alternatives as a result of supply constraints. See Perry et al., "Child Care Preferences, Beliefs, and Past Experiences of Welfare Mothers."

16. Ken Auletta, *The Underclass* (New York: Random House, 1982), p. xiii.

17. Chapter 3 in Bane and Ellwood, *Welfare Realities*.

18. Fuller et al., "Rich Culture, Poor Markets"; National Center for Educational Statistics, *The Educational Progress of Hispanic Students* (Washington, D.C.: U.S. Department of Education, 1995).

19. The anthropologist Robert LeVine has argued that (1) cultural models pertaining to how to raise children are reflective of particular local demands (economic and social); and (2) contextual demands and prevalent cultural models change over time, influenced by new institutions and social networks that penetrate the original community. See Robert A. LeVine, Suzanne Dixon, Sarah LeVine, Amy Richman, P. Herbert Leiderman, Constance H. Keefer, and T. Berry Brazelton, *Child Care and Culture: Lessons from Africa* (Cambridge, England: Cambridge University Press, 1994).

Index

Abuse: child, 11, 22, 28, 56, 160, 225; mothers and, 63, 139; sexual, 19, 56–57, 73, 93, 128, 161, 173; verbal, 130

Affirmative action, 8

African-Americans, 5, 8, 23, 24, 77–78, 112, 161; attitude toward education, 133–134, 135, 137; compared with Latinos, 224–225; and discipline, 118–119; and kinship, 17, 99; and moving out of poverty, 19, 23, 31, 207, 210; and racial identity, 14, 104–105, 166. *See also* Children: African-American; Mothers: African-American

Aid to Families with Dependent Children (AFDC), 11, 34, 41, 70; and child care, 45, 156, 163, 165–166, 173, 175, 181; and cultural scripts, 5, 13, 18, 19, 161, 163, 204, 205, 222, 223; and pregnant women, 22, 42, 165, 204; and welfare reform, 10, 207, 214

Alexander, Karl, 134

Anderson, Elijah, 17

Auletta, Ken, 222

Ayers, William, 178

Baumrind, Diana, 118–119

Becker, Gary, 152

Behavior, children's: conceptions of, 76, 78–94, 95; mothers' explanations of, 85–89, 95

Biculturalism, 97–102; and children's identity, 104; and choice, 112–113; and language, 170, 186, 195, 197, 221

Blau, Judith, 210

Bloom, Benjamin, 15

Bryk, Anthony, 116

Bush, George, 208

Busing, 19, 84, 148, 174. *See also* Metco busing program

Child care: availability of, 155, 176, 214; and business leaders, 213; and choice, 11, 21, 34, 35, 151–157, 160–176, 206, 207, 219–220; and community activism, 44–45, 212–213; cost of, 71–72, 74, 80, 157, 176; decisions about, 35, 151, 167–171; family (home-based), 55–56, 64, 79, 94, 104, 141, 163–165, 167–169, 170, 175, 203, 205, 208–209, 212, 216, 217, 218, 219; improvement in, 171–176; quality of, 4, 35, 37, 152, 153, 171, 175, 176, 216, 217–218, 220; role of, in education, 136–137, 177; and sexual abuse, 19, 56–57, 73; and social skills, 86, 87, 184–189, 192; stability of, 71, 74; studies of, 17–18; supply of, 4, 155, 216; vouchers for, 9, 22, 42, 80, 152, 157, 160, 166–167, 168, 171–172, 175, 204, 208, 219, 220; and welfare reform, 216, 225